SCENES IN DIALECT
FOR YOUNG ACTORS

A Smith and Kraus Book
Published by Smith and Kraus, Inc.
177 Lyme Road, Hanover, NH 03755

Cover and Text Design by Julia Gignoux, Freedom Hill Design

First Edition: April 2002
10 9 8 7 6 5 4 3 2 1

The Library of Congress Cataloging-In-Publication Data
Scenes in dialect for young actors / edited by Kimberly Mohne Hill.
p. cm. — (Young actors series)
Includes bibliographical references.
ISBN 1-57525-251-1
1. Drama. 2. English language—Dialects. 3. English language—Pronunciation by foreign speakers. I. Hill, Kimberly Mohne. II. Young actors series.
PN2080 .S265 2001
822.008—dc21
    2001055037

SCENES
IN DIALECT
FOR
YOUNG ACTORS

Edited by Kimberly Mohne Hill

YOUNG ACTORS SERIES

A SMITH AND KRAUS BOOK

FOR CRAIG SLAIGHT, DEBORAH SUSSEL,
AND MY GRANDMA, LOIS BOHLIN,
WHO BELIEVED IN ME

CONTENTS

Note: The numbers in parentheses after titles show the number of selections from that title.

SECTION THREE: RUSSIAN

SECTION FOUR: AMERICAN (NEW YORK)

SECTION FIVE: AMERICAN (SOUTHERN)

APPENDIX: CLASSROOM EXERCISES

DEEPENING CHARACTER
THROUGH DIALECT

As an instructor of dialects at the American Conservatory Theater (A.C.T.), I have found that young actors are especially adept at the creation and application of dialects with their characters. There seems to be a sense of abandon in young actors where their voice and speech is concerned, and they seem to enjoy the instant gratification they feel when they observe such a strong difference in their own vocal patterns. Dialects can instantly transform you into another person by affecting the very essence of who you are to the world — your speech. Dialects, for many actors, are enjoyable, useful tools.

The students at A.C.T. are taught that dialects are not to be taken lightly, as some silly voices they put on to "be different." Just as the essence of who you are is revealed in your personal speech pattern, so are your characters' souls revealed in *their* speech patterns. Dialects are to be respected. We study the region of the dialect region to understand its place and its context. This deeper understanding makes us take responsibility for creating as true and realistic and deep a dialect as we possibly can. We strive to move beyond stereotype and generality.

After the students have researched the dialect and the region in which it occurs, they listen to tapes and study the actual sound changes that occur in the dialect. Through practice sentences and improvisations, they begin to feel the difference of the sounds in their bodies, and they work to feel free in the dialect, attempting to develop a personal attachment to the sounds they are making so that the dialect becomes a necessity for their characters rather than an option. Then they work with scenes.

The scenes represented in this collection are not necessarily written *in* a particular dialect; but rather, serve to give the actor a feel for the rhythm, emotion, society, or history of the *people* or *place* of the dialect being studied. These scenes will work when you speak them in dialect, but they may not necessarily have been written specifically for performance in dialect.

The introductions to the scenes have been written to help the readers learn and apply the dialect of the section. The dialect of a character is directly related to who they are in the world and what their world has been all their lives. In this regard, approach each dialect as a character study. Find out where your character lives — not just a town on a map, but the buildings in the town, the weather of the town, the people of the town, etc. Find out what country the character lives in and what cultural, social, historical, geographical, and religious influences the country has experienced. Find out about the education level and social circle of your character. Find out about your character's dreams and fears, challenges, and triumphs. All these "character" questions are actually the way to develop a strong, nonstereotypical dialect. You become invested in the way you speak because you know your character has no other choice but to speak in the way he or she always has. You are not simply putting on a funny accent and trying to make it seem real, it *is* real, because it is who you are in this scene/world/play.

As you begin to speak the dialects aloud, it is important to remember that you are a human being, and that your speech is as malleable as your mind. Most likely, you have found yourself in the position of talking with someone who has a real dialect, and by accident, you find yourself slipping into it. That is normal! If it happens to you, speaking the native dialect *you* speak, of course it can happen to your characters when they speak their native dialects. I am giving you permission to be not perfect at these dialects. Speech is not a perfect science. Speech (and dialect) is ever changing, depending on the speaker and the person speaking to the speaker. So approach this work with a lightness of heart and tongue, and you will be fine!

Of course, there are some basic precepts that need to be maintained when speaking a dialect. Just as you have permission to be not perfect at the dialect at hand, you must always remain consistent. Consistency in dialect means that when you pronounce a word a certain way, take a proper name for example, you *always* pronounce it that way. Sometimes your stage directions will tell you to pronounce something in a certain way, just so that another character can later correct you. Consistency also means maintaining the flavor and rhythm of your dialect even when the others onstage are speaking in different dialects. This is probably one of the hardest things to do as an actor, but the stronger your character research is, the stronger your connection to your dialect will be; and even if you slip into someone else's dialect onstage, your character can justify it!

I have included in each section a reference source to help actors find the actual sounds of the dialect being studied. It is important to listen to as many primary sources of the dialects as possible to get an idea of how it sounds aloud. Seeing the sound changes on a page can only do so much, you must hear and see real people speaking the sounds.

For those students who know the International Phonetic Alphabet (IPA), I have left a space beside each of the phonetically spelled sound changes for you to mark the IPA equivalent.

In the Appendix are improvisations and exercises I have found effective in getting students to free themselves of the head work that comes from drilling sounds off a page — the improvisations allow them to play with the sounds and characters in their bodies, under the safe umbrella of acting and play. Everything they do is right and accepted; every sound they make is correct. With this freedom comes confidence in their ability to speak the dialect and create real, truthful "regionally enhanced" characters. Some of the improvs can be used with any of the dialects, and some work best only with the dialects described. Some of the improvisations work best with groups, and some are private, personal exercises. All are fun!

SECTION ONE

BRITISH

(STANDARD AND COCKNEY)

STANDARD BRITISH INTRODUCTION

A merican actors are fortunate that the study of the British dialect is made easier because so many British films are shown in American movie theaters and are available in video stores. We need only rent a Merchant-Ivory film to hear and see the British world right in our living rooms. We can practice imitating a British actor by rewinding the videotape and repeating the actor's lines over and over until our mimicry has made it "just right" in our mouths. However, this is only one beginning step in the quest for authentic British characters — we have much deeper work to do in order to do our characters justice.

Most American actors will have to do Standard British (also called Received Pronunciation, London, or BBC) at some point in their careers. An incredible amount of amazing British theatrical literature and wonderful classic British characters keep American audiences challenged and entertained, calling for American actors to take command of the British rhythm and sounds.

For our purposes, we will be focusing on the sound changes and elements of Standard British spoken by the relatively educated, neutral London population. I use the term *neutral* not in the political sense, but in the sense that there are no regional enhancements to the general speech pattern we will study. The education system in Great Britain is such that, even with a bare minimum of education, elocution will have been taught at some point. Also, the BBC national news and other forms of visual and audio media will use a general, nonregional accent, and this carries over to the listeners. As with all forms of language, this is evolving, and more and more Britons are laying claim to their original regional dialects.

It is important to know that there exists in Britain (and indeed in each area of dialect we will study) a wide variety of dialects that are based on the region's economic, social, and geographic conditions. For example, the Northumberland region of England, the farm country remoteness, coupled with the presence of the nearby Scottish border creates a speech pattern that can sound completely different than the one heard in London. As an actor, it is up to you to find out where your character is from and research the dialect needs of that particular region.

Standard British dialect is called English for a reason: They invented the language! Of course, it takes its roots from a variety of sources, but the finished product is a form of speech that we tend to consider a heightened form of American English. The sounds tend to be more precisely made, but with an ease and sense of confidence that comes from having spoken the language since its creation.

The people of England are class-conscious and focus intently on their speech as a symbol of their status in the community at large. Even in Standard British, there are some people who are higher status and some who are less so, both qualities being exhibited in their speech.

What follows are some key points about Standard British and the important sound changes/elements.

- As an American (Californian) actor doing a British accent, I have noticed that I must make my mouth rounder than it normally is — indeed, when I look at British people speaking, the corners of their mouths seem to come close together in an almost frowning way. That is not to say that British people do not smile — they do — but the placement of their sound has an element of roundness to it quite consistently.

- A precision about the British sounds requires some conscious effort, but must appear to be completely easy and relaxed when we speak.

- If a word is unimportant in a sentence (usually articles, conjunctions, pronouns, linking verbs), the British barely give it any notice at all. They go for the image words and the operative (important) words of the sentence, which helps with the British rhythm.

- The British dialect stresses only one syllable per word, even if the word has more than one syllable. For example, we (in California) say "SEK ra tair ree" (secretary), and they would say "SEK reh trih." We tend to pay attention to every syllable of a word, and they focus on the stressed syllable only.

- The tone/sound of the British dialect uses the forward muscles of the face (rounded lips), but there is great openness and roundness at the base of the tongue near the throat — imagine the sounds coming out already formed perfectly way down in the center of your body.

- Even though the British dialect has a different inflection rhythm when they ask a question (they tend to raise the pitch and inflection on the second to last word in the sentence, i.e., "Do you WANT some?"), it's important to keep the inflection under check so as not to become too sing-song. Just remind yourself to *mean* what you say.

- Try not to smile, and practice over-rounding your lips when you first begin playing with the sound changes.

- We *like* hearing them talk. There is a reason for that. They know how to make speech sound good, eloquent, and flawless. There is power to that awareness — you can *know* people will listen to you!
- Please do not use your new British dialect on Shakespeare (unless directed to). It is a "bad acting" cliché.

Standard British Film, Television, and Audio References

Film

Mansfield Park	Cast
Four Weddings and a Funeral, Notting Hill	Hugh Grant
The Sound of Music, Victor/Victoria, Mary Poppins, Thoroughly Modern Millie	Julie Andrews
Sense and Sensibility	Cast
Hamlet (Film and CD)	Kenneth Branagh's version
Shakespeare in Love	Dame Judi Dench, Joseph Fiennes, Gwyneth Paltrow
A Room with a View, Howard's End, Remains of the Day (Merchant-Ivory films)	Cast
Mrs. Dalloway	Cast
Truly, Madly, Deeply	Juliet Stevenson, Alan Rickman
The Princess Bride	Cary Elwes, Robin Wright
Sliding Doors, Emma	Gwyneth Paltrow
Dirty Rotten Scoundrels	Michael Caine
Arthur (I and II)	Dudley Moore, John Gielgud
Milo and Otis	Dudley Moore
Bedknobs and Broomsticks	Angela Lansbury, Roddy McDowell
The Parent Trap, Pollyanna	Hayley Mills

Dialect Tapes and Books

(These tapes and books are available through Drama Books or Samuel French or in the libraries of any university with a theater department.)

Standard British	Gilian Lane-Plescia
Stage Dialects	Jerry Blunt
English Accents and Dialects	Hughes and Trudgill
Dialects for the Stage	Evangeline Machlin
Acting with an Accent, Standard British	David Alan Stern
IDEA website	www.ukans.edu/~idea/index.html

For a more complete and detailed list of films/resources, see Ginny Kopf's book The Dialect Handbook.

Standard British
Elements and Sounds

- The dropped *r:* The British dialect drops the *r* sound at the ends of words and when the *r* precedes a consonant. The *uh* you see in the substitutions below is actually really subtle. It's a little off-glide of sound. Pay attention to the first part of the change (the pure vowel) and the rest should take care of itself. If you overdo the *uh* sound, you will go to a Brooklyn dialect, so be careful! Keep the essence of *r* in there and pretend you are still saying it.

ear → ih uh	here, we're, dear →	hih uh, wih uh, dih uh
air → eh uh	where, their, fare →	weh uh, theh uh, feh uh
oor → oo uh	sure, boor, moor →	shoo uh, boo uh, moo uh
ore → oh uh	you're, more, door →	yoh uh, moh uh, doh uh
are → ah	far, car, yard →	fah, kah, yahd
er → eh	girl, word, heard →	gehl, wehd, hehd

- The round sounds: These will take some effort and an ear for you to hear the difference. Most Americans do not make these sounds naturally (except Brooklyn New Yorkers) and so you will have to retrain your mouth and your mind to get them to be natural. You must really round your lips and drop your jaw open (two fingers wide) to shape these sounds, but remember to imagine the sound coming from the center of your body already perfectly formed.

  ah → aw (rounded almost to an *oh* sound)

          law, all, fall hall → law, awl, fawl, hawl

  ah → o (rounded and "popped" like the sound in the word "pop")

          hot, top, stop → hot, top, stop

  ow → ah oh   how, now, brown → hahoh, nahoh, brahohn

  oh → uh oh   go, slow, road, show → guhoh, sluhoh, ruhohd, shuhoh

- The liquid *u:* Much the way the word "music" has a *y* sound after the consonant "m," the British dialect inserts a *y* sound before the long *u* sound after the letters *t, d,* and *n*. Note: if the word has an *o* in the spelling, do not use the liquid *u*.

  Duke, duty, dubious → Dyuke, dyuty, dyubious

new, nude, newer → nyew, nyude, nyewer

tune, Tuesday, tutor → tyune, Tyuesday, tyutor

- The pure Anne sound: The short *a* in the word *Anne* (and others) can tend to be flattened and blended into the consonant that changes the *a* into an *ay* sometimes. In the British dialect, you must pay attention to the vowel (all vowels) before you move on to the consonant. The *a* sound is made with a wide open, smiling mouth (like you are biting into an apple). Make the vowel sound purely, and *then* say the consonant that follows it.

  Anne, can, and → A nne, ka n, a nd

- Prefixes: Keeping with the tradition of stressing only one syllable in a word, the British dialect uses the pure, short sound *ih* on prefixes/suffixes (where we, especially in California, would say *ee*).

  believe, prepare, rehearse → bih lieve, prih pare, rih hearse

- Suffixes: When words end with *ed*, *y*, or *ly*, the British dialect will not stress it or make it a full *ee* or *ed* sound, but will rather substitute the precise *ih* sound instead.

  wanted, lovely, wordy → wan tihd, love lih, wuh dih

- The voiced *th*: In the word *with*, the British dialect voices the *th* sound (like in the word *this*).

- The ask list: One of the main errors made by American actors learning the British dialect is the overuse of the *ah* sound whenever a word is spelled with an *a*. The "ahsk list" seeks to eliminate that tendency by listing all the words that substitute the *ah* sound instead of the *a* sound. If it is not on the list, use the pure Anne sound. For the complete ask list, see pages 81 to 83 of *Speak with Distinction.* by Skinner, Mansell, and Monich.

Standard British
Practice Sentences

ear → ih uh:
> Here dear, the cheer is near to tears. We're fearful of deers.

air → eh uh:
> Where there is care, share the fare. The lair of the bear is fairly scary.

oor → oh uh:
> The poor do-er of newer sewers was sure pure. Fewer pure boors swim moors.

ore → oh uh (very rounded):
> The door was shorter than before the war. More than the four lowered the floor.

are → ah:
> Park your car and start your heart. The part of the art was hard to cart.

er → eh:
> The girl's birth was the first in the world. Hurl the churl to the earth.

ah → aw (very rounded):
> All the tall law books fall in the hall. Always call after the Ball.

ah → o (rounded and popped):
> The hot copper coffee pots popped their tops. Not in the pot, Colin!

ow → ah oh:
> How now brown cow? Round and round without a sound, they found the ground.

uh → uh oh:
> Don't go to the road show, it's slow. Joe and Rose know the flow of the crow.

Pure Anne:

Anne can stand to fan with her hand the man's back. Plan to scram.

Liquid *u:*

Tuesday, the Duke and the Tutor played new tunes on the Tuba.

Prefixes:

The rehearsal was believed to be preparing the delivery of delight.

Suffixes:

It's lovely and sunny in the newly renovated terrace. Calmly study the Wanted List.

COCKNEY BRITISH INTRODUCTION

Most students of dialect have a good deal of fun with the Cockney British dialect. Just as American actors can relax their speech a little to create the essence of a Southern dialect, so too can we relax our British dialect a bit to create the Cockney sounds.

The Cockney dialect is an evolving dialect. Historically attributed to undereducated, working-class people from the crowded lower suburbs of London, the Cockney sounds have been making an appearance in the speech patterns of some prominent and highly educated British citizens (namely, the current Prime Minister, Tony Blair). Much as street slang in America finds its way into the general speech patterns of *all* races and classes, the Cockney sounds contain the same allure and hip qualities people like to sprinkle throughout their speech. It's fun. It's accessible. It makes one seem more as if one belongs to the group.

The Cockney dialect was originally so deeply ingrained in the Cockney people, that it made them completely unintelligible to the upper-class citizens of nearby London proper — and that is the way the Cockneys wanted it. Almost in direct rebellion against their more privileged neighbors, the Cockneys would maintain their distinctive dialect to create a sense of separate identity and status over the stuffy, aristocratic Londoners who looked down on them. They went so far in their plan to distance themselves from the Standard British speakers that they created what is still called "rhyming slang" — a secret code language that only they know.

Using words and phrases that rhymed with what they meant to say (i.e., "apples and pears" for "stairs," sometimes shortened to "apple"), the Cockneys could communicate in a mystifying language. While not as prevalent among the greater speakers of Cockney nowadays, the rhyming slang can still be observed among the wholesale grocers, traders, and workers is specialized areas of industrial London. (The PBS documentary *The History of English* contains great samples of this particular speech pattern.)

When an upper-class or middle-class Briton speaks with the elements of the Cockney dialect, the dialect they speak moves toward what is now being called Estuary English. If your character needs a British dialect with a hint of working-class, Cockney elements, chances are you will be speaking Estuary English. To do a true Cockney dialect on stage would make you almost entirely unintelligible, and that is not what you want to do!

If you do all the sound changes and elements that follow at the same time, you will have a strong Cockney dialect. Use just a few key sounds and you will have a slightly working-class version of the General British accent — Estuary English. Have fun!

- Like New Yorkers, you will find in a later section, the Cockney people have a certain energy of attack on words and phrases — the energy of living in a crowded, bustling metropolitan area.
- The Cockneys are a proud group of people who are devoted to maintaining a sense of themselves and their traditions. To give over to the standardized British pronunciation of words would seem to the proud Cockneys something of a sellout.
- Whereas the Standard British sounds are produced by a rounding of the mouth and a dropping of the resonance into the chest and throat, the Cockney sounds are much flatter in the back of the mouth and resonate in the nose.
- As mentioned before, true Cockney can be fast, mumbled and almost totally unintelligible — be careful.
- There are more sound changes and substitutions in this dialect than in the Standard British, so you must concentrate on maintaining a sense of what the original word is. For example, when you say "wiv" instead of the word "with," we must still know what you meant to say. Keep thinking of the original word and its correct spelling, that way you still keep an essence of the correct pronunciation, and we can then understand you.
- There is a sense of mischief in the Cockney dialect that comes through in the way you carry yourself. It is much more relaxed than the Standard British. It can be cool and hip.
- Cockneys have little lip movement, but the vowels stay rounded and the sounds come out of a more open mouth.
- Like Eliza Doolittle in the film *My Fair Lady,* there can be a tendency to drag out operative syllables of words: "gaaaooohhh ooonnn" ("go on"). Again, it's very nasalized and whiny sounding.
- Cockneys are not quiet.

COCKNEY BRITISH FILM, TELEVISION, AND AUDIO REFERENCES

FILMS

The Very Thought of You	All levels of British
Beautiful People	Multiple levels throughout cast
The Limey	Terence Stamp
Monty Python and the Holy Grail, *Monty Python and the Meaning of Life*	Cast
My Fair Lady	Eliza and her father
Oliver	Cast
Chitty Chitty Bang Bang	Most of the cast
Remains of the Day	Anthony Hopkins's father
Willy Wonka and the Chocolate Factory	Cast
A Fish Called Wanda	Michael Palin

TELEVSION
"East Enders"

DIALECT TAPES AND BOOKS
(Available through Drama Books, Samuel French, or any library of a university with a theater department.)

Cockney for Actors	Gillian Lane-Plescia
Stage Dialects	Jerry Blunt
English with an Accent	BBC Record
Dialects for the Stage	Evangeline Machlin
Acting with an Accent (Cockney)	David Alan Stern

COCKNEY BRITISH
ELEMENTS AND SOUNDS

- The dropped *r* and the intrusive *r*: As with the British dialect, the Cockneys drop the *r* at the ends of words and before consonants. When a word ends with an *r* and the next word starts with a vowel ("car and driver"), they will pronounce that final *r*. Sometimes, this rule makes them overcompensate on words that do not have an *r* in the spelling, and they will accidentally put one in there ("law and order" would become "lawr and ohduh"). This is called an intrusive *r*.
- They always use the liquid *u:*
  Duke, new, tune → dyuke, nyu, tyun
- They drop the *h* at the beginnings of words. Be careful not to make a "glottal attack" (slamming your vocal chords together on the initial vowel of the word), and say the word as if you are silently producing the *h*.
  Harry, he, hit → 'arry, 'ee, 'it
- They drop the *g* on *-ing* endings.
  running, flying, walking → runnin', floyin', walkin'
- The consonant combination *th* changes to either *v* or *f* depending on whether it is voiced or unvoiced.
  mother, father these → muvvuh, fahvuh, veez
  thanks, both, Goth → fanks, buhohf, Gof
- The final *l* in words is not done with the tongue against the roof of the mouth, but rather with a shaping of the lips into almost an *oo* sound (think Elmer Fudd).
  well, bill, careful → weh oo, bi oo, keh foo
- Unique and important to the Cockney dialect is the glottal stop (symbol is ʔ): Instead of your articulators (tongue, teeth, lips) coming together to make a sound (the consonant *t* or *k*), your throat does a little catch and you pretend to have made the sound. In simple terms, you are dropping the *t* and *k* sound in certain instances. The glottal stop only happens when the *t* is in the middle of two vowel sounds, or at the end of a word, and when the *k* sound is at the end of a word.
  little, late, bit, glottal → liʔoo, lyʔ, biʔ, gloʔoo
  like, lake, make → loyʔ, lyʔ, myʔ

- The [ay] (long a) sound becomes [eye] and will be represented with a [y] like in the word [my].

   take, may, gray, paper → ty?, my, gry, pypuh
- The [y/eye] sound becomes [oy].

   while, kite, fly, my → woyl, koy?, floy, moy
- The pure Anne sound (a) becomes very nasalized and can almost become an [eh] sound.

   man, stand, ran → man/mehn, stand/stend, ran/ren
- The [oh] sound gets an open glide into it so it becomes almost like [a-oh].

   go, show, no → ga-oh, sha-oh, na-oh
- The [ow] sound becomes more nasalized and sounds like [ah-ow].

   how, now, brown → hah-ow, nah-ow, brah-own
- The [ee] (long e) sound becomes [ay]. Remember to keep the essence of the real word you are saying in there.

   he, me, free → 'ay, may, fray
- The [eh] sound becomes a lazier [ih] sound.

   get, them, dens → gi?, vim, dinz
- The [aw] sound becomes *very* rounded and sounds almost like [ooaw].

   all, law, fall, call → ooawl, looaw, fooawl, cooawl
- The pure [oo] sounds get a lazy schwa glide into it so it becomes [uh-oo].

   blue, grew, food → bluhoo, gruhoo, fuhood

COCKNEY BRITISH
PRACTICE SENTENCES

[ay] → [y]:

> The rain in Spain stays mainly in the plain. They came from the same place.

[y/eye] → [oy]:

> While I was flying, my wife left in the night. Liza likes to fight the right battle.

[oh] → [a-oh]:

> I told the old goat to grow the gold coat. The boat is slow for the rowers and Joe.

[ow] → nasalized [ah-ow]:

> The cow of the town was brown around the crown. They found them downtown.

[ee] → [ay]:

> We three better see if the meat is free. The tree pleases me.

[eh] → [ih]:

> Get them in the den with the men of Trent. The kennel of leopards is second to none.

[aw] → very rounded [ooaw]:

> They fall all over Paul when he calls. I thought the law was fraught with awful rules.

[oo] → [uh-oo]:

> The blue shoe is for the youth movement. They threw the computer off the roof.

[h] dropped:

> Harry was his biggest hero. The heckler got his hand chopped off by Horace.

[g] dropped on [-ing] endings:

> Getting off the rolling bus was scaring me. The laughing hyenas were boring.

[th] → [f/v]:

> Me mother was thinking of thanking me father. This is something.

[l] in final position:

> Well, Bill, the little call to the hall will tell you. They can tell if the spell is well.

[ʔ] the glottal stop:

> With a little bit of kittle, the cake will be better. The glottal stop is a little bit of fun.

ALMOST GROWN
by Richard Cameron

Cockney British: Two Males

THE PLAY: The events of childhood are revealed to have lasting impacts on three young men. We see their lives play out in their late teens as they take their separate paths, but we are also swept back to the days when they were careless schoolboys playing practical jokes on classmates. A tragic twist of fate brings the former friends face-to-face once more.

THE SCENE: Dave (17) and Scott (17) play out their fantasies of what their futures will be like — college for Scott, immediate work for Dave — and reminisce about the past.

TIME AND PLACE: Present. A town in England, near a river. Scott's bedroom.

Nine months ago. Scott's bedroom.

SCOTT: *(In career officer's voice.)* Now then, lad, let's see. Who are you?

DAVE: David Marshall, sir.

SCOTT: Well now, David, have you had a think about your future?

DAVE: Sir?

SCOTT: What do you want to be, lad? What do you want to do with your life?

DAVE: I wanna be . . . erm . . .

SCOTT: *(Singing and playing guitar blues.)*
  I wanna be a hoochie coochie man
  Play my mojo all night long.
  I said I wanna be a hoochie coochie man,
  Play my mojo all night long.
  Gonna find me a loving woman now,
  A woman that will do me no wrong.
  (Pause.)

DAVE: Yea. *(Pause.)* So I told him what everybody else was telling him. I want to be a mechanical engineer, sir.

SCOTT: *(Pretending to write it down.)* David Marshall. Apprentice prat.

DAVE: Only thing that came into my head. I couldn't tell him I wanted to be a poet, could I? Can't get a job as a poet.

SCOTT: You should have waffled him like I did. I don't know what I want to do. I just want to be famous. Fast cars. That's all. I'm not bothered how I get there.

DAVE: No, I've got to take this job now. I've got to contribute a bit at home, with me Dad gone. Our Elaine still at school, and that. You're all right. Your folks can afford to let you go to college. You even get a load for passing your exams.

SCOTT: Yea. That's for my lessons. Putting in for my test next year. Won't need many. I can drive anyway. Been driving an MG.

DAVE: I might try to do evening classes. Get my Maths this time. I would have liked to have gone. Anyway, I'd never pass.

SCOTT: No. You're thick.

DAVE: Get lost.

SCOTT: All the revision you did.

DAVE: Yea, well.

SCOTT: I didn't do any.

DAVE: Yea, we know. You pass everything and what I don't fail, I scrape through by the skin of my teeth.

SCOTT: You've either got it or you ant.

DAVE: Yea, well. I'm out in the *real* world now, as me Mam says.

SCOTT: Plenty of talent at college.

DAVE: I heard all the women at this place where I'm going, they initiate you, like.

SCOTT: How?

DAVE: Get your pants down. Tub of grease round your tackle.

SCOTT: Get out.

DAVE: I'm telling you.

SCOTT: Who told you that?

DAVE: Somebody that used to work there.

SCOTT: Bloody hell.

DAVE: I know.

    (Pause.)

SCOTT: You're not going to stop there, though, are you?

DAVE: No. Till I sell one of my stories. Then I'm off.

SCOTT: "I was raped by twenty sex-crazed women. Apprentice tells of his rite of passage."

    (Pause.)

    I wonder what we'll be doing in ten years' time?

DAVE: Won't be in this place for a start.

SCOTT: True.

DAVE: Maybe come back to do a book-signing session in town.

SCOTT: Yeah. I'll come back and drive up and down the high street in my open top sports car. Saturday afternoon. Blonde next to me. All the old mob out shopping, pushing prams. "Hey, look, Scott Carey. He's making films now." Stop at the lights and they all mob me for my autograph.

DAVE: Who's the blonde?

SCOTT: Some film actress I'm working with.

DAVE: Not Stella, then?

SCOTT: Do me a favour, Dave.

DAVE: I thought she were, you know . . .

SCOTT: She is. She's all right. But, you know, you move on, don't you? You meet new people. Will be doing. College and that. Otherwise it just gets stale.

DAVE: Yea.

SCOTT: I've only kept it going 'cos I fancy her Mam.

DAVE: Do you?

SCOTT: Yea.

DAVE: How old is she?

SCOTT: Forty?

DAVE: Forty? Have you . . . you know . . . anything ever . . .

SCOTT: No.

DAVE: One of my fantasies, that.

SCOTT: Me too.

DAVE: Hitch-hiking somewhere and this woman stops, gives me a lift. Takes me all the way.

SCOTT: Yea. I think she fancies me.

DAVE: Who?

SCOTT: Stella's Mam. I were stacking bails of straw one day for 'em. Stella weren't there. She'd gone with her Dad to take the horse to the vet's. Her Mam come in the barn with a drink for me. Gives it to me, sits next to me.

DAVE: Jesus. Yea, go on.

SCOTT: I didn't have a shirt on. She couldn't take her eyes off. Had this skirt on. I'm telling you.

DAVE: What?

SCOTT: I knew what she were thinking.

DAVE: What?

SCOTT: She were like . . . trembling.

(Dave gives a low moan.)

SCOTT: I knew she felt as scared as I did. I should have made a move.

DAVE: You should have. I would have.

SCOTT: You?

DAVE: Yea.

SCOTT: I'm sure.

DAVE: I would.

SCOTT: Like when I set it up for you with our Melanie?

DAVE: That were different. I never thought about her that way.

SCOTT: Not much.

DAVE: I never.

SCOTT: Slept with her bra for a month.

DAVE: Yea, all right, Scott.

    (Scott laughs.)

    You got it for me.

SCOTT: I got fed up of you asking me to nick it for you.

DAVE: Yea, all right. And then you went and told her.

    (Scott laughs.)

    She thinks I'm a right perv now.

SCOTT: You are.

DAVE: I've never dared look at her since.

SCOTT: Remember when you brought it to school?

DAVE: Leave off.

SCOTT: What did you do with it?

DAVE: You chucked it down that old lime kiln. Pretended it were Stella's. Last summer. That day we stuck Roberts down.

SCOTT: Scared him silly.

DAVE: Telling me.

SCOTT: We give him some aggravation, didn't we? Him being new.

DAVE: Everybody did. He deserved it, though, didn't he? Going on about army cadets and stuff. Always bragging.

SCOTT: Yea. Funny kid, really.

DAVE: Yea. I tried to talk to him and that. I give up.

SCOTT: Yea, I know what you mean.

DAVE: Never see him around anywhere outside school, do you?

SCOTT: No.

    (Pause.)

DAVE: Served him right. He asked for it.

SCOTT: What?

DAVE: When we left him. Him bragging about how he could climb down with that rope we found.

SCOTT: I know.

DAVE: He must have been a bit thick, not to twig we'd untie it from the tree once he were down.

SCOTT: Yea. Mind you, it was a bit cruel, leaving him.

DAVE: Only to see where Stella and Tommy had got to. We came back.

SCOTT: Yea, after a couple of hours.

DAVE: Chucking lighted grass down to see if we could see him.

SCOTT: We thought he were dead.

DAVE: Well, he wouldn't speak, would he?

SCOTT: We thought he'd blacked out or something.

DAVE: Tried to climb out and fallen back down.

SCOTT: Yea.

DAVE: Then he starts cursing and swearing.

SCOTT: Tied it back to the tree and ran off.

(Pause.)

Funny, that day.

DAVE: What?

SCOTT: The way Tommy left.

DAVE: I knew he were leaving.

SCOTT: Yea, but not saying anything to anybody. He goes off down the river with Stella to the stream to fill the bottle . . . they get some water and then he just goes off . . . that's it . . . leaves her to come back on her own.

DAVE: Yea, well, he didn't want to talk about it, did he?

SCOTT: I know, but never saying "see you" or anything. Just going like that. *(Pause.)* I wonder what he's up to now?

DAVE: In nick probably.

SCOTT: Probably.

DAVE: I've seen his brother Eddie a couple of times. He doesn't know anything.

(Fade out.)

ALMOST GROWN
by Richard Cameron

Cockney British: Two Males

THE PLAY: Traversing time, the events of childhood are revealed to have lasting impacts on three young men. As we see their lives play out in their late teens and they carve out their separate paths, we are also swept back to the days when they were careless schoolboys playing practical jokes on classmates. A tragic twist of fate brings the former friends face-to-face once more.

THE SCENE: Tommy (18) and Eddie (18) attend their mother's funeral and attempt to honor her memory by trying to figure out why her life had been so bad. The brothers' distant connection is rekindled and a sense of family is renewed on this solemn day.

TIME AND PLACE: Present. A city in England. A funeral home.

Three weeks ago. A back garden. Eddie and Tommy in suits. Eddie passes Tommy a piece of paper. Tommy reads it.

TOMMY: What's that mean, then?
EDDIE: It's medical for what caused it.
TOMMY: Oh, right.
    (Gives it back. Pause.)
EDDIE: It went all right, didn't it? *(Pause.)* Tommy?
TOMMY: Eh?
EDDIE: It went off all right.
TOMMY: Yea.
EDDIE: You OK?
TOMMY: Yea. *(Pause.)* You getting married, then?
EDDIE: Eh?
TOMMY: You and . . .
EDDIE: Christine.
TOMMY: Yea.
EDDIE: No.
TOMMY: She's all right.
EDDIE: Yea.

TOMMY: I wonder what Mam would have thought of her?

EDDIE: *(Puzzled.)* Dunno. She would have liked her.

(Tommy looks at him.)

Maybe not. *(Pause.)* Never had much of a life, did she?

TOMMY: No, not much.

EDDIE: Better off where she is.

TOMMY: Bin brain dead for years anyway.

EDDIE: Yea. I don't know, I suppose she cared about us in her own way.

TOMMY: Never got round to showing it.

EDDIE: Just too far gone with everything. Couldn't say anything worthwhile any more. I'm sure she wanted us around.

TOMMY: No, she didn't.

EDDIE: It was him.

TOMMY: Yea, well, I never went back and saw her, so that's that. *(Pause.)* If he cleared off once he found out she was ill, why didn't she send for you? She knew where you were, didn't she?

EDDIE: I think by then she didn't know much about anything.

TOMMY: What is he? What's in his brain to make her block us out, made her so she didn't have any sons any more? How can a woman be so scared of losing him, scared of him being there, she goes along with it when he kicks me out?

EDDIE: Go from one bloke that frightens 'em to death to another, some women. Maybe she thought that was what love was all about. Never knew any other kind, with Dad, with him.

TOMMY: Yea. He was mental. When you left it was . . .

EDDIE: I had to.

TOMMY: I know.

EDDIE: Should have took you with me. *(Pause.)* Anyway, you've done all right.

TOMMY: Have I?

EDDIE: I keep hearing bits and pieces. The legend of Tommy Fallon lives on.

TOMMY: Huh. I thought I were given a wide berth last night. Parting of the Red Sea in that pub.

EDDIE: Yea. Good feeling, though.

TOMMY: You get a reputation you have to keep living up to it.

EDDIE: What do you mean?

TOMMY: I am what they want me to be. What they always had me marked down for even before I did anything. So I don't disappoint 'em. I act the part they want to see.

EDDIE: Tough little shit.

TOMMY: Yep.

EDDIE: Even this afternoon. Nothing on your face.

TOMMY: For her? Why should I cry for her?

EDDIE: What did you come back for? *(Pause.)* Good to see you, anyway. Two years nearly.

TOMMY: Something like that.

(Pause.)

EDDIE: After you ran away from home I got to know some of what went on. Saw some of your mates.

TOMMY: What mates?

EDDIE: David Marshall. The lad you stopped with the night you left.

TOMMY: What did he say?

EDDIE: He told me about Spawnail coming at you with a knife

TOMMY: He was mental. Did Dave tell you about the dog?

EDDIE: What dog?

TOMMY: Spawnail's Alsatian.

EDDIE: No. What?

TOMMY: What he did to it.

EDDIE: What?

TOMMY: To prove to me Mam how much he loved her. Another row they'd had. She told him she'd had enough, wanted him out. He'd smacked her a good 'un. So he's pleading with her, saying sorry, saying how much he loves her and needs her, and then he says he'll prove it. His dog, his best friend . . . It were chained up in the yard. Couldn't get away. Went out wi' a kitchen knife and stuck it in its belly. And me Mam fell for it. Holding on to each other, crying their eyes out, while the dog bled to death.

(Pause.)

EDDIE: I got him for you.

TOMMY: What?

EDDIE: When I heard how he'd been knocking you about. I got hold of him.

TOMMY: What did you do?

EDDIE: I collared him one night, coming down the backs. He never knew what hit him.

TOMMY: What did?

EDDIE: Clumped him with a coal shovel. I hurt him. Broke a few bits. Bloodied his best shirt for him.

(Pause.)

ALMOST GROWN
by Richard Cameron

Cockney British: Two Males

THE PLAY: Traversing time, the events of childhood are revealed to have lasting impacts on three young men. As we see their lives play out in their late teens and they carve out their separate paths, we are also swept back to the days when they were careless schoolboys playing practical jokes on classmates. A tragic twist of fate brings the former friends face-to-face once more.

THE SCENE: Dave's (18) little sister Elaine was hit by a car and remains in a coma in the hospital. Tommy (18) makes a surprise return to the town where he was raised to visit with Dave and see Elaine.

TIME AND PLACE: Present. A town in England, near a river. Dave's house.

Dave's house. Three days ago.

DAVE: You were kept on the register till Christmas.
TOMMY: Was I?
DAVE: We kept saying you'd left, but they wouldn't believe it.
TOMMY: Too good to be true.
    (Pause.)
DAVE: How long are you about, then?
TOMMY: Just till I get a few things sorted.
DAVE: Yea, I expect there's a bit to do.
    (Pause.)
TOMMY: I went down the river the other day. Up as far as the lime kiln.
DAVE: Yea?
TOMMY: Do you get down?
DAVE: Not much, not been in ages.
TOMMY: Still the same.
DAVE: Yea. Can't mess about much with a river, can they? Messed about everywhere else.
TOMMY: Yea, a few changes. Different shops and that. I see the Co-op's somebody else now.

DAVE: It's been about six different shops since you left.

TOMMY: Has it? I broke in there once.

DAVE: Did you?

TOMMY: Years ago. I got in through this skylight. Dropped down into this room. When I put the light on, it was empty, nothing I could use to get back out. I had to break a door down, get these big cardboard boxes, full of Persil or something, drag 'em into the room and stack 'em up so I could climb back out. I never got a thing. *(Pause.)* Mad.
(Dave smiles.)

TOMMY: What?

DAVE: Everybody knew you were thieving, we all knew, but you never involved us, it were never mentioned, all that, was it? We never talked about it. Like, being mates was something else.

TOMMY: Yea. *(Pause.)* You wouldn't believe some of the stuff I nicked.

DAVE: I don't want to know.

TOMMY: I never kept a thing. Never sold it, never give it away, just took it, walked through the streets like I was invisible, and dumped it all.

DAVE: What?

TOMMY: All of it. Off the bridge into the river. *(Pause.)* It was all so easy. Maybe I was wanting to get caught. I think to start with it was just somewhere to break in to stop the night. Sleep on a shop floor rather than go home.

DAVE: No wonder you were always falling asleep at school.

TOMMY: Yes. *(Pause.)* So you don't reckon you're going to stick it out where you are?

DAVE: No, not much longer.

TOMMY: Do you know what you're going to do?

DAVE: No. I just know I've had enough. There's got to be something else. My own fault, really.

TOMMY: Why?

DAVE: Taking books to read in my dinner hour. They always took the piss. I come back from break one afternoon and they'd been in my bag, taken my books out and drilled holes through 'em all.

TOMMY: Yea, well, bit of a daft thing to do, what do you expect?

DAVE: Yea, I suppose.

TOMMY: Chucking darts at that Bible in the youth club.

DAVE: Yea.

TOMMY: See who could throw the furthest in.

DAVE: Yea.

TOMMY: I won. Got all the way to Deuteronomy. *(Pause.)* You always had your head in a book.

DAVE: Yea.

TOMMY: Get a job in a library.

DAVE: Yea, I wouldn't mind.

TOMMY: You never got round to writing your masterpiece, then?

DAVE: No.

TOMMY: You ought. You were the only one of us I thought would actually finish up doing it, what they wanted to do. *(Pause.)* You ought.

DAVE: I might. One day.

TOMMY: You ought.

DAVE: Yea.

(Pause.)

TOMMY: Our Eddie's doing all right.

DAVE: Is he?

TOMMY: Got a welding job. Been doing it a bit.

DAVE: Yea?

TOMMY: Got hisself a girl. Be getting married next.

DAVE: Eddie, settling down?

TOMMY: I know. She's all right, though. I like her. Christine. It's her flat I'm stopping at. Well, their flat I suppose.

DAVE: Oh, right.

(Pause.)

TOMMY: You're not with anybody, then?

DAVE: No. Well, sort of. Not really, just seeing somebody.

TOMMY: Who?

DAVE: Melanie Carey. Scott's sister. Remember?

TOMMY: The one you always fancied at school? You finally scored, then?

DAVE: I've only taken her out a couple of times.

TOMMY: Weren't she . . . Int she a bit young?

DAVE: No. Seemed like it then, I suppose. So you lot always used to tell me, anyway. Two years difference then is like, well, it's not like two years now. You know what I mean?

TOMMY: Yea. So how's Scott, then? You still see him?

DAVE: No.

TOMMY: I always thought he'd finish up in a big name band. I wonder if he still plays?

DAVE: Dunno.

TOMMY: He was good.

DAVE: Yea.

TOMMY: Well he seemed good to me.

DAVE: He was.

TOMMY: If you see him, you'll have to say you've seen me.

DAVE: I don't see him.

TOMMY: When we used to go up the river, camping, lighting fires. Sitting in the dark, him on guitar, you on harmonica, me hitting two sticks together.

DAVE: Yea.

TOMMY: Some good sessions.

DAVE: Yea.

TOMMY: Who cares what it sounds like when it's the middle of a wood, middle of the night?

DAVE: I've still got the tapes somewhere of us in his shed, when we recorded ourselves that time.

TOMMY: Have you?

DAVE: Somewhere.

TOMMY: We thought we were ace, didn't we?

DAVE: We were ace.

TOMMY: We were. *(Pause.)* Well, I'll get off then.

DAVE: Oh, right. Good to see you, anyway.

TOMMY: Yea, you too. Look after yourself.

DAVE: Thanks for coming round.

TOMMY: I might go up and see Elaine while I'm here.

DAVE: Yea, right.

TOMMY: Get that book written, you. I'm waiting to see myself in print.

DAVE: Right.

TOMMY: I'll get off, then.

DAVE: I'll come down with you.

(They go. Fade out.)

ARCADIA
by Tom Stoppard

Standard British: One Male and One Female

THE PLAY: Two separate but entwined stories are played out in the same house, but in two different eras. The mysteries left by a nineteenth-century family are investigated and solved by the twentieth-century scholars that converge at the family estate.

THE SCENE: Precocious beyond her years, Thomasina Coverley (13) is being tutored by Septimus Hodge (22) in mathematics, and, much to his chagrin, the world of love and carnality.

TIME AND PLACE: Derbyshire, England. 1809. April. The study room/library of a large country estate.

A room on the garden front of a very large country house in Derbyshire in April 1809. Nowadays, the house would be called a stately home. The upstage wall is mainly tall, shapely, uncurtained windows, one or more of which work as doors. Nothing much need be said or seen of the exterior beyond. We come to learn that the house stands in the typical English park of the time. Perhaps we see an indication of this, perhaps only light and air and sky.

The room looks bare despite the large table which occupies the centre of it. The table, the straight-backed chairs and, the only other item of furniture, the architect's stand or reading stand, would all be collectable pieces now but here, on an uncarpeted wood floor, they have no more pretension than a schoolroom, which is indeed the main use of this room at this time. What elegance there is, is architectural, and nothing is impressive but the scale. There is a door in each of the side walls. These are closed, but one of the French windows is open to a bright but sunless morning.

There are two people, each busy with books and paper and pen and ink, separately occupied. The pupil is Thomasina Coverly, aged thirteen. The tutor is Septimus Hodge, aged twenty-two. Each has an open book. Hers is a slim mathematics primer. His is a handsome thick quarto, brand new, a vanity production, with little tapes to tie when the book is closed. His loose papers, etc, are kept in a stiff-backed portfolio that also ties up with tapes.

Septimus has a tortoise which is sleepy enough to serve as a paperweight. Elsewhere on the table there is an old-fashioned theodolite and also some other books stacked up.

THOMASINA: Septimus, what is carnal embrace?

SEPTIMUS: Carnal embrace is the practice of throwing one's arms around a side of beef.

THOMASINA: Is that all?

SEPTIMUS: No . . . a shoulder of mutton, a haunch of venison well hugged, an embrace of grouse . . . *caro, carnis*; feminine; flesh.

THOMASINA: Is it a sin?

SEPTIMUS: Not necessarily, my lady, but when carnal embrace is sinful it is a sin of the flesh, QED. We had *caro* in our Gallic Wars — "The Britons live on milk and meat" — *"acte et carne vivunt."* I am sorry that the seed fell on stony ground.

THOMASINA: That was the sin of Onan, wasn't it, Septimus?

SEPTIMUS: Yes. He was giving his brother's wife a Latin lesson and she was hardly the wiser after it than before. I thought you were finding a proof for Fermat's last theorem.

THOMASINA: It is very difficult, Septimus. You will have to show me how.

SEPTIMUS: If I knew how, there would be no need to ask *you*. Fermat's last theorem has kept people busy for a hundred and fifty years, and I hoped it would keep you busy long enough for me to read Mr. Chater's poem in praise of love with only the distraction of its own absurdities.

THOMASINA: Our Mr. Chater has written a poem?

SEPTIMUS: He believes he has written a poem, yes. I can see that there might be more carnality in your algebra than in Mr. Chater's "Couch of Eros."

THOMASINA: Oh, it was not my algebra. I heard Jellaby telling cook that Mrs. Chater was discovered in carnal embrace in the gazebo.

SEPTIMUS: *(Pause.)* Really? With whom, did Jellaby happen to say?

(Thomasina considers this with a puzzled frown.)

THOMASINA: What do you mean, with whom?

SEPTIMUS: With what? Exactly so. The idea is absurd. Where did this story come from?

THOMASINA: Mr. Noakes.

SEPTIMUS: Mr. Noakes!

THOMASINA: Papa's landskip architect. He was taking bearings in the garden when he saw — through his spyglass — Mrs. Chater in the gazebo in carnal embrace.

SEPTIMUS: And do you mean to tell me that Mr. Noakes told the butler?

THOMASINA: No. Mr. Noakes told Mr. Chater. *Jellaby* was told by the groom, who overheard Mr. Noakes telling Mr. Chater, in the stable yard.

SEPTIMUS: Mr. Chater being engaged in closing the stable door.

THOMASINA: What do you mean, Septimus?

SEPTIMUS: So, thus far, the only people who know about this are Mr. Noakes the landskip architect, the groom, the butler, the cook, and, of course, Mrs. Chater's husband, the poet.

THOMASINA: And Arthur who was cleaning the silver, and the bootboy. And now you.

SEPTIMUS: Of course. What else did he say?

THOMASINA: Mr. Noakes?

SEPTIMUS: No, not Mr. Noakes. Jellaby. You heard Jellaby telling the cook.

THOMASINA: Cook hushed him almost as soon as he started. Jellaby did not see that I was being allowed to finish yesterday's upstairs' rabbit pie before I came to my lesson. I think you have not been candid with me, Septimus. A gazebo is not, after all, a meat larder.

SEPTIMUS: I never said my definition was complete.

THOMASINA: Is carnal embrace kissing?

SEPTIMUS: Yes.

THOMASINA: And throwing one's arms around Mrs. Chater?

SEPTIMUS: Yes. Now, Fermat's last theorem —

THOMASINA: I thought as much. I hope you are ashamed.

SEPTIMUS: I, my lady?

THOMASINA: If you do not teach me the true meaning of things, who will?

SEPTIMUS: Ah. Yes, I am ashamed. Carnal embrace is sexual congress, which is the insertion of the male genital organ into the female genital organ for purposes of procreation and — pleasure. Fermat's last theorem, by contrast, asserts that when x, y, and z are whole numbers each raised to power of n, the sum of the first two can never equal the third when n is greater than two.

(Pause.)

THOMASINA: Eurghhh!

SEPTIMUS: Nevertheless, that is the theorem.

THOMASINA: It is disgusting and incomprehensible. Now when I am grown to practice it myself I shall never do so without thinking of you.

SEPTIMUS: Thank you very much, my lady. Was Mrs. Chater down this morning?

THOMASINA: No. Tell me more about sexual congress.

SEPTIMUS: There is nothing more to be said about sexual congress.

THOMASINA: Is it the same as love?

SEPTIMUS: Oh no, it is much nicer than that.

(Pause.)

THOMASINA: When you stir your rice pudding, Septimus, the spoonful of jam spreads itself round making red trails like the picture of a meteor in my astronomical atlas. But if you stir backward, the jam will not come together again. Indeed, the pudding does not notice and continues to turn pink just as before. Do you think this is odd?

SEPTIMUS: No.

THOMASINA: Well, I do. You cannot stir things apart.

LA DISPUTE
by Marivaux

Standard British: Two Females

THE PLAY: A classic study of the moral fiber of men versus women. *La Dispute* seeks to answer the question "who cheated first?"

THE SCENE: Adine (18) and Eglé (18) have been raised in isolation in separate parts of a forest by servants hired by the local king. They are part of the king's experiment, and are finally, on their eighteenth birthdays, let out of their homes to roam around and come upon each other. So far, the young women have met one man each and have fallen madly in love with that man — thinking that they are the only people on the earth. This is the first time either of the young women have ever met another young woman.

TIME AND PLACE: Present. Any forest.

Eglé, Adine.

ADINE: What's this?

EGLÉ: Oh, this seems to be yet another person.

ADINE: A new object. I'll get closer and have a look.

EGLÉ: The person's studying me with care, but it doesn't seem to feel admiration for me. This is not another Azor. *(She looks at herself in the mirror.)* Nor is it an Eglé, no, definitely not. And yet, it seems to be making comparisons.

ADINE: I don't know what to think of that face. It lacks something; it's rather insipid.

EGLÉ: There's something about this person I don't like.

ADINE: Does it have a language? Let's see. Hm, hm. Are you a person?

EGLÉ: Yes, I am very much a person.

ADINE: Well? *(Pause.)* Have you nothing to say to me?

EGLÉ: No. People are usually eager to speak to me.

ADINE: But aren't you delighted by me?

EGLÉ: By you? I am the one who delights others.

ADINE: What? You're not overjoyed to see me?

EGLÉ: Neither overjoyed nor particularly displeased. Why should I care whether I see you or not?

ADINE: This is very strange. I show myself to you, you look at me. And yet you feel nothing. You must be looking somewhere else by mistake. Gaze upon me with a little more care. Now. How do you find me?

EGLÉ: You, you, you. Who cares about you? I've already told you that I'm the one who is gazed upon. I'm the one who's spoken to and told about the impression I've made. That's how it is. How can you ask me to look at you when I myself am here?

ADINE: Surely it's the one who is the more beautiful who waits for others to notice her and gaze upon her in astonishment.

EGLÉ: Then what are you waiting for? Be astonished.

ADINE: Didn't you hear me? I said it was the more beautiful one who waits for the admiration of others.

EGLÉ: And I've told you the more beautiful one is waiting.

ADINE: If I am not that one, then where is she? There are three people in this world and they are all lost in admiration of me.

EGLÉ: I know nothing about these people of yours, but there are three who are enchanted with me and who treat me as I deserve to be treated.

ADINE: I know that I am beautiful, so beautiful I delight myself every time I look at myself. You see how things are.

EGLÉ: What is this tale you're telling me? I who am speaking to you can never look at myself without becoming totally enraptured.

ADINE: Enraptured? I admit you're quite passable, even rather pleasant. You see that I'm not like you and that I'm making an effort to be fair.

EGLÉ: *(Aside.)* I'd like to beat her with her fairness.

ADINE: You're not seriously thinking of entering into a dispute with me over who is the more beautiful, are you? Why, one need only look.

EGLÉ: But it's by looking that I find you rather ugly.

ADINE: That's because you can't help finding me beautiful and you're jealous.

EGLÉ: The only thing that prevents me from finding you beautiful is your face.

ADINE: My face? Oh, you can't vex me that way. I've seen my face. Go and ask the waters of the stream about my face. Ask Mesrin who adores me.

EGLÉ: The waters of the stream are making fun of you and they've already told me that there is nothing more beautiful than my own face. I know nothing about this Mesrin of yours but he will need only catch a glimpse of my face to stop looking at you. Furthermore I have an Azor who's worth much more than your Mesrin, an Azor I love and who is almost as enchanting as I am. And he says I am his life. You're nobody's life. *And* I have a mirror which confirms everything the stream and Azor have already told me. Can anything beat that?

ADINE: *(Laughing.)* A mirror? You have a mirror as well? What can a mirror do for you except make you look at yourself. Hahaha.

EGLÉ: Hahaha. I knew I wouldn't like her.

ADINE: Here. Take a look at this mirror which tells the truth. Learn to know yourself better and to keep quiet.

EGLÉ: Why don't you take this one and look at yourself in there. It will teach you how mediocre you are and to adopt a tone of modesty when speaking to me.

ADINE: Go away. I have no use for you if you will persist in your refusal to admire me. I'm turning my back on you. There.

EGLÉ: As for me, I don't even know you're here.

ADINE: What a madwoman.

EGLÉ: She's deluded. What world can such a person have come from? There's Carise, I'll ask her.

INVENTING A NEW COLOUR
by Paul Godfrey

Standard British: Two Males

THE PLAY: Through a series of monologues and scenes, the lives of a family trying to maintain a semblance of normalcy amidst the cruelties and unknowns of war are revealed.

THE SCENE: Peter (17) is sent away from London to live as a refugee with Francis' (16) family in Devon, England during World War II. They are meeting for the first time.

TIME AND PLACE: Devon, England. 1942. The kitchen of Francis's home.

In the kitchen: February. Francis comes in. Peter is waiting. He has his things.

FRANCIS: Is this you, just arrived then? Peter. The evacuee.
PETER: Me. Yes. Here, here in the country.
FRANCIS: Oh.
PETER: So much green here. It's all green, the countryside round here, isn't it?
FRANCIS: Exeter's not exactly like that.
PETER: Ah, but Exeter's so old.
FRANCIS: What's left.
PETER: My father said it was a place to have property, Devon. I'd really like to have property round here.
FRANCIS: Why here? When you've come from London.
PETER: I mean to retire to, I'd give anything to be rich enough to retire down here.
FRANCIS: It's damp you know, here. If you retired here, you'd die of rheumatism. Wettest valley in England, brilliant place to retire to this.
PETER: I was told we have to go and work in the fields out of term.
FRANCIS: Yes. We can walk back each day though, or cycle, along the canal.
PETER: There's no tram?
FRANCIS: Look, I'd better tell you now. My parents, they're at the funeral. My grandmother she died this week. You've not come to a happy house.
PETER: Should I do something? What should I do?

FRANCIS: Nothing; just don't worry if they act out of the ordinary when they get back.

PETER: Oh, dear.

FRANCIS: It's all right, don't expect them to be normal that's all.

PETER: No one's parents are normal: My mother she's Italian.

FRANCIS: That must be strange.

PETER: It's difficult sometimes, but I don't mind it.

FRANCIS: Is that all you've brought?

PETER: Yes.

FRANCIS: You've brought quite a lot with you.

PETER: I'm late, I should've registered by five. Is that the time?

FRANCIS: It'll do.

PETER: Perhaps I can do it tomorrow.

FRANCIS: Would you like to see the river?

PETER: Why, is it interesting?

FRANCIS: There's a weir.

PETER: Oh I've seen that, from the train.

Did she die in the bombing then your granny. Was it a bomb?

FRANCIS: Not a bomb, old age. She wasn't bombed. She was very old. You shouldn't laugh.

PETER: You are.

FRANCIS: She was my granny. I cried earlier. She was more than eighty. On Monday my dad found her in bed asleep; dead.

PETER: Where do I stay?

FRANCIS: My father asked me to clear half of my room and he's brought in another bed. Yours is going to be the one under the window, and there's a desk, but you could use this table for your homework.

PETER: There's going to be a lot of that, isn't there?

FRANCIS: School certificates you mean. Are you taking them too?

PETER: That's why they sent me. I missed them last year.

FRANCIS: But you look grown-up. Too old to be an evacuee.

PETER: I'm only seventeen. These exams are important. Aren't you a bit young to be taking them?

FRANCIS: I've been sixteen for a long time. How many are you taking?

PETER: Six, six is all you'll ever need. You?

FRANCIS: Eleven: Maths, English, language and literature, history, French, Latin, Greek, chemistry, and physics.

PETER: That's only nine.

FRANCIS: R.I. and art too.

PETER: You're the smart one. There's no straw in your hair.

FRANCIS: The only way to face these things is head on.

PETER: What? Exams.

FRANCIS: Head on and by the throat!

PETER: Don't you know there's a war on?

FRANCIS: Half measures is no good. To the hilt or not at all.

PETER: But why condemn yourself to all this rubbish then? Where does it get you?

FRANCIS: You'll see.

PETER: When we get back to work?

FRANCIS: When we get back to school.

PETER: Do you think I'll get on all right?

FRANCIS: You will.

PETER: Now tell me your name.

FRANCIS: Francis.

PETER: Francis: the original Devon pirate.

INVENTING A NEW COLOUR
by Paul Godfrey

Standard British: Two Males

THE PLAY: Through a series of monologues and scenes, the lives of a family trying to maintain a semblance of normalcy amidst the cruelties and un-knowns of war are revealed.

THE SCENE: Peter (17) and Francis (16) have overcome the rough beginnings of their "forced" friendship and have begun to truly trust each other. The effects of the raging war have landed on Francis, who reveals his macabre plan for his school.

TIME AND PLACE: Devon, England. 1942. Francis's bedroom.

In the bedroom, late at night. Francis is still awake. Peter comes in.

FRANCIS: You're late, the all-clear was hours ago.
PETER: They say it was the worst raid yet, Eric sent me home, he's still out.
FRANCIS: How did you get on with him?
PETER: All right. He's a good chap, I like him. And I suppose I learnt a lot, mechanical things, that'll be helpful in the Force. Some of the devices are quite simple. Eric showed me one, it was just eight pieces. I reckon I could take one apart in no time and rebuild it. It'd not be difficult. And they're not all big either. I saw another; it would fit in my bicycle basket.
FRANCIS: You know what your mother wrote?
PETER: You read my letter?
FRANCIS: Yes. I found it.
PETER: Francis!
FRANCIS: "I hope you have an uneventful journey." I can't understand how anyone can wish someone that. It's too dull. Life shouldn't be that dull.
PETER: I don't agree.
FRANCIS: An uneventful journey.
PETER: How can you say that? Christ, *four* raids this week.
FRANCIS: Choose. Choose now. Eventful or uneventful. I choose the pro-foundly eventful.
PETER: Oh Francis, just now: I'm away from home. Bombs drop. People die

and kill. My mother wished me an uneventful journey. That's not unnatural.

FRANCIS: But we have no choice, do we?

PETER: I try to get on with you, you know, but there you go, acting up all the time. I'm so tired. Tell me what you mean. What do you *mean?* You need to smarten up your ideas, Francis.

FRANCIS: It's my house you live in.

PETER: Thanks, it's the middle of the night, that's marvellous.

FRANCIS: I'm glad you're grateful, City Boy.

PETER: Local yokel! Ha Ha Ha!

FRANCIS: Goodnight! *(Goes to sleep.)*

PETER: Francis, wake up. *(Francis wakes up.)*

FRANCIS: I like the rustic impressions. *(Pause.)* I mean what I say. We have no uneventful journey. *(Pause.)*

PETER: Are we friends? We are friends. Aren't we?

FRANCIS: Yes. I think so. *(Pause.)*

PETER: It means a lot to me. I've been very lonely, but if I know that you are my friend then I can carry on and do it all, because I know you'll be there, and I can talk to you. Let's meet when we're old, shall we? Will you come to my funeral if it's first? I'll go to yours. *(Pause.)*

FRANCIS: You are a silly old thing. I didn't know at all.

PETER: I'm sorry. *(Pause.)*

FRANCIS: I was waiting for you. Will you help me?

PETER: Yes, of course.

FRANCIS: It's serious. You know you help my father now to collect pieces of the dismantled UXB's. I'd like to get enough pieces to make a bomb. I'd like to blow up the school. No more exams then!

PETER: That would be terrible.

FRANCIS: I don't see.

PETER: Francis, some things are good and some bad, everyone knows that. This is bad! Lots of people could be killed.

FRANCIS: Not if we timed it right.

PETER: Buildings destroyed, Francis.

FRANCIS: That's the idea.

PETER: Why now? Francis, making a bomb is wrong.

FRANCIS: We go out and do it to the Germans.

PETER: That's very different. The school is not our enemy, not like the Germans.

FRANCIS: Oh yes?

PETER: Look we know we're right, on the side of good, but the Nazis are wrong.

FRANCIS: Exactly. The things we like and agree with are good and those we dislike and disagree with are bad. Got it?

PETER: It's not so simple.

FRANCIS: Millions and millions of bombs drop every day, yesterday, tomorrow. How does one extra tip the balance. Right or wrong? We hate these exams, yes? You do.

PETER: Yes.

FRANCIS: Most of them will be no use. You want to be a soldier, yes?

PETER: Yes, I suppose so.

FRANCIS: And to me, well, they're a joke — a bad joke. None of us knows why we go through this charade. Who knows if the war will end, even if we win. So, let's choose; to sweep it all away. You're not convinced.

PETER: People might be killed, you and me.

FRANCIS: Look, I've worked it out. We assemble it under the stage in the hall, then we help to stack chairs one day and stay to switch the lights off and one of us goes to set it. After prayers the hall is always empty for an hour. Peter, no one will get hurt. It's a miracle the school's not been hit already. It's monstrous, how could they have missed?

PETER: Are you really serious?

FRANCIS: I'm asking you to help me, as my friend, Peter.

PETER: Does this mean friends for ever then whatever happens?

FRANCIS: Yes.

PETER: I'll go with you.

FRANCIS: Everyone will be so sorry. Poor boys, no exams. Tragic, and they worked *so* hard. Enforced school holiday.

PETER: How long have you been planning this?

FRANCIS: How often will you go out with him on the defusing lark?

PETER: Three nights a week from now on, perhaps. As many nights as there are raids.

FRANCIS: Can you start collecting pieces, without him noticing?

PETER: Yes.

FRANCIS: You and I. Together. Soon.

INVENTING A NEW COLOUR
by Paul Godfrey

Standard British: Two Males

THE PLAY: Through a series of monologues and scenes, the lives of a family trying to maintain a semblance of normalcy amidst the cruelties and unknowns of war are revealed.

THE SCENE: While Francis (16) thinks it was Hitler's bomb that just destroyed his home, Peter (17) knows the real truth. The revelation of Peter's secret serves to deepen the boys' friendship, and marks the beginning of the end of all things "normal" for the young men.

TIME AND PLACE: Devon, England. 1942. An allotment shed (temporary housing) following a bombing.

Next day. An allotment shed. Peter curled up. Francis comes in.

FRANCIS: Hello, Peter. We thought we'd lost you.

PETER: How did you find me?

FRANCIS: I knew you'd be here.

PETER: That easy?

FRANCIS: Transparent.

PETER: What's happened?

FRANCIS: You know.

PETER: What now, then?

FRANCIS: They're all upset, it's horrible. We stay in a shelter tonight and go to my grandmother's tomorrow. It's miles out. The house has not been touched since she died. You must come.

PETER: Forget about me boy.

FRANCIS: Well sir, since Hitler, perhaps the only wholly evil man in the world, dropped a bomb on Salmon Pool Lane, you have nowhere else.

PETER: It wasn't Hitler's bomb.

FRANCIS: What?

PETER: It was ours. You know, the pieces. I put them together, like your dad showed me.

FRANCIS: In the house?

PETER: In the kitchen.

FRANCIS: The kitchen!

PETER: During the raid. And they worked, the last thing I expected. The timer gave me thirty seconds and I ran. I got your revision notes. *(Hands them to Francis. Francis takes the pile of papers and throws them on the ground.)*

FRANCIS: Gone! All gone. Whooah! Rubbish house, room, street! All gone! Whooah! No more exams, Peter!

PETER: We have to tell your parents, you know.

FRANCIS: No, we must never do that. No one must know.

PETER: But they're upset, it was their home. They took me in, you're their son.

FRANCIS: I'm still here.

PETER: How can we not tell?

FRANCIS: Because it would make nothing easier. Things would be more painful that way.

PETER: You're a coward.

FRANCIS: This will be more difficult. No one but you and me must ever know.

PETER: How can we go on as if we'd done nothing? Won't they know, won't they guess something's up? They know you too well, Francis.

FRANCIS: Everything is different now, we are no longer in that house. All the changes in our behavior, they will account to what's happened.

PETER: I don't know if I can do this at all.

FRANCIS: Look, I'll help you. We're lucky not to be dead; if you are wise you will work, as I shall. We have to keep doing the messages too.

PETER: You make it sound very easy.

FRANCIS: Soon, you'll get your call-up. What? Two and a half months, less. That's what you want, isn't it? You are not as tied as I am.

PETER: So we plug on and say nothing?

FRANCIS: Yes.

PETER: I'll try Francis, I promise you that.

FRANCIS: Come on, let's go.

PETER: Your revision notes, better take them. We will still have to go to school, take exams.

FRANCIS: Do you think so?

PETER: The school is still there. What reason is there not to? You said I should work as you will. Isn't that what you meant?

FRANCIS: I don't know. I didn't think.

PETER: Not like you Francis.

FRANCIS: You're not so stupid Peter. Did you take anything of yours when you left?

PETER: No, I don't care about that. It's all a mess. In London, my sister may be dead, my mother gone, and I did this here.

FRANCIS: It was our idea remember? My fault as much as yours. Perhaps our house would have gone anyway.

PETER: Perhaps. Perhaps you're right.

THE IMPORTANCE OF BEING EARNEST
by Oscar Wilde

Standard British: Two Males

THE PLAY: In this, one of Oscar Wilde's most famous plays, the lives of the hysterically superficial aristocracy are revealed for all their quirks and foibles. In the Victorian era of manners and romance, Mr. Wilde pokes fun at the mores and constraints of the time in intelligent and surprising ways.

THE SCENE: John (Earnest) Worthing (29) has just proposed to the honorable Gwendolyn Fairfax, Algernon Montcrief's (23 to 25) cousin. John has been informed by Miss Fairfax's mother, Lady Bracknell, that he is not a suitable choice for her daughter.

TIME AND PLACE: London, England. 1800s, Algernon Moncrief's flat.

Lady Bracknell sweeps out in majestic indignation.

JACK: Good morning! *(Algernon, from the other room, strikes up the Wedding March. Jack looks perfectly furious and goes to the door.)* For goodness' sake don't play that ghastly tune, Algy! How idiotic you are!
(The music stops and Algernon enters cheerily.)
ALGERNON: Didn't it go off all right, old boy? You don't mean to say Gwendoline refused you? I know it is a way she has. She is always refusing people. I think it is most ill-natured of her.
JACK: Oh, Gwendoline is as right as a trivet. As far as she is concerned, we are engaged. Her mother is perfectly unbearable. Never met such a Gorgon . . . I don't really know what a Gorgon is like, but I am quite sure that Lady Bracknell is one. In any case, she is a monster, without being a myth, which is rather unfair . . . I beg your pardon, Algy, I suppose I shouldn't talk about your own aunt in that way before you.
ALGERNON: My dear boy, I love hearing my relations abused. It is the only thing that makes me put up with them at all. Relations are simply a tedious pack of people who haven't got the remotest knowledge of how to live, nor the smallest instinct about when to die.
JACK: Oh, that is nonsense!

ALGERNON: It isn't.

JACK: Well, I won't argue about the matter. You always want to argue about things.

ALGERNON: That is exactly what things were originally made for.

JACK: Upon my word, if I thought that, I'd shoot myself. . . . *(A pause.)* You don't think there is any chance of Gwendoline becoming like her mother in about a hundred and fifty years, do you, Algy?

ALGERNON: All women become like their mothers. That is their tragedy. No man does. That's his.

JACK: Is that clever?

ALGERNON: It is perfectly phrased! and quite as true as any observation in civilized life should be.

JACK: I am sick to death of cleverness. Everybody is clever nowadays. You can't go anywhere without meeting clever people. The thing has become an absolute public nuisance. I wish to goodness we had a few fools left.

ALGERNON: We have.

JACK: I should extremely like to meet them. What do they talk about?

ALGERNON: The fools? Oh! about the clever people, of course.

JACK: What fools.

ALGERNON: By the way, did you tell Gwendoline the truth about your being Ernest in town, and Jack in the country?

JACK: *(In a very patronizing manner.)* My dear fellow, the truth isn't quite the sort of thing one tells to a nice, sweet, refined girl. What extraordinary ideas you have about the way to behave to a woman!

ALGERNON: The only way to behave to a woman is to make love to her, if she is pretty, and to someone else, if she is plain.

JACK: Oh, that is nonsense.

ALGERNON: What about your brother? What about the profligate Ernest?

JACK: Oh, before the end of the week I shall have got rid of him. I'll say he died in Paris of apoplexy. Lots of people die of apoplexy, quite suddenly, don't they?

ALGERNON: Yes, but it's hereditary, my dear fellow. It's a sort of thing that runs in families. You had much better say a severe chill.

JACK: You are sure a severe chill isn't hereditary, or anything of that kind?

ALGERNON: Of course it isn't!

JACK: Very well, then. My poor brother Ernest is carried off suddenly, in Paris, by a severe chill. That gets rid of him.

ALGERNON: But I thought you said that . . . Miss Cardew was a little too much interested in your poor brother Ernest? Won't she feel his loss a good deal?

JACK: Oh, that is all right. Cecily is not a silly romantic girl, I am glad to say. She has got a capital appetite, goes on long walks, and pays no attention at all to her lessons.

ALGERNON: I would rather like to see Cecily.

JACK: I will take very good care you never do. She is excessively pretty, and she is only just eighteen.

ALGERNON: Have you told Gwendoline yet that you have an excessively pretty ward who is only just eighteen?

JACK: Oh! one doesn't blurt these things out to people. Cecily and Gwendoline are perfectly certain to be extremely great friends. I'll bet you anything you like that half an hour after they have met, they will be calling each other sister.

ALGERNON: Women only do that when they have called each other a lot of other things first. Now, my dear boy, if we want to get a good table at Willis's, we really must go and dress. Do you know it is nearly seven?

JACK: *(Irritably.)* Oh! it always is nearly seven.

ALGERNON: I'm hungry.

JACK: I never knew you when you weren't . . .

ALGERNON: What shall we do after dinner? Go to a theatre?

JACK: Oh, no! I loathe listening.

ALGERNON: Well, let us go to the Club?

JACK: Oh, no! I hate talking.

ALGERNON: Well, we might trot round to the Empire at ten?

JACK: Oh, no! I can't bear looking at things. It is so silly.

ALGERNON: Well, what shall we do?

JACK: Nothing!

ALGERNON: It is awfully hard work doing nothing. However, I don't mind hard work where there is no definite object of any kind.

THE IMPORTANCE OF BEING EARNEST
by Oscar Wilde

Standard British: Two Females

THE PLAY: In this, one of Oscar Wilde's most famous plays, the lives of the hysterically superficial aristocracy are revealed for all of their quirks and foibles. In the Victorian era of manners and romance, Mr. Wilde pokes fun at the mores and constraints of the time in intelligent and surprising ways.

THE SCENE: Cecily Cardew (18) meets a visitor to her country home for the first time. Gwendoline Fairfax (19 to 22) has arrived at her fiancé's home to discover the young Miss Cardew in the garden, preparing for tea. Beneath a mask of manners lurk the true thoughts of the young ladies as they size each other up.

TIME AND PLACE: Hertfordshire, England. 1800s. July. The garden at Manor House, Woolton.

CECILY: My name is Cecily Cardew.

GWENDOLINE: *(Center.)* Cecily Cardew! *(Moving to her and shaking hands.)* What a very sweet name. Something tells me that we are going to be *great friends*. I like you already more than I can say. My first impressions of people are never wrong.

CECILY: How nice of you to like me so much after we have known each other such a comparatively short time. *(Pause.)* Pray sit down.

GWENDOLINE: *(Still standing up front center chair.)* I may call you Cecily, may I not?

CECILY: With pleasure.

GWENDOLINE: And you will always call *me* Gwendoline, won't you?

CECILY: If you wish.

GWENDOLINE: Then that is all settled, is it not?

CECILY: I hope so. *(Pause. They both sit together, Cecily lower center, Gwendoline center.)*

GWENDOLINE: Perhaps this might be a favorable opportunity for my mentioning who I am. My father is Lord Bracknell. You have never heard of papa, I suppose.

CECILY: I don't think so.

GWENDOLINE: Outside the family circle, papa, I am glad to say, is entirely unknown. I think that is quite as it should be. The home seems to me to be the proper sphere for the man. Cecily, mamma, whose views on education are remarkably strict, has brought me up to be extremely short-sighted. It's part of her system, so you do not mind my looking at you through my glasses?

CECILY: Oh, not at all, Gwendoline. I am very fond of being looked at.

GWENDOLINE: *(Long pause. After examining Cecily carefully through lorgnette.)* You are here on a short visit, I suppose?

CECILY: Oh, no! I live here.

GWENDOLINE: *(Severely.)* Really? Your mother no doubt, or some female relative of advanced years, resides here also.

CECILY: Oh, no! I have no mother, nor, in fact, any relations.

GWENDOLINE: Indeed?

CECILY: My dear guardian, with the assistance of Miss Prism, has the arduous task of looking after me.

GWENDOLINE: Your guardian?

CECILY: Yes, I am Mr. Worthing's ward.

GWENDOLINE: Oh! It is strange he never mentioned to me that he had a ward. How secretive of him. He grows more interesting hourly. I am not sure, however, that the news inspires me with feelings of unmixed delight. *(Rises and walks right center.)* I am very fond of you, Cecily. I have liked you ever since I met you. But I am bound to state that, now I know that you are Mr. Worthing's ward, I cannot help expressing the wish that you were — well, just a little older than you seem to be — and not quite so very alluring in appearance. In fact, if I may speak candidly — *(Returning center.)*

CECILY: Pray do! I think that whenever one has anything unpleasant to say, one should always be quite candid.

GWENDOLINE: Well, to speak with perfect candor, Cecily, I wish that you were fully forty-two — *(Sits on sofa, right of Cecily.)* — and more than usually plain for your age. Ernest has a strong, upright nature. He is the very soul of truth and honor. But even men of the noblest possible moral character are extremely susceptible to the influence of the physical charms of others.

CECILY: I beg your pardon, Gwendoline. Did you say Ernest?

GWENDOLINE: Yes.

CECILY: Oh, but it is not Mr. Ernest Worthing who is my guardian. It is his brother — his elder brother.

GWENDOLINE: Ernest never mentioned to me that he had a brother.

CECILY: I am sorry to say they have not been on good terms for a long time.

GWENDOLINE: Ah, that accounts for it. And now I think of it, I have never heard any man mention his brother. The subject seems distasteful to most men. Of course you are quite, quite sure that it is not Mr. Ernest Worthing who is your guardian?

CECILY: Quite sure. *(Pause.)* In fact, *I* am going to be *his.*

GWENDOLINE: *(Inquiringly.)* I beg your pardon?

CECILY: *(Rather shy and confidingly.)* Dearest Gwendoline, there is no reason why I should make any secret of it to you. Our little county newspaper is sure to chronicle the fact next week. Mr. Ernest Worthing and I are engaged to be married.

GWENDOLINE: *(Quite politely, rising, crossing right center.)* My darling Cecily, I think there must be some slight error. Mr. Ernest Worthing is engaged to *me.* The announcement will appear in the *Morning Post* on Saturday at the latest.

CECILY: *(Very politely, rising and moving right center.)* I am afraid you must be under some misconception. Ernest proposed to me exactly ten minutes ago. *(Shows diary.)*

GWENDOLINE: *(Examines diary through her lorgnette carefully.)* It is certainly very curious, for he asked me to be his wife yesterday afternoon at five-thirty. If you would care to verify the incident, pray do so. I never travel without my diary. One should always have something sensational to read in the train. *(Produces her diary.)* I am so sorry, dear Cecily, if it is any disappointment to you, but I am afraid I have the prior claim.

CECILY: It would distress me more than I can tell you, dear Gwendoline, if it caused you any mental or physical anguish, but I feel bound to point out that since Ernest proposed to *you* he has clearly changed his mind.

GWENDOLINE: *(Meditatively.)* If the poor fellow has been entrapped into any foolish promise, I shall consider it my duty to rescue him at once, and with a *firm hand. (Moves a little right center.)*

CECILY: *(Thoughtfully and sadly, moving slowly left.)* Whatever unfortunate entanglement my dear boy may have got into, I will never reproach him with it after we are married. *(Moves down center.)*

GWENDOLINE: *(Moving center.)* Do you allude to me, Miss Cardew, as an entanglement? You are presumptuous. On an occasion of this kind, it becomes more than a moral duty to speak one's mind — it becomes a pleasure.

CECILY: *Moving up center to Gwendoline.)* Do you suggest, Miss Fairfax, that I entrapped Ernest into an engagement? How dare you? This is no time for wearing the shallow mask of manners. When I see a spade I call it a spade.

HAYFEVER
by Noel Coward

Standard British: One Male and One Female

THE PLAY: Noel Coward gives us a look into the country life of an eclectic, artistic family over the course of a weekend. Led by the patriarch author and the matriarch actress, the Bliss family invites unwitting guests and admirers to their country home for a quiet, uneventful weekend. What the guests soon learn, though, is that there is no such thing as "uneventful" when one is referring to the Blisses!

THE SCENE: Attempting to regain her sense of peace and reality after a maddening weekend with the Bliss family, Miss Jackie Coryton (20 to 22) finds a comrade in the equally distraught Mr. Sandy Tryell (20 to 22).

TIME AND PLACE: Corkham, England. Present. The hall of the Bliss Estate.

> *It is Sunday morning, about ten o'clock. There are various breakfast dishes on a side table, and a big table is laid down center.*
>
> *Sandy appears at the top of the stairs. On seeing no one about, he comes down quickly and furtively helps himself to eggs and bacon and coffee, and seats himself at the table. He eats very hurriedly, casting occasional glances over his shoulder. A door bangs somewhere upstairs, which terrifies him; he chokes violently. When he has recovered, he tears a bit of toast from a rack, butters it and marmalades it and crams it into his mouth. Then, hearing somebody approaching, he darts into the library. Jackie comes downstairs timorously; her expression is dismal, to say the least of it. She looks miserably out the window at the pouring rain, then, assuming an air of spurious bravado, she helps herself to some breakfast and sits down and looks at it. After one or two attempts to eat it, she bursts into tears.*
>
> *Sandy opens the library door a crack and peeps out. Jackie, seeing the door move, screams. Sandy re-enters.*

JACKIE: Oh, it's only you — you frightened me!
SANDY: What's the matter?
JACKIE: *(Sniffing.)* Nothing.
SANDY: I say, don't cry.
JACKIE: I'm not crying.

SANDY: You were — I heard you.

JACKIE: It's this house. It gets on my nerves.

SANDY: I don't wonder — after last night.

JACKIE: What were you doing in the library just now?

SANDY: Hiding.

JACKIE: Hiding?

SANDY: Yes; I didn't want to run up against any of the family.

JACKIE: I wish I'd never come. I had horrible nightmares with all those fearful dragons crawling across the wall.

SANDY: Dragons?

JACKIE: Yes; I'm in a Japanese room — everything in it's Japanese, even the bed.

SANDY: How awful!

JACKIE: I believe they're all mad, you know.

SANDY: The Blisses?

JACKIE: Yes — they might be.

SANDY: I've been thinking that, too.

JACKIE: Do you suppose they know they're mad?

SANDY: No; people never do.

JACKIE: It was Mr. Bliss asked me down, and he hasn't paid any attention to me at all. I went into his study soon after I arrived yesterday, and he said, "Who the hell are you?"

SANDY: Didn't he remember?

JACKIE: He did afterwards; then he brought me down to tea and left me.

SANDY: Are you really engaged to Simon?

JACKIE: *(Bursting into tears again.)* Oh, no — I hope not!

SANDY: You were, last night.

JACKIE: So were you — to Sorel.

SANDY: Not properly. We talked it over.

JACKIE: I don't know what happened to me. I was in the garden with Simon, and he was being awfully sweet, and then he suddenly kissed me, and rushed into the house and said we were engaged — and that hateful Judith asked me to make him happy!

SANDY: That's exactly what happened to me and Sorel. Judith gave us to one another before we knew where we were.

JACKIE: How frightful!

SANDY: I like Sorel, though; she was jolly decent about it afterwards.

JACKIE: I think she's a cat.

SANDY: Why?

JACKIE: Look at the way she lost her temper over that beastly game.

SANDY: All the same, she's better than the others.

JACKIE: That wouldn't be very difficult.

SANDY: Hic!

JACKIE: I beg your pardon?

SANDY: *(Abashed.)* I say — I've got hiccoughs.

JACKIE: Hold your breath.

SANDY: It was because I bolted my breakfast.
  (He holds his breath.)

JACKIE: Hold it as long as you can.
  (There is a pause.)

SANDY: *(Letting his breath go with a gasp.)* I can't any more — hic!

JACKIE: Eat a lump of sugar.

SANDY: *(Taking one.)* I'm awfully sorry.

JACKIE: I don't mind — but it's a horrid feeling, isn't it?

SANDY: Horrid — hic!

JACKIE: *(Conversationally.)* People have died from hiccoughs, you know.

SANDY: *(Gloomily.)* Have they?

JACKIE: Yes. An aunt of mine once had them for three days without stopping.

SANDY: How beastly.

JACKIE: *(With relish.)* She had to have the doctor, and everything.

SANDY: I expect mine will stop soon.

JACKIE: I hope they will.

SANDY: Hic! — There!

JACKIE: Drink some water the wrong way round.

SANDY: How do you mean — the wrong way round?

JACKIE: *(Rising.)* The wrong side of the glass. I'll show you. *(She goes to side table.)* There isn't any water.

SANDY: Perhaps coffee would do as well.

JACKIE: I've never tried coffee, but it might. *(She pours him out some.)* There you are.

SANDY: *(Anxiously.)* What do I do?

JACKIE: Tip it up and drink from the opposite side, sort of upside down.

SANDY: *(Trying.)* I can't reach any —

JACKIE: *(Suddenly.)* Look out — somebody's coming. Bring it into the library — quick . . .

SANDY: Bring the sugar — I might need it again — hic! Oh God!

JACKIE: All right.
  (They go off into the library hurriedly.)

LOW LEVEL PANIC
by Clare McIntyre

Cockney British: Two Females

THE PLAY: A disturbing look into the lives of young, single, working women in present-day London as they deal with feeling like prey for the men in the world, *Low Level Panic* is an intense, contemporary one-act with mature language and theme.

THE SCENE: Jo (20 to 22) and Mary (20 to 22) are roommates getting ready to go out. The main obstacle to their evening's enjoyment, however, is the sexual assault that Mary experienced a few weeks earlier. Jo tries to get Mary back into the world again.

TIME AND PLACE: Present. London. A flat (apartment) in a populated area of the city. Early evening. The bathroom of the flat (not the toilet, which is separate).

JO: Put some music on.
MARY: *(Going out.)* Like what?
JO: *(Off.)* Something boppy.
MARY: *(Off.)* What?
JO: *(Off.)* Anything.
MARY: *(Off.)* Name something.
JO: *(Off.)* Anything. Use your head.
> *(Jo comes in. She is also in her party gear. Both women are dressed in things they have bought specifically to go out in. Jo is also nearly dressed and doing the finishing touches. Mary has put on a record: it is something good to dance to. Jo has painted her nails and the varnish is drying.)*
> Shit. I meant to do my toes . . . Louder! . . . Mary . . . Turn it up.
> *(Jo goes out. Mary turns up the music. It is incredibly loud. Jo comes back on with a mirror which she props up against the bathroom wall. Mary comes in.)*
MARY: How do I look?
JO: What?
> *(Mary goes out to turn down the music. She comes back on.)*
MARY: What do you think?

JO: Brilliant.

MARY: Do I need anything else?

JO: It suits you down to the ground.

MARY: Do you think?

JO: I *know* it does.

MARY: Doesn't it need something round the neck?

JO: No. It looks exactly right as it is. Don't play around with it.

MARY: I don't know I like it.

JO: Oh Mary don't say that. We spent hours finding it.

MARY: I know.

JO: You liked it in the shop.

MARY: I know.

JO: You did didn't you?

MARY: Yes.

JO: So what's happened?

MARY: I don't know.

JO: It's just 'cos it's not what you're used to buying.

MARY: Ummn.

JO: But it looks terrific on you.

MARY: I don't know.

JO: Honestly.

MARY: I thought I might . . .

JO: It suits you. Believe me.

MARY: I'd never have bought it if you hadn't been there.

JO: I know. You wouldn't even have tried it on.

MARY: Would you wear it?

JO: I couldn't get into it could I?

MARY: These shoes are killing me. No wonder you never wear them.

JO: Take them off when you get there. You won't want to dance in them anyway will you? No one in their right mind dances with their shoes on . . .
You should have worn them round the house, broken them in a bit.

MARY: Haven't you ever worn them?

JO: Yes . . . no. They're too small.

MARY: Were they expensive?

JO: Not really.

MARY: They look expensive.

JO: I know. I love them.

MARY: Christ! *(She takes one off.)*

JO: Put bits of plaster on where they hurt.

MARY: They're killing me. I can't walk.

JO: They're flattering though. They make your feet look right. If I get shoes that make my feet look small, they make me look enormous. Those look perfect on me and I can't bloody walk in them.

MARY: They're agony.

JO: Are they?

MARY: Ummn.

JO: Shit . . . Seriously?

MARY: I think so.

JO: They're not too small are they?

MARY: I don't think so. They just hurt.

JO: Where?

MARY: Here.

JO: Stick bits of cotton wool in there. They'll soften up. So long as they're not too small you'll be all right.

MARY: No they're not too small. They're definitely not too small.

JO: They'll soften up. All you've got to do is stand around in them.

MARY: They're the right sort of thing aren't they?

JO: They're perfect.

MARY: I'll just have to grin and bear it then.

JO: Take some cotton wool with you in case. We look brilliant.

MARY: Yeah.

JO: Fucking ace.

MARY: Mnn.

JO: We'll knock 'em dead.

MARY: Ummn . . . Do you like the colour?

JO: Oh God yes. You can wear stuff like that . . . I don't look right in a mirror.

MARY: You look fine.

JO: Do I?

MARY: Yeah. You look great.

JO: Sure?

MARY: Yes. Now stop looking at yourself or you'll start wanting to change everything.

JO: Right . . . This really is what you need to know. You need to get yourself out of yourself, forget who you are and have a good time . . . *Do* I look all right in this?

MARY: Course you do.

JO: Do I?

MARY: Yeah.

JO: I'm not sure.

MARY: Well if it's not comfortable don't wear it.

JO: It is comfortable. I mean it fits. I got the right size. It's not too small. I just don't know I like it . . . on me. Does it make me look attractive?

MARY: I don't know. It looks nice enough.

(Jo goes out to turn up the music. Mary stays looking at herself in the mirror.)

MARY: Jo!

JO: *(Off.)* What?

MARY: Come here a minute.

JO: *(Off.)* Where's you perfume?

MARY: Come in here.

JO: *(Comes back on.)* Where is it?

MARY: I don't want to go.

JO: What?

MARY: Really I don't.

JO: Why?

MARY: I feel sick.

JO: You look really nice.

MARY: *(Takes her dress off and sits down holding it.)* I hate it.

JO: You can take the shoes off when you get there.

MARY: It's not the shoes.

JO: You've got to go.

MARY: I haven't.

JO: You can't.

MARY: I can.

JO: But why?

MARY: You go.

JO: For fuck's sake. *(She goes out. Mary shouts after her. She turns off the music.)*

MARY: *(As Jo comes in with a bottle of wine.)* I feel like a tart. I feel disgusting.

JO: You don't look like a tart.

MARY: I feel it.

JO: What's a tart anyway?

MARY: I don't know.

JO: You don't look like a tart. You look French.

MARY: So what?

JO: Why didn't you say any of this in the shop?

MARY: I can never think straight in clothes shops . . . You can see straight through it.

JO: You can't. You can't see anything. I'd have told you.

MARY: We're going to walk down the street and get whistled at by blokes who'd stick their fingers up your vagina as soon as look at you and they don't even know who I am.

JO: We'll get a taxi.

MARY: I feel like somebody else.

(Pause.)

JO: Those blokes were dickheads. It was just one of those things. It's never happened before. It won't happen again. And why let it wreck this evening?

MARY: They're not just anything. They're out there in their thousands and their heads are full of rubbish and you don't know who the hell they are.

JO: You can't stop yourself having fun. It'll drive you mad.

MARY: I am mad.

JO: You're not. You're screwed up. We're all screwed up.

MARY: What's the point? What are we going for?

JO: Fun.

MARY: What fun?

JO: Anything.

MARY: Like what?

JO: Oh come on.

MARY: What?

JO: What the hell do you go to parties for? You know.

MARY: Yes.

JO: Have a bop. Meet someone.

MARY: It's all the same thing.

JO: It's not the same thing. They were stupid idiots.

MARY: Why me?

JO: Because you were there.

MARY: My body was there but I was somewhere else.

JO: You were all right though weren't you? Nothing broken? Nothing spoilt?

MARY: No.

JO: They wanted to frighten you.

MARY: I wasn't frightened.

JO: Take the piss out of you.

MARY: I was angry.

JO: Right.

MARY: I was terrified.

JO: They didn't know what they were doing.

MARY: I wouldn't know them if I passed them in the street.

JO: It's not everyone: not by a million miles it's not everyone.

MARY: I don't even dress up much.

JO: That's got nothing to do with it. You've just got to be born female.

MARY: Great.

JO: You're one in a million.

MARY: Everyone's one in a million.

JO: It won't happen again.

MARY: What if they'd had a knife?

JO: They didn't . . . Now something nasty's happened to you, it'll happen to someone else next.

MARY: It wasn't nasty enough.

JO: You might fall out of a helicopter next, get drowned in a boat. Why worry?

MARY: I'm a sitting duck.

JO: You've sailed along so far.

MARY: I'm going to sit in this bathroom for the rest of my life and go out every so often for a sandwich. *(Jo crosses to the door.)* Where are you going?

JO: I'm going to watch telly: some American rubbish with people in big cars who live by the sea. *(She goes out.)*

MARY: Fat lot of good that'll do you. *(She takes a couple of large swigs from the wine bottle, which she hangs onto for the rest of the scene.)*

JO: *(Coming in.)* If you don't come to this party I'll kill you.

MARY: It was because I was dressed up.

JO: We've been over this before, Mary: you weren't dressed up.

MARY: I was more dressed up than usual.

JO: You were wearing a skirt.

MARY: For me I was dressed up.

JO: You weren't dressed up at all. You never dress up. And what if you were?

MARY: I remember being all dolled up.

JO: I can't remember ever seeing you all dolled up.

MARY: I am now.

JO: Apart from now I don't.

MARY: I was wearing those enamel bracelets I've got. I can't remember why . . . but I was looking nice. I know I was. I just felt it. Sometimes you do feel that don't you? Sometimes you just know you're looking okay. It's not like I was looking like anything in particular. I just felt nice. That's more it. I'd felt nice when I'd been cycling to work: all cool and breezy. I don't remember what I looked like but I remember how I felt.

JO: But you weren't dressed up.

MARY: I wasn't concentrating.

JO: You weren't.

MARY: No.

JO: You always wore a skirt didn't you?

MARY: Had to.

JO: You were just dressed ordinary.

MARY: They didn't think so.

JO: Boys like that don't think, not with their brains that is. They might think a bit with their dicks but not with their brains they don't. Not at all. They don't even know where their brains are.

MARY: I'm sure I was looking nice . . . for me, that is.

JO: You are nice looking.

MARY: I must have been looking sexy but I didn't know it. They must have thought I was looking all dressed up and sexy.

JO: What's wrong with looking sexy?

MARY: I want to look like I feel.

JO: You do. You must do. You just look natural.

MARY: Not in a bloody party dress I don't. Not all done up in a party dress. It makes me feel like I did then, all flimsy and open and . . .

JO: And women love it.

MARY: What?

JO: Being sexy.

MARY: Do they?

JO: Course they do.

MARY: And what's being sexy?

JO: Oh come on.

MARY: Feeling like this?

JO: Yes. What's wrong with that?

MARY: It feels horrible.

JO: Why can't you enjoy it?

MARY: Because . . .

JO: You won't let yourself will you? Just relax.

MARY: I'm trying.

JO: You've got to feel good about yourself or nothing'll happen.

MARY: Nothing like what?

JO: I'm going to count to ten and then I'm going to *scream.*

MARY: So this looks sexy does it? *(Holding the dress up against her.)*

JO: Course it does . . . No, it doesn't. It doesn't look sexy at all. Okay?

MARY: No. I feel like someone else. I feel funny and peculiar and a million miles from confident and that's fine and terrific and just as it should be and I'm to go out and enjoy myself. Right?

JO: Yes.

MARY: That's what you want me to do?

JO: Yes. 'Cos you will. You're just nervous. I'm nervous for Heaven's sake.

MARY: Are you?

JO: Yes. No.

MARY: Which?

JO: I don't know.

MARY: But what . . .

JO: Stop asking questions. You'll disappear up your own bum.

MARY: I think I'm in a coma.

JO: Well rally round or we'll be late.

MARY: "Pornography's the tip of the iceberg." Somebody said that.

JO: Oh my God. Cut my wrists. Cut my wrists.

MARY: They were right.

JO: And we've all got to learn to live with it.

MARY: I can't . . .

LOW LEVEL PANIC
by Clare McIntyre

Cockney British: Two Females

THE PLAY: A disturbing look into the lives of young, single, working women in present-day London as they deal with feeling like prey for the men in the world, *Low Level Panic* is an intense, contemporary one-act with mature language and theme.

THE SCENE: Jo (20 to 22) has just returned from the party she had taken her roommates to, and she finds Mary (20 to 22) dyeing her dress and sheets in the bathtub in the middle of the night.

TIME AND PLACE: Present. London. A flat (apartment) in a populated area of the city. Middle of the night. The bathroom of the flat (not the toilet, which is separate).

Later that night after the party. Jo comes in to the bathroom which is in virtual darkness. Any light there is in the room is coming through the window from outside as the light in the room itself is out. Jo switches on the light to reveal Mary kneeling beside the bath with both her arms in the tub. She is wearing daytime clothes and has on a pair of rubber gloves. Jo is still in her party clothes.

JO: Jesus Christ you gave me a fright!
MARY: Hello.
JO: What are you doing?
MARY: Umnn?
JO: What are you doing?
MARY: Seeing what my sheets'll look like in the dark.
JO: What?
MARY: I'm just seeing what my sheets'll look like in the dark.
JO: What on *earth* are you doing?
MARY: I'm dyeing my sheets.
JO: Bloody Hell. (*She goes out switching off the light as she goes. Mary swirls the sheets round. Jo comes back. She has changed into her slippers.*)
  Do you know what time it is?

MARY: No.

JO: It's the middle of the bloody night.

MARY: Is it?

JO: Just thought I'd mention it.

MARY: I couldn't sleep.

> *(Pause.)*

JO: God I always do it. I always bloody do it. I always guffaw at parties. Always. I don't know why I can't seem to keep a check on myself. I can't seem to see what a twit I'm being until I'm out on the street, on my own, on my way home. Then I have instant, total recall of every stupid, awful, embarrassing thing I said . . . I wish I didn't have such a loud laugh. It's deafening. Even in a room full of people shouting it's deafening. I can't seem to keep quiet and enigmatic and let other people do the approaching. But what if nobody does? What then? What if everyone avoids me all evening . . . ? Nobody talks more than me at parties. As soon as I feel unrelaxed my mouth opens and out come a million questions. I just come across as terribly, terribly interested in everyone there. That's why people want me to go to their sodding parties. At least I'll talk. Am I terribly loud?

MARY: No.

JO: Do I act the fool?

MARY: I don't think so. *(She holds up her party dress out of the bath. She has been dyeing it along with the sheets.)* What do you think?

JO: Is that your . . . ?

MARY: Yeah. I've dyed it.

JO: So I see.

MARY: What do you think?

JO: You're ruined it.

MARY: Why?

JO: Look at it.

MARY: I haven't ruined it.

JO: What have you gone and done that for?

MARY: I didn't like it.

JO: Ask a silly question get a silly . . .

MARY: It's a nice colour isn't it?

JO: What are you trying to prove?

MARY: What do you mean?

JO: That we shouldn't have bought it?

MARY: No.

JO: Sure?

MARY: Yes. I'm not trying to prove anything.

JO: Aren't you?

MARY: No.

JO: It might be a nice colour. You can't really tell when it's wet . . . *(Feeling her armpits.)* God I'm sweating. There's a swamp up here. Was I sweating like this all evening?

MARY: I'm going to wear it with a sweatshirt over it. It'll just look like a skirt.

JO: I must have been sweating nonstop. Look at the tidemarks.

MARY: It'll look all right.

JO: That's nerves you know.

MARY: What is?

JO: Sweating like this.

MARY: Is it?

JO: You should have got someone to do it properly if you wanted to do it. You can never get the colour even yourself and it's "dry clean only" isn't it?

MARY: I don't know. I didn't look.

JO: That sort of thing always is.

MARY: Never mind.

JO: I'd never have let you buy it if I'd known you'd . . .

MARY: God I'll wear it now. I'd never have worn it again like it was.

JO: I really thought you'd wear it.

MARY: No way. Clingy party dresses aren't really my thing are they?

JO: They could be.

MARY: I'm going to look like I feel, not like someone else's idea of what they think I'm feeling like.

JO: Come again.

MARY: Ummn?

JO: You're going to look like your idea . . .

MARY: If you're comfy in jeans and a T-shirt wear jeans and a T-shirt. Why make yourself miserable trying to be something you're not.

JO: Ah yes. Now that sounds more like it.

MARY: More like what?

JO: You *are* trying to make a point.

MARY: Who to? I've dyed the dress so I'll wear it because I'd never have worn it how it was because I don't like wearing things that make me feel naked.

JO: Did you hate it?

MARY: What?

JO: The party?

MARY: It was okay.

JO: What you don't like in the world isn't going to go away because you go and do something weird like dye a party dress.

MARY: Why are you trying to turn this into some kind of big gesture?

JO: Well it is isn't it?

MARY: No.

JO: It looks like a big gesture to me.

MARY: Why?

JO: 'Cos it's such a bizarre thing to be doing. It's the middle of the night and you're sloshing this stuff around in the bath, in the dark and you've gone and deliberately ruined a very nice dress.

MARY: Will you stop saying that. It's going to look fine. You wait.

JO: It is a weird thing to do though you must admit.

MARY: I suppose so.

JO: I mean I don't usually come back from a party and throw my dress into a bath full of dye.

MARY: Nor do I.

JO: I suppose it might look all right with a sweatshirt.

MARY: It will. I know it will. *(She wrings the dress out and puts it on a hanger.)*

JO: Well I did my best. I got you all glammed up and looking fabulous and . . .

MARY: Oh I enjoyed the party. I mean it was all right. I didn't hate it or anything. 'Cept there wasn't any food.

JO: You only stayed ten minutes.

MARY: No I didn't. Honestly I stayed . . .

JO: Twenty.

MARY: Did you enjoy it?

JO: I didn't meet anyone if that's what you mean. Nothing happened. I don't know if anyone met anyone but I know I didn't. There didn't seem to be anyone there that I could see: nobody that you'd want to . . .

MARY: No.

JO: *(Inspecting her face in the mirror.)* People are different now aren't they? Maybe parties aren't where you meet people any more.

MARY: It was very loud.

JO: Maybe you've got to join a club or have hobbies or something. It's weird to think about isn't it?

MARY: What?

JO: Whether to be worried or not . . . Whether to do it or not. Mind you I don't know what I'm talking about 'cos there wasn't anyone there to do it with was there?

MARY: Now admit it it looks all right.

JO: Maybe.

MARY: Not a streak in sight.

JO: No but it's shrunk.

MARY: Has it?

JO: But you'll wear it. I can see you wearing it. You've gone and wrecked it but you'll wear it won't you?

MARY: Yup.

JO: And you're happy now aren't you?

MARY: Yup.

JO: It's still a shame.

MARY: I don't think so.

JO: You looked so good in it. *(She is inspecting her face in the mirror.)*

MARY: Where would you be without a mirror?

JO: Dunno.

MARY: You'd really be at a loose end wouldn't you?

JO: Shut your trap. You're getting as bad as Celia.

MARY: She met someone.

JO: What?

MARY: She met someone.

JO: How do you know?

MARY: She came back with him.

JO: How do you know?

MARY: She did.

JO: You're kidding.

MARY: Sh.

JO: Jesus.

MARY: Shh.

JO: *Jesus.*

MARY: Shut up.

JO: Who?

MARY: I don't know. Some bloke.

JO: Who?

MARY: How should I know?

JO: I don't believe it . . . Really . . . ? You're taking the piss.

MARY: Yes. Really.

JO: But there wasn't anyone there . . . Bloody hell. She wouldn't even have been there if it hadn't been for me, if I hadn't invited her. I don't know why I did. Sometimes I feel sorry for her I suppose.

MARY: There's no need to feel sorry for Celia.

JO: How did she meet someone? There wasn't anyone there apart from a bunch of pricks.

MARY: Maybe she met a prick.

JO: Are they noisy?

MARY: I don't know.

JO: Go on.

MARY: I don't know. Why don't you go down and ask them?

JO: Go on say.

MARY: Say what?

JO: *(Opens the door and listens.)* I wonder if you can hear them from here.

MARY: I don't know.

JO: If they were really noisy you could.

MARY: I'll bet they can hear you.

JO: Sh.

MARY: You're the one who's making all the noise.

JO: Listen.

MARY: Why are you so interested?

JO: I'm not.

MARY: You could have fooled me.

JO: Sh.

MARY: You're jealous.

JO: Course I am.

MARY: Beats me.

JO: Sh. Sh.

MARY: Don't be so childish.

JO: What beats you?

MARY: What makes you tick?

JO: Why?

MARY: You don't know what you do want do you?

JO: Oh come off it. I'm not jealous really. All the men at that party were repulsive.

MARY: Exactly.

JO: But . . .

MARY: But what?

JO: Nothing.

MARY: What?

JO: Sometimes I'd rather be with anybody than nobody I suppose. That's all.

MARY: You wouldn't really.

JO: Yes I would. Believe me I would.

MARY: Even somebody you didn't like?

JO: Yes.

MARY: Even somebody from that party?

JO: Yes.

MARY: Somebody you didn't even find attractive?

JO: Yes.

MARY: You don't mean that.

JO: I do.

MARY: Why?

JO: Because I would.

MARY: How can you possibly say that? You wouldn't enjoy that at all.

JO: I would.

MARY: How?

JO: You're so bloody naive, Mary.

MARY: I don't understand you at all.

THE MILL ON THE FLOSS
by George Eliot; adapted by Helen Edmundson

Standard British: One Male and One Female

THE PLAY: Set in Victorian England, *The Mill on the Floss* is an adaptation of the famous novel of the same name. Using the device of actors playing multiple characters, and multiple actors playing *one* character, the story of family loyalty and love between rivals is brought to life. Maggie is played by three different actresses representing three distinct periods in her lifetime. As she grows up, and the events of her life propel her forward and force certain restrictions on her, the Maggies of the past come into her consciousness and remind her of herself.

THE SCENE: After the death of her father, and the curse he laid on Phillip's family, Maggie becomes more spiritual and introspective, shedding the skin of the bold and outspoken child she once was. Her favorite place of solace is the forest called the Red Deeps (named after the Scotch fir trees). In this scene, Maggie (14 to 15) is startled to see Phillip (17 to 18) in her part of the forest. Her feelings for him are forbidden by the wishes of her family, and she must struggle to keep them in check.

TIME AND PLACE: Victorian England. Near the Tewkesbury Mill on the River Avon (the Floss is a fictional river, but many think that Eliot was referring to the river near her home). The Red Deeps forest. Daytime.

Maggie is walking in the Red Deeps. Phillip appears. He raises his hat, then holds out his hand to her. She takes it.

MAGGIE: You startled me. I never meet anyone here.

PHILLIP: Forgive me. I needed to see you. I've been watching our house for days to see if you would come out. I followed you.

MAGGIE: I'm glad. I wished very much to have an opportunity of speaking to you. Shall we talk?
(They do so. It is as if they are in a dream.)
I like the light here. And the Scotch firs. It is so different from the other scenery about.

PHILLIP: Yes. I remember coming here once, as a child.

MAGGIE: I was frightened to come. The Red Deeps . . . I thought all kinds of devils and wild beasts lurked here. *(Pause.)* I have often thought of you.

PHILLIP: Not so often as I have thought of you.

MAGGIE: I wasn't sure you would remember me.

(Phillip takes a miniature case from his pocket and hands it to her.)

PHILLIP: It's a picture I painted of you on the last day of your visit. In the study . . .

MAGGIE: I remember my hair like that, and that pink frock. I really was like a gypsy. I suppose I still am. Am I how you expected me to be?

PHILLIP: No. You are very much more beautiful.

(Pause.)

MAGGIE: Phillip, you must go now and we must not see each other again. I wish we could be friends . . . I wish it could have been good and right for us, but it is not. I have lost everything I loved when I was little; the old books went, and Tom is different and my father — it is like death. But that is how it must be. I wanted you to know that if I behave as if I had forgotten you, it is not out of pride or — any bad feeling.

PHILLIP: I know what there is to keep us apart, Maggie. I would always want to obey my father but I will not, cannot obey a wish of his that I do not feel to be right.

MAGGIE: I don't know . . . I have sometimes thought that I shouldn't have to give up anything and I've gone on thinking that until it seems I have no duty at all. But that is an evil state of mind. I would rather do without anything than make my father's life harder. He is not at all happy.

PHILLIP: Neither am I. I am not happy.

MAGGIE: I am very sorry that you say that. I have a guide now, Phillip — Thomas à Kempis. Perhaps you have read him. His words are the only ones that make sense to me. I have been so much happier since I gave up thinking about what is easy and pleasant and being discontented because I couldn't have my own way. Our life is determined for us and it makes the mind very free when we give up wishing and only think of bearing what is laid upon us.

PHILLIP: For goodness sake, Maggie. I can't give up wishing. How can we give up wishing and longing while we are thoroughly alive? *(Pause.)* I'm sorry. I have no friend . . . no one who cares enough for me. If I could only see you now and then and you would let me talk to you and show me that you cared for me and that we may always be friends in our hearts — then I might come to be glad of my life.

MAGGIE: Oh, Phillip . . .

PHILLIP: If there is enmity between those who belong to us we ought to try to mend it with our friendship. You must see that.

(Pause.)

MAGGIE: I can't say either yes or no. I must wait and seek for guidance.

PHILLIP: Let me see you here once more. If you can't tell me when, I will come as often as I can until I do see you.

MAGGIE: Do so, then. *(Pause. They smile.)* How were you so sure that I would be the same Maggie?

PHILLIP: I never doubted you would be the same. I don't know why I was so sure; I think there must be stores laid up in our natures that our understandings can make no inventory of. It's like music; there are certain strains which change my whole attitude of mind. If the effect would last I might be capable of heroisms.

MAGGIE: I know what you mean — or at least, I used to. I never hear music now except the organ at church.

PHILLIP: You can have very little that is beautiful in your life. *(Taking a book from his pocket.)* Have this. I've finished with it.

MAGGIE: I've given up books. Except Thomas à Kempis and The Christian Year and the Bible. *(He offers it again.)* Don't Phillip.

(She walks on quickly.)

PHILLIP: Maggie, don't go without saying good-bye. I can't go on any farther, I think.

MAGGIE: Of course. Good-bye. What a beautiful thing it seems that God made your heart so that you could care about a strange little girl you only knew for a few weeks. I think you cared more for me than Tom did.

PHILLIP: You would never love me so well as you love your brother.

MAGGIE: Perhaps not . . . but then, the first thing I remember in my life is standing with Tom by the side of the Floss, while he held my hand; everything before that is dark to me.

PHILLIP: I kept that little girl in my heart for five years; didn't I earn some part in her too?

THE MILL ON THE FLOSS
by George Eliot; adapted by Helen Edmundson

Standard British: One Male and One Female

THE PLAY: Set in Victorian England, *The Mill on the Floss* is an adaptation of the famous novel of the same name. Using the device of actors playing multiple characters, and multiple actors playing *one* character, the story of family loyalty and love between rivals is brought to life. Maggie is played by three different actresses representing three distinct periods in her lifetime. As she grows up, and the events of her life propel her forward and force certain restrictions on her, the Maggies of the past come into her consciousness and remind her of herself.

THE SCENE: After the death of her father, and the curse he laid on Phillip's family, Maggie becomes more spiritual and introspective, shedding the skin of the bold and outspoken child she once was. Her favorite place of solace is the forest called the Red Deeps (named after the Scotch fir trees). In this scene, Maggie (14 to 15) has told Phillip (17 to 18) that she mustn't see him again, and yet he still pursues her. She attempts to break it off, and then the spirit of her younger self takes over.

TIME AND PLACE: Victorian England. Near the Tewkesbury Mill on the River Avon (the Floss is a fictional river, but many think that Eliot was referring to the river near her home). The Red Deeps forest. Daytime.

Phillip is there. His face lights up when he sees Maggie.

PHILLIP: Maggie . . .

MAGGIE: This is the last time, Phillip. I don't like to conceal anything from my family. I won't do it. I know their feelings are wrong and unchristian but it makes no difference. We must part.
(Pause.)

PHILLIP: Then stay with me for a while and let us talk together. Will you take my hand? *(She does so. They walk.)*

PHILLIP: I have begun another painting of you. In oils, this time. You will look like a spirit creeping from one of the fir trees.

MAGGIE: Phillip, did you mean it when you said you are unhappy and that your life means nothing to you?

PHILLIP: Yes.

MAGGIE: But why? You have so much . . . your painting, your music, your books. You can travel . . .

PHILLIP: Oh yes, I have a great number of interests. I flit from one to the other at will. I daresay that would be enough for me if I were like other men. But I am not, am I? The society at St. Oggs sickens me. I am sure it is sickened by me. My life sickens me.

MAGGIE: I understand what you mean. Sometimes it seems to me that life is very hard and unbearable. But, Phillip, I think we are only like children, and someone who is wiser is taking care of us.

PHILLIP: Ah yes. You have your guide to show you the way.

MAGGIE: Yes I do. Are you mocking me, Phillip?

PHILLIP: No. I only wonder how long you can go on with this.

MAGGIE: I have found great peace this last year — even joy in subduing my will.

PHILLIP: No you haven't.

MAGGIE: I have resigned myself. I bear everything . . .

PHILLIP: You are not resigned. You are only trying to stupefy yourself. It is stupefaction to shut up all the avenues by which you might engage in life.

MAGGIE: I don't want to engage in life.

PHILLIP: You were so full of life when you were a child. I thought you would be a brilliant woman — all wit and imagination. And it flashes out in your face still — there! But then you draw that veil across.

MAGGIE: Why do you speak so bitterly to me?

PHILLIP: Because I care. I can't bear to see you go on with this self-torture.

MAGGIE: I will have strength given me.

PHILLIP: No one is given strength to do what is unnatural. You will be thrown into the world someday and then all your needs will assault you like a savage appetite.

MAGGIE: How dare you shake me in this way. You are a tempter.

PHILLIP: No, I am not. But love gives insight. Maggie.

(Pause. Maggie is confused and shocked.)

Do you really want to get up every day for the rest of your life and have no company but that of your parents, nothing to do but to read your Bible? Day after day. Think about it. *(Pause.)* I suppose you will never agree to see me now. *(Pause.)* What if I came to walk here sometimes, and met you by chance? You would not have agreed to meet me. There would be no concealment in that.

(She looks at him. There is some relief in her eyes, but she says nothing. Phillip goes, feeling he has cause for hope.)

(The crowd has gathered above. They repeat some of the gestures used in testing the witch.)

(Maggie falls to her knees, and begins to pray. First Maggie enters and tries to interrupt her prayer. Second Maggie moves away and keeps praying. First Maggie follows her — Second Maggie moves. This goes on for some time until she cannot go on with her prayer. She turns to First Maggie and embraces her.)

SECOND MAGGIE: Go then.

(First Maggie runs to Phillip who is waiting in the Red Deeps. She throws her arms around him. They laugh.)

PHILLIP: Maggie, you promised you would kiss me when you met me again. Do you remember? You haven't kept your promise yet.

(She kisses him. It is the same simple, childish kiss. Phillip looks lovingly at Second Maggie, as he and First Maggie walk away together, hand in hand. Music.)

ROSENCRANTZ AND GUILDENSTERN ARE DEAD
by Tom Stoppard

Standard or Cockney British: Two Males

THE PLAY: The brilliant Mr. Stoppard gives us a witty, behind the scenes look into the lives of Hamlet's friends, Rosencrantz and Guildenstern, before and after they meet up with Hamlet at Elsinore.

THE SCENE: While waiting to meet up with Hamlet, Rosencrantz (20 to 22) and Guildenstern (20 to 22) attempt to distract themselves from the odd events occurring at the castle.

TIME AND PLACE: Two Elizabethans passing the time in a place without any visible character.

ROSENCRANTZ: We could play at questions.

GUILDENSTERN: What good would that do?

ROSENCRANTZ: Practice!

GUILDENSTERN: Statement! One — love.

ROSENCRANTZ: Cheating!

GUILDENSTERN: How?

ROSENCRANTZ: I hadn't started yet.

GUILDENSTERN: Statement. Two — love.

ROSENCRANTZ: Are you counting that?

GUILDENSTERN: What?

ROSENCRANTZ: Are you counting that?

GUILDENSTERN: Foul! No repetitions. Three — love. First game to . . .

ROSENCRANTZ: I'm not going to play if you're going to be like that.

GUILDENSTERN: Whose serve?

ROSENCRANTZ: Hah?

GUILDENSTERN: Foul! No grunts. Love —one.

ROSENCRANTZ: Whose go?

GUILDENSTERN: Why?

ROSENCRANTZ: Why not?

GUILDENSTERN: What for?

ROSENCRANTZ: Foul! No synonyms! One — all.

GUILDENSTERN: What in God's name is going on?

ROSENCRANTZ: Foul! No rhetoric. Two — one.

GUILDENSTERN: What does it all add up to?

ROSENCRANTZ: Can't you guess?

GUILDENSTERN: Were you addressing me?

ROSENCRANTZ: Is there anyone else?

GUILDENSTERN: Who?

ROSENCRANTZ: How would I know?

GUILDENSTERN: Why do you ask?

ROSENCRANTZ: Are you serious?

GUILDENSTERN: Was that rhetoric?

ROSENCRANTZ: No.

GUILDENSTERN: Statement! Two — all. Game point.

ROSENCRANTZ: What's the matter with you today?

GUILDENSTERN: When?

ROSENCRANTZ: What?

GUILDENSTERN: Are you deaf?

ROSENCRANTZ: Am I dead?

GUILDENSTERN: Yes or no?

ROSENCRANTZ: Is there a choice?

GUILDENSTERN: Is there a God?

ROSENCRANTZ: Foul! No *non sequiturs,* three — two, one game all.

GUILDENSTERN: *(Seriously.)* What's your name?

ROSENCRANTZ: What's yours?

GUILDENSTERN: I asked you first.

ROSENCRANTZ: Statement. One — love.

GUILDENSTERN: What's your name when you're at home?

ROSENCRANTZ: What's yours?

GUILDENSTERN: When I'm at home?

ROSENCRANTZ: Is it different at home?

GUILDENSTERN: What home?

ROSENCRANTZ: Haven't you got one?

GUILDENSTERN: Why do you ask?

ROSENCRANTZ: What are you driving at?

GUILDENSTERN: *(With emphasis.)* What's your name?!

ROSENCRANTZ: Repetition. Two — love. Match point to me.

GUILDENSTERN: *(Seizing him violently.)* WHO DO YOU THINK YOU ARE?

ROSENCRANTZ: Rhetoric! Game and match! *(Pause.)* Where's it going to end?

GUILDENSTERN: That's the question.

ROSENCRANTZ: It's *all* questions.

GUILDENSTERN: Do you think it matters?

ROSENCRANTZ: Doesn't it matter to you?

GUILDENSTERN: Why should it matter?

ROSENCRANTZ: What does it matter why?

GUILDENSTERN: *(Teasing gently.)* Doesn't it *matter* why it matters?

ROSENCRANTZ: *(Rounding on him.)* What the *matter* with you?
   (Pause.)

GUILDENSTERN: It doesn't matter.

ROSENCRANTZ: *(Voice in the wilderness.)* . . . What's the game?

GUILDENSTERN: What are the rules?
   *(Enter Hamlet behind, crossing the stage, reading a book — as he is about
   to disappear Guildenstern notices him.)*

GUILDENSTERN: *(Sharply.)* Rosencrantz!

ROSENCRANTZ: *(Jumps.)* What!
   (Hamlet goes. Triumph dawns on them, they smile.)

GUILDENSTERN: There! How was that?

ROSENCRANTZ: Clever!

GUILDENSTERN: Natural?

ROSENCRANTZ: Instinctive.

GUILDENSTERN: Got it in your head?

ROSENCRANTZ: I take my hat off to you.

GUILDENSTERN: Shake hands.

SECTION TWO
IRISH

IRISH INTRODUCTION

With its enchanting musical inflection and the colloquial use of colorful expressions, it is no wonder that the Irish dialect is one of the most popular dialects in today's theater scene. Indeed, with the abundance of Irish works being staged all over America, many actors are hurrying to the nearest dialect coach to develop an Irish accent. Not only can the dialect be heard on many American stages, but it can also be found in many popular films in our video stores and movie theaters.

Just as there are many dialect variations of Standard British, there are many dialect variations of Irish. Northern Ireland, a separate nation, has a distinctly different dialect than its near neighbor, Northwest Ireland. The West Ireland dialect (namely Galway) differs greatly from the more metropolitan (lighter) dialect of Dublin (located in Eastern Ireland). Then there's County Cork, thought by some to contain the most lyrical and "traditional" of the Irish dialects. What Americans tend to do when they fake an Irish accent is a bad version of County Cork sounds.

For our purposes, we will apply some general, consistent sound changes that should give you a general, mostly West Ireland–sounding dialect.

The Irish dialect can trace its roots to the original speakers of the Celtic language — the Pagans who originally inhabited Ireland. Because their religious rituals were not written down, they passed on their traditions and stories by singing. As the language evolved, and the social structure of Ireland evolved (due to the conquering peoples which took over the land), the dialect evolved into a singing version of English.

The music of the Irish dialect is key to its reproduction, but it can become too singsong if you are not careful. Always remember the point of the sentence, not the notes.

The Irish people are warm, hospitable, and generous, and they are masters at conversation. Their speech is filled with proverbs, metaphors, clichés and quotations from plays, songs, or films. There is a joy in speaking that comes through in the delivery. This is not to say that there are no sad people in Ireland; indeed, there is always a sense of deep-seated sorrow at the core of the Irish, but this sorrow is masked in the twinkling of the "Irish eyes."

As with any dialect, you must first know your character's life circumstances to accurately reproduce his or her speech patterns. With the Irish, this is important to avoid overgeneralizing your approach to the material and playing simply a singsong action on your lines. Subtler is better with the Irish dialect.

- When telling a story or personal anecdote, the music of the Irish dialect is more present than when simply speaking a normal sentence. For example, if you were to tell your parents about an incident that happened to you at school that really affected you, your voice would become more animated and energized. The same is true for the strength of the Irish dialect. When they are narrating a story, they color it with all the vocal colors they can. The music plays in their voices.

- Due perhaps in part to the origins of the Irish culture (Celtic, Pagan tribes), and the exceedingly harsh conditions (cold, rural, isolated, semi-barren land) in which they have lived over the past hundreds of years, the Irish have a tendency to be a spiritual people. Although the dominant religion at this time is Catholicism, the Irish have been known to believe in (or tell stories about) things that are of a more fantastical or imaginary nature (i.e., fairies, banshees, and leprechauns). Historically, the Irish needed to explain their tragedies away, and belief in the supernatural sometimes seemed the only comfort.

- The Irish dialect is musical. The music comes from extending the length of the vowel sounds and moving the pitch/note of the sound up and down.

- Again, due to environmental conditions (cold, fog, wind) there is a lack of mouth opening and movement when the Irish produce sounds.

- Because the Irish use so many quotations, proverbs, and clichés in their everyday speech, they tend to speak faster than the average person. They compose their thoughts quickly and with the skill of old, professional orators.

- When the Irish *do* pause to compose a thought, the nonverbal interjection they use instead of our American *um* is *am*.

- More noticeably than with the English accents, the Irish have colloquialisms that are more rhythmic in their literature. Usually these phrases, words or interjections are not to be taken literally but poetically as part of the natural rhythm of the line.

- The Irish do a few vowel sounds with a sense of tightening and closing of the lips. These sounds are traditionally diphthongs (two vowel sounds made in the time of one), but they make only the first sound of the diphthong and hold it for a longer time. To master these sounds, you must first observe what your mouth does when it makes these sounds normally. It is called "Irish lengthening" in the section that follows.

Irish Film, Television, and Audio References

Films

Rural West Ireland:
Riders to the Sea
The Butcher Boy
Waking Ned Devine
Angela's Ashes

Rural North Ireland (Donegal):
Dancing at Lughnasa
The Field
The Secret of Roan Inish
The Closer You Get

North Ireland (Belfast):
Michael Collins
In the Name of the Father
The Crying Game
Titanic Town

South Ireland (Dublin):
My Left Foot
The Commitments
Circle of Friends

Americanized Irish (actors doing Irish accents):
The Brothers McMullen
Far and Away

Television
PBS Special: "The Irish in America"

Dialect Tapes and Sources
Irish   Gillian Lane-Plescia
Stage Dialects and More Stage Dialects Jerry Blunt
Dialects for the Stage   Evangeline Machlin
Acting with an Accent — Irish   David Alan Stern
IDEA website   www.ukans.edu/~idea/index.html

For a more complete and detailed list of films/resources, see Ginny Kopf's book The Dialect Handbook.

Irish Elements and Sounds

- The *r* of the Irish: Unlike the Standard British dialect, the Irish produce what we call a hard *r*. The hard *r* sound is produced with the tongue arching up towards gum ridge behind the top teeth. The *r* is not trilled like the Scots, but just pronounced.

- The Irish lengthening: When producing these sounds, always make sure that your voice stays supported and well placed, otherwise the tension may cause some vocal exhaustion.

  [oh] → [o:] don't, go, show, slow, road → do:n't, go:, sho:, slo:, ro:d (round your lips to make the [oh] sound and then keep them there, don't let them move as you say [o:] out loud. Add some time to it and hold the sound now.)

  [ay] → [eh] take, name, face, Kate, plate → te:k, ne:m, fe:s, Ke:t, ple:t (smile and prepare to make the [ay] sound but keep your mouth in position and lengthen the first half of the sound only.)

- Other Irish vowel/consonant changes:

  [ih] → [eh] hill, different, dig, quick, thick → hehll, dehfrent, dehg, quehck, thehck

  [uh] → [u] (the schwa sound becomes more like the [u] sound as in the word "put" or "took") mother, from, love, button, won → muther, frum, luv, buttn, wun

  [th] → [t] thirty, cathedrals, thanked, theater → tairty, catedrals, tanked, teater

  [th] → [dh] this, them, those, weather → dhis, dhem, dhose, weadher

  [ing] → [in] drop the *g* on -ing endings

  [er/ir] → [air] girl, heard, bird → gairl, haird, baird

[or] → [are] word, storm, forth → ward, starm, farth

[ow] → [uh-oo] now, town, without → nuh-oo, tuh-oon, wit uh-oot

[oy] → [y] boy, joy, noise, toys → by, jy, nyz, tyz
(occasional change)

[y] → [oy] Ireland, my, kite → oyrland, moy, koyt
(occasional change)

[t]/[d] → [t(h)/d(h)] better, door, drink, what, write → bet(h)er,
d(h)oor, d(h)rink, what(h), wroyt(h)
The consonant [t] and [d] sounds are dentalized (meaning your tongue is
touching the back of your top teeth) and lots of air falls off those sounds.
In some Irish plays, this element of the dialect is spelled out in the script
writing by adding an [h] after the [t] or [d] (i.e., "better" would be written
"betther"). Just think of the [h] symbol as a clue to have a bit more air
come out after you make the consonant sound.

[a] becomes not as crisp as the Pure Anne sound. Round your lips and say
"ah" and then smile to make this sound in the words like "grand," "Pat,"
"and," etc. Another way to think of this sound is to imagine the American
Southern way of saying "I."
Words: grand, fan, pat, wrap, flat, cat, Anne, Adam, stand, ran, land

IRISH PRACTICE SENTENCES

[r]

Here where their car started the yard parted. Park your car and start your heart.

[o:]

Go slow near the show by the road, Joe. The crow ate the doe.

[e:]

You can take me name but you can't take me face. Stay Kate, stay and play with Kay.

[ih] → [eh]

The hills look different when you dig. Quick, pick up the stick, ya thick!

[uh] → [u]

Me mother loves me brother more. I won a button from London.

[th] → [t]

The thirty cathedrals thought the theater was through. Thanks for the oath of thinking.

[ing] → [in]

The crying working man was drinking and thinking about skiing.

[er/ir] → [air]

The first bird is early and dirty.

[or] → [are]

Work is the worst when it hurts.

[ow] → [uh-oo]

Now the sound of the round crowd fills the town. The crown fell down on the ground.

[oy] → [y]

Me boy's toys make a load of noise. The joy is noisy in the Toy Shoppe.

[y] → [oy]

Ireland is the right bright light. At night the sky is ripe with flying spies.

[t/d] → [t(h)/d(h)]

You'd better not drink that water. Don't drink drunk. Take that tired talk home.

THE CRIPPLE OF INISHMAAN
by Martin McDonagh

Irish: One Male and One Female

THE PLAY: Set on the remote Aran Island of Inishmaan, this rich, poignant story of a young man dreaming to escape the boundaries of his island life is at once compelling, humorous, and ultimately stark and tragic.

THE SCENE: Cripple Billy (18) has just returned from his adventures in America, where he went to become an actor. He got to America, in part, by deceiving the villager Babbybobby. Upon his return, Babbybobby exacts his revenge by beating him with a lead pipe. His village friend, and object of his affection, Slippy Helen (18) comes by to see his wounds, prompting Billy to summon up the courage to finally speak his mind.

TIME AND PLACE: Inishmaan, Aran Islands. Ireland. 1934. Early evening. Billy's Aunties' store/home.

Helen pulls up Billy's bandages to look under them.

BILLY: Hurts a bit that picking does, Helen.
HELEN: Ar don't be such a fecking girl, Cripple Billy. How was America?
BILLY: Fine, fine.
HELEN: Did you see any girls over there as pretty as me?
BILLY: Not a one.
HELEN: Or almost as pretty as me?
BILLY: Not a one.
HELEN: Or even a hundred times *less* pretty than me?
BILLY: Well, maybe a couple, now.
    (Helen pokes him hard in the face.)
BILLY: *(In pain.)* Aargh! Not a one, I mean.
HELEN: You just watch yourself you, Cripple Billy.
BILLY: Do ya have to be so violent, Helen?
HELEN: I do have to be so violent, or if I'm not to be taken advantage of anyways I have to be so violent.
BILLY: Sure, nobody's taken advantage of you since the age of seven, Helen.
HELEN: Six is nearer the mark. I ruptured a curate at six.

BILLY: So couldn't you tone down a bit of your violence and be more of a sweet girl?

HELEN: I could, you're right there. And the day after I could shove a bent spike up me arse. *(Pause.)* I've just lost me job with the egg man.

BILLY: Why did you lose your job with the egg man, Helen?

HELEN: D'you know, I can't for the life of me figure out why. Maybe it was me lack of punctuality. Or me breaking all the egg man's eggs. Or me giving him a good kick whenever I felt like it. But you couldn't call them decent reasons.

BILLY: You couldn't at all, sure.

HELEN: Or me spitting on the egg man's wife, but you couldn't call that a decent reason.

BILLY: What did you spit on the egg man's wife for, Helen?

HELEN: Ah the egg man's wife just deserves spitting on. *(Pause.)* I still haven't given you a good kick for your taking your place in Hollywood that was rightfully mine. Didn't I have to kiss four of the film directors on Inishmore to book me place you took without a single kiss?

BILLY: But there was only *one* film director on Inishmore that time, Helen. The man Flaherty. And I didn't see you near him at all.

HELEN: Who was it I was kissing so?

BILLY: I think it was mostly stable boys who could do an American accent.

HELEN: The bastards! Couldn't you've warned me?

BILLY: I was going to warn you, but you seemed to be enjoying yourself.

HELEN: You do get a decent kiss off a stable boy, is true enough. I would probably go stepping out with a stable boy if truth be told, if it wasn't for the smell of pig-shite you get off them.

BILLY: Are you not stepping out with anyone at the moment, so?

HELEN: I'm not.

BILLY: *(Pause.)* Me, I've never been kissed.

HELEN: Of course you've never been kissed. You're a funny-looking cripple boy.

BILLY: *(Pause.)* It's funny, but when I was in America I tried to think of all the things I'd miss about home if I had to stay in America. Would I miss the scenery, I thought? The stone walls, and the lanes, and the green, and the sea? No, I wouldn't miss them. Would I miss the food? The peas, the praities, the peas, the praities and the peas? No, I wouldn't miss it. Would I miss the people?

HELEN: Is this speech going to go on for more long?

BILLY: I've nearly finished it. *(Pause.)* What was me last bit? You've put me off . . .

HELEN: "Would I miss the people."

BILLY: Would I miss the people? Well, I'd miss me aunties, or a *bit* I'd miss me aunties. I wouldn't miss Babbybobby with his lead stick or Johnnypateen with his daft news. Or all the lads used to laugh at me at school, or all the lasses used to cry if I even spoke to them. Thinking it over, if Inishmaan sank in the sea tomorrow, and everybody on it up and drowned, there isn't especially anybody I'd really miss. Anybody other than you, that is, Helen.

HELEN: *(Pause.)* You'd miss the cows you go staring at.

BILLY: Oh that cow business was blown up out of all proportion. What I was trying to build up to, Helen, was . . .

HELEN: Oh, was you trying to build up to something, Cripple Billy?

BILLY: I was, but you keep interrupting me.

HELEN: Build up ahead so.

BILLY: I was trying to build up to . . . There comes a time in every fella's life when he has to take his heart in his hands and make a try for something, and even though he knows it's a one in a million chance of him getting it, he has to chance it still, else why be alive at all? So, I was wondering, Helen, if maybe sometime, y'know, when you're not too busy or something, if maybe . . . and I know well I'm no great shakes to look at, but I was wondering if maybe you might want to go out walking with me some evening. Y'know, in a week or two or something?

HELEN: *(Pause.)* Sure what would I want to go out walking with a cripple boy for? It isn't out walking you'd be anyways, it would be out shuffling, because you can't walk. I'd have to be waiting for ya every five yards. What would you and me want to be out shuffling for?

BILLY: For the company.

HELEN: For the company?

BILLY: And . . .

HELEN: And what?

BILLY: And for the way sweethearts be.

A HANDFUL OF STARS
by Billy Roche

Irish: One Male and One Female

THE PLAY: Life in a small town for a young man with ambitions and dreams can be a study in frustration and resignation. Jimmy is on the cusp of his future in a small town in Ireland, and all his hometown heroes are still home in the small town pool hall, drinking, playing, and dreaming their lives away. The memory of a good moment in his life gives him hope that he may find the same sense of joy and completion—perhaps with his love, Linda. But soon, the desperation of his existence becomes too much for him to bear, and he explodes in a rampage that sets his future in stone.

THE SCENE: Jimmy and his girlfriend Linda (both 17) sneak into the local pub/pool hall for a private evening together. Jimmy's tale of his escape from the law gains mythic proportions as he retells it with pride to Linda.

TIME AND PLACE: The present. A small town in Ireland. A scruffy pool hall. Late night.

The Club in darkness. There is some commotion off stage and soon Jimmy comes into view, coming out of the toilet door. He goes across to the front door and opens it up. Linda steps in, Jimmy closing the door gently behind her and switching on the light. Linda stands just inside the door, looking around at the place, seemingly unimpressed. Jimmy goes across to the pot-bellied stove and starts banking it up with coal.

LINDA: I thought you said you had your own key.

JIMMY: No I said meself and Tony had our own private entrance.

LINDA: *(Moving a little deeper into the club.)* Oh! . . . How did you get in as a matter of interest?

JIMMY: What? There's a window broken in the jacks. It's been like that this ages. Meself and Tony let ourselves in and out of here whenever we've no place else to go. It's queer handy.

LINDA: Won't someone see the light shinin' from the street?

JIMMY: No. We checked that out. I had Tony stand down there one night and look up. Once those shutters are drawn you can't tell a thing.

LINDA: You have it well planned. All the same I think I'd prefer to be some-where else.

JIMMY: Look stop fussin'. I told yeh it was all right. *(Jimmy rubs his hands to-gether and stands up.)* A bit of heat now and we'll be elected. Poor Paddy will be hoverin' over this yoke tomorrow night, tryin' to figure out where all the coal is gone. I'm not coddin' yeh, meself and Tony were often here breakin' our hearts laughin' and Paddy looking at the half-empty bucket and scratchin' himself. We'd be after usin' all the coal up on him.

LINDA: Oh now you're a right pair of chancers.

(Jimmy sits on the bench. He watches her ramble around the club, touching the cues, caressing the table and finally coming to a standstill in front of the glass panel. She tries to see in but it is too dark.)

JIMMY: What do yeh think of it?

(Linda looks over her shoulder at him but doesn't bother to respond.)

LINDA: What's in there? The auld fella's office or somethin'?

JIMMY: What? No that's where the whatdoyoucallit go . . . the élite.

LINDA: The élite?

JIMMY: Yeah. Conway and all.

(She cups her hands and peers in. Jimmy rambles over closer to her, standing behind her.)

That's Tony's main ambition, yeh know?

LINDA: What is?

JIMMY: To get inside there.

LINDA: *(Ponders on the remark.)* Why don't he just break in there some night when the pair of yeh have the run of the place?

JIMMY: That's what I said. But no, that wouldn't do him at all.

LINDA: Why not?

JIMMY: *(Thinks about it.)* Tony's waitin' to be invited in.

LINDA: Invited? Who's goin' to invite him?

JIMMY: *(Putting on a deep voice.)* The men. *(He steps up to the slot machine and puts some money in, banging away at it.)* It's not just gettin' in there that matters to him yeh know? It's ah . . . I don't know.

LINDA: He wants to be accepted I suppose?

JIMMY: Yeah.

LINDA: *(Sarcastically.)* By the men?

JIMMY: I suppose so.

(Linda smirks at the very idea.)

LINDA: *(Taking down a cue, awkwardly taps around with a few loose balls that have been left on the table.)* And what about you?

JIMMY: Me? What about me?

LINDA: You mean to tell me you don't dream about gettin' in there too?

JIMMY: (Smiles at this remark.) Naw . . . I don't belong in there.

LINDA: Where do you belong then?

JIMMY: What? Where? I don't know. Not in there anyway that's for sure.

> (Jimmy is standing close to her now and the intimacy seems to make Linda uneasy. She breaks away, placing the cue across the table.)

LINDA: What's in there?

JIMMY: The jacks.

> (Linda backs out of the doorway, cringing at the stink of the place. She spots a cutting from a newspaper pinned up on the door that leads to the back room. She goes across to read it. Jimmy picks up the cue and starts to show off, taking up an exaggerated stance sprawling himself across the table.)

LINDA: "Chase over rooftops." (She glances towards him.)

JIMMY: (Takes his shot.) "A dramatic chase took place last Sunday night over rooftops on the South Main Street when a young man who was suspected of breaking and entering was pursued by Detective Garda Swan. The drama occurred when Detective Swan slipped and went tumbling down the slanted roof. Eye witnesses said that he was dangling from a considerable height, holding on to the gutter by the tips of his fingers. Ah . . ."

LINDA: "His cries for help . . ."

JIMMY: Oh yeah . . . "His cries for help were answered when the young man that he was chasing came back to assist him, a factor that later contributed to the leniency of the sentence." That's a deadly word ain't it? Leniency.

LINDA: "The judge said summing up that the defendant James Brady was a nuisance and a danger to the public. He resisted arrest and was constantly in trouble with the police. "The sooner he grows up the better for all of us."

JIMMY: Hey don't forget. "The probation act was applied."

LINDA: What did you do Jimmy, learn it off by heart or somethin?

JIMMY: The whole town has it off by heart. I'm famous sure. They don't know whether I should be crucified or ascended into heaven. I have about twelve of those cuttings at home. Every time Paddy rips one down I stick another up. Conway is ragin' . . . I don't know what you're lookin' at me like that for, I did it for you.

LINDA: (Baffled.) For me?

JIMMY: Yeah. I was skint. If I was goin' to take you somewhere I needed some money fast didn't I? I mean I couldn't turn up with no money again could I?

LINDA: And that's why you broke into the shop?

JIMMY: Ah I've been knockin' off that place for ages. It was a cinch. In through the window and the money was always left in the same drawer. The only thing was they had a trap set for me. There was all this dye or ink or somethin' all over the money and it stained all me hands and clothes. So when he picked me up he knew straight away that I was the one.

LINDA: And that's when you took off up onto the roof?

(Jimmy nods.)

I mean you must have known that you couldn't get away? It was stupid.

JIMMY: Yeah I suppose it was.

LINDA: Why did you do it then?

JIMMY: I don't know. I just felt like it at the time.

(He goes across to the cue stand.)

LINDA: You just felt like it?

JIMMY: Yeah. It seemed like a good idea . . . *(He puts up the cue.)* at the time.

(Linda shakes her head and smiles in disbelief. He smiles across at her.)

Look, I've always enjoyed knockin' off stuff. Ever since I was a young lad and I'd rob me Da's pockets while he was asleep in the chair. He'd have come in stocious drunk and gave me poor Ma a couple of belts and maybe broke the place up too into the bargain. Then he'd flop down into the armchair and demand his dinner. When he was asleep, snorin' his big head off, I'd rifle his coat pockets. He'd wake up dyin' and not a penny to his name.

LINDA: You'd rob your own Da?

JIMMY: Yeah. Why not? If somebody has somethin' I want I'll take it.

LINDA: What, anybody?

JIMMY: No, not anybody. Yeah though, anybody. Why not?

LINDA: Aw I can't believe that. What, even Tony yeh mean.

JIMMY: Yeah, if he had somethin' I wanted.

LINDA: *(Shakes her head.)* I can't . . . I mean I know your brother Dick real well and he's terrible nice.

JIMMY: Yeah well Richard follows me Ma.

LINDA: And who do you follow?

JIMMY: *(Shrugs.)* Naw I wouldn't rob Tony though. The fucker never has anythin' worth talkin' about anyway.

LINDA: But yeh would rob your Da?

JIMMY: *(Nods that he would.)* If your Da was like mine you'd rob him too.

LINDA: *(Shakes her head in disbelief.)* Your poor Ma must be addled between the two of you.

(Jimmy falls silent. He is sitting up on the pool table now, his legs dangling over the edge.)

JIMMY: I once caught them kissin' yeh know. Me Ma and Da I mean. I was only a little lad at the time. I ran out to tell Richard and when we got back Da was singin' at the top of his voice and the two of them were waltzin' around the little kitchen. Me and Richard just stood starin' at them. "There they are now," says me Da. "James the Less and his brother Jude." He had his good suit on him and a gleamin' white shirt and the smell of Brycreem off him would nearly knock you down. Me Ma was breakin' her heart laughin' at the face of us, her own face lit up like a Christmas tree. I'm not coddin' you she looked absolutely . . . radiant. *(Pause.)* Richard says he doesn't remember that happenin' at all. Me Ma don't either. Maybe it was just a whatdoyoucallit . . . a mirage.

(Linda has come closer to him now. She picks softly at his shirt, pulling at the loose threads.)

Richard kicked me Da out of the house yeh know when I was away with the F.C.A. that time.

LINDA: I never knew you were in the F.C.A.

JIMMY: Yeah I used to be. They threw me out of it. I got fed up of your man shoutin' at me. Whatshisname . . . yeh know your man lives up by you there . . . Brown! I told him to go and cop on himself. Anyway when I got home I found me Da stayin' down in that auld hostel. I felt terrible. He was just lyin' there, readin' a war book or somethin', a couple of those army blankets tossed across his feet. I wanted to burn the place down. I told him to get his things and come on home but he wouldn't. Well let's face it fellas like meself and me Da don't have a ghost of a chance do we? Like when I went looking for a job at your place. What did your man O'Brien ask me? What Brady are you then? Well that was me finished before I even started wasn't it?

LINDA: Aw he was probably only . . .

JIMMY: Yes he was yeah. He wrote me off straight away. Even if I had never been in trouble I was out. I wouldn't mind but he was knockin' off stuff all over the place himself. They found the generator in his car didn't they?

LINDA: Yeah.

JIMMY: And I heard they found a load of more stuff up in his garage — stuff belongin' to the firm. And he didn't even get the sack out of it did he?

LINDA: He's still down there anyway.

(Jimmy shakes his head and smirks at the idea.)

JIMMY: It's just as well I didn't get a job down there anyway. I'd never have been able to stick that Conway. I can't stomach that fella I'm not coddin' yeh. Did you know he's after talkin' Tony into gettin' married?

LINDA: To who? Not to that young one surely?

JIMMY: Yeah. She's up the pole sure. And now Conway is preachin' to him that the decent thing to do is marry her.

LINDA: Well if it's his child . . .

JIMMY: Look Conway never stopped at him when Tony started goin' out with her first. Did you do this yet and did you do that yet? Badgerin' and jeerin' the chap and makin' a holy show of him in front of everyone. And now all of a sudden he's preachin' about what's right and what's wrong. All of a sudden she's a grand little girl . . . Tony don't want to marry her anyway.

LINDA: Poor Tony. He's real nice. (She studies Jimmy's face.) What would you do if you were in his shoes?

JIMMY: I'd run for the hills.

LINDA: Aw you wouldn't.

JIMMY: No not half wouldn't I.
       (Linda watches him carefully, trying to see if he is only joking.)
       (Earnestly.) I would.

LINDA: *(Disappointed, turns away.)* Let's get out of here Jimmy. This place is stinkin'.

JIMMY: We only just got here.

LINDA: I know but . . .

JIMMY: *(Going to her, putting his arms around her, kissing her gently.)* What's wrong with yeh?

LINDA: Nothin'. I'd just prefer to be somewhere else that's all.

JIMMY: Yeah well we're not somewhere else are we? We're here.

LINDA: I know but I'd prefer to go someplace else.

JIMMY: Where?

LINDA: I don't know.

JIMMY: Do you want to go to the dance?

LINDA: How can we go to the dance when you're barred from the hall?

JIMMY: Yeah well you can go in on your own can't yeh? I don't mind.

LINDA: Look Jimmy if I'm goin' with a fella I'm goin' with him.

JIMMY: I know that. I just thought you liked dancin' that's all.

LINDA: I do like dancin'.

JIMMY: Well then?

LINDA: I'll just have to live without it won't I?
       (Jimmy sighs and winces.)
       What's wrong?

JIMMY: You'll have to live without goin' to the pictures too.

LINDA: Why, what did you do up there?

JIMMY: I asked the auld fella do be on the door how much would he charge to haunt a house? Did you ever see the face on him. He's like a ghost ain't he? *(Jimmy is laughing and so is Linda in spite of herself. Jimmy kisses her, hugs her, wraps his arms around her. Linda responds. Jimmy gradually caresses her all over, her hair, her face, her neck. Eventually he tries to slip his hand up her jumper. She stops him.)*

JIMMY: *(Whispers.)* What's wrong?

LINDA: I don't want you runnin' for the hills do I?

JIMMY: I said if I was in Tony's shoes I'd run for the hills. I'm not.

LINDA: You're in James Brady's shoes are yeh?

JIMMY: Yeah.

> *(Linda considers his answer.)*
>
> Well they're me brother Richard's shoes actually but . . .
>
> *(This makes Linda smile. This time she takes the initiative and kisses him, running her fingers through his hair.)*
>
> *(Lights down.)*

A HANDFUL OF STARS
by Billy Roche

Irish: One Male and One Female

THE PLAY: Life in a small town for a young man with ambitions and dreams can be a study in frustration and resignation. Jimmy is on the cusp of his future in a small town in Ireland, and all his hometown heroes are still home in the small town pool hall, drinking, playing, and dreaming their lives away. The memory of a good moment in his life gives him hope that he may find the same sense of joy and completion—perhaps with his love, Linda. But soon, the desperation of his existence becomes too much for him to bear, and he explodes in a rampage that sets his future in stone.

THE SCENE: Linda (17) has grown tired of Jimmy (17) and his limitations. She arrives at the pool hall to confront him for a final time. His once-proud façade begins to melt a bit as he realizes his dream is beginning to slip away.

TIME AND PLACE: The present. A small town in Ireland. A scruffy pool hall. Early evening.

Linda throws Tony a dirty look. Tony is embarrassed and turns away from the row.

LINDA: Jimmy I know where you were at quarter to seven tonight. You were here. And I know where you were this afternoon too.

JIMMY: Where?

LINDA: You were drinkin' down in the Shark.

JIMMY: Yeah, well, I wasn't supposed to meet you this afternoon was I?

LINDA: I know you were with Maureen Carley.

JIMMY: Yeah Maureen was there.

LINDA: You were with her, drinkin' with her. You were seen.

JIMMY: Who saw me?

LINDA: Conway saw you. And he was only too glad to tell me about it in front of everyone. He said you left the bar with her.

JIMMY: Yeah well I couldn't stick listenin' to him yappin' any longer. I had to get out.

LINDA: And she had to go with you I suppose?

JIMMY: She was goin' home.

LINDA: You needn't think you're going to make an eejit out of me at all boy.

JIMMY: She was goin' home. She went one way and I went the other.

LINDA: The whole feckin' place was laughin' at me down there. They all thought it was very funny.

JIMMY: You can't blame me for that, Linda.

LINDA: *(Sighs.)* Anyway that's why I came down here tonight.

JIMMY: Why?

LINDA: Just in case you were laughin' at me too.

JIMMY: I'm not laughin'. Do you see me laughin'?

LINDA: Yeah well you might take me for a fool and I'm not. I know who you were with and what you were up to. Okay?

(Jimmy nods.)

So the best thing you can do now is to stay away from me in the future. I don't want to see you again. Right?

JIMMY: Hang on Linda . . .

LINDA: There's no hangin' on Jimmy. Every time we had a date you was either drunk or late or else you didn't even bother to turn up at all.

JIMMY: There was only one other time, as far as I can remember, that I didn't turn up and that was the night . . .

LINDA: Look I don't care. I'm sick of yeh. I'm gettin' nothin' only hassle over yeh anyway.

JIMMY: From who?

LINDA: From me Ma and Da. From the girls at work. We can't go to the pictures, we can't go to a dance . . . You're bad news Jimmy.

JIMMY: Yeah well maybe I am bad news and all the rest of it but let's talk about it. I'll get me coat and we'll go somewhere.

LINDA: Where?

JIMMY: We'll go for a walk somewhere.

LINDA: *(Sarcastically.)* A walk?

JIMMY: Look, Linda, Tony is gettin' married in the mornin'. We're supposed to be goin' to the weddin'.

LINDA: Tony don't need me to get married. He don't need you either.

JIMMY: Hang on and I'll get me coat.

LINDA: Don't bother. I don't want to talk about it anyway.

JIMMY: Well I do.

LINDA: And I don't. That's not why I came down here. I never had to follow any fella in me life and I'm not goin' to start with you.

JIMMY: I know that.

(Jimmy move in closer to her, glancing over her shoulder to make sure that Tony is not watching or listening. He tenderly caresses her face with the back of his hand and whispers.)

JIMMY: Give us a chance Linda will yeh?

LINDA: *(Sighs and grows a little tender.)* There's no point Jimmy, you'll only end up soft-soapin' me. I'll go home tonight delighted with meself but tomorrow or the next day I'll wake up to find we're back where we started . . . Conway's right about you Jimmy, you're not goin' to change.

(Pause.)

LINDA: Go back to your game will yeh before Tony has a heart attack there.

A HANDFUL OF STARS
by Billy Roche

Irish: Two Males

THE PLAY: Life in a small town for a young man with ambitions and dreams can be a study in frustration and resignation. Jimmy is on the cusp of his future in a small town in Ireland, and all his hometown heroes are still home in the small town pool hall, drinking, playing, and dreaming their lives away. The memory of a good moment in his life gives him hope that he may find the same sense of joy and completion—perhaps with his love, Linda. But soon, the desperation of his existence becomes too much for him to bear, and he explodes in a rampage that sets his future in stone.

THE SCENE: Jimmy (17) has gone on a rampage and has robbed, vandalized, and assaulted people and establishments in his small town. Everyone is looking for him. His rage and frustration finally exhausts him to the point of wanting to give himself up. He calls on his best friend Tony (17) to meet him at the pool hall to discuss the "surrender" plan.

TIME AND PLACE: The present. A small town in Ireland. A scruffy pool hall. Late night.

The Club. Lights come up on Jimmy who is sitting in a moody half light. He is ruffled-looking and his hand is bleeding. The glass panel behind him is smashed, with "'Jimmy" crawled in chalk on the door. Tony enters through the front door, which has been left ajar.

TONY: Jimmy, Jimmy, where are yeh?

JIMMY: I'm over here. Come in and close the door after yeh.

TONY: *(Closing the door gently.)* What did yeh leave it open like that for? I could have been anybody. *(The sight of the smashed glass panel stops Tony in his tracks.)* What happened here? Aw Jaysus Jimmy there was no need to go and do that . . .

JIMMY: Give it a rest will yeh.

(Tony looks down at Jimmy in disgust.)

JIMMY: What are you lookin' at me like that for? You'd think I was after pissin' on a shrine or somethin' the way you're goin' on. That's only a room in there Tony. It's just a room.

(Tony hangs his head, disappointed that Jimmy has abused the back room. Jimmy eyes his woebegone friend.)

JIMMY: Look if you're worried about gettin' the blame for this don't. I'll tell them you had nothin' to do with it. Okay?

TONY: That doesn't matter.

JIMMY: Yes it does matter. When I get out I expect you to be a staunch member here with your own key and everything. Sure you've already got the ingredients to be a miniature Conway. Money in the Credit Union and a set of bicycle clips now and you'll be away with it.

TONY: There's nothin' wrong with Conway, Jimmy, he's all right.

JIMMY: Oh I know he's all right. You can bet your sweet life on that. The Creep.

TONY: So he's a creep and you're a fuckin' ejit. What's the difference?

JIMMY: None I suppose. But if I had a choice I'd prefer to be an ejit than a creep.

TONY: Why?

JIMMY: I don't know. I just would.

TONY: *(Sighs.)* Look what do you want to do Jimmy?

JIMMY: What? I don't know.

TONY: Well you'd better make up your mind. I'm gettin' married in the mornin' don't forget.

JIMMY: I don't think so Tony. I think I just got you a reprieve.

TONY: What are you talkin' about?

JIMMY: Listen I want you to do me a favour. I want you to go up to the barracks and tell them where to find me.

TONY: *(Flabbergasted.)* Haw? What do you think I am, a squealer or somethin'? I couldn't do that . . .

JIMMY: Look I'm askin' you to go . . . as a favour. I don't want them burstin' in here after me like they were the Sweeney or somethin'.

(Tony paces up and down nervously, shaking his head.)

TONY: You're landin' me right in the middle of it all. Supposin' Swan decides to hold on to me for the night too. What if one of those bastards feels like takin' it out on me? They might try and implicate me just because I was with you earlier on tonight . . .

(Jimmy is sitting there biting his nails, a frightened, hunted look in his eyes. Tony sees that Jimmy is afraid and stops talking. Tony sighs and there is a long silence while Tony thinks it over.)

What do you want me to say?

JIMMY: Tell them where I am. Tell them the door will be wide open and the lights full on. And don't forget to say that I'm unarmed.

TONY: The door will be wide open and the lights full on. And he's unarmed.

JIMMY: Yeah. Go to Swan himself.

TONY: Where is the gun anyway?

JIMMY: Tell them you don't know where it is.

TONY: What? Now they're goin' to want to know where that gun is.

JIMMY: That's their hard luck.

TONY: Aw come on Jimmy I'm supposed to be gettin' married in the mornin'. I don't fancy gettin' the ears boxed off me half the night over you. What's the point anyway?

JIMMY: The point is you never know when you might need a gun. You might be glad of it one day to blow your brains out.

TONY: What are you on about? Gettin' me a reprieve. And me blowing me brains out. Anyone would think that it was me who was in trouble or somethin'. Jimmy you're the one that's goin' up the river not me.

JIMMY: Never mind about that. I know well enough where I'm goin'. But you've been shanghai'd in your sleep Tony. You're on a slow boat to China or somewhere boy and yeh don't even realize it.

TONY: *(Angry and hurt.)* At least I never went berserk over a girl anyway.

JIMMY: This has nothin' to do with her.

TONY: Oh yeah? Pull the other one Jimmy. Linda gave you the shove and you went berserk. Admit it.

JIMMY: She didn't give me the shove. We had a bit of a row that's all.

TONY: Oh yeah? Well then why don't yeh get her to do your dirty work for yeh. Why don't you ask her to go up and see Swan . . . No, you won't do that will yeh? 'Cause yeh have the auld gom here. Well you needn't think now for one minute that I'm goin' up there until I know exactly where that gun is 'cause I'm not.

(Jimmy shakes his head and smiles. Tony becomes furious and moves in closer to Jimmy.)

What's so funny, Jimmy?

JIMMY: You. You'd give it all up just like that wouldn't yeh? You'd hand it to them on a plate. Well not me. I want to see them runnin' around, like blue-arsed flies. And when I'm up in that courtroom and somebody mentions a gun I'll say, "Gun? What gun? I don't see no gun."

TONY: And what about the rest of us? What about me?

JIMMY: What about yeh?

TONY: They're goin' to assume that I know where it is. That you told me.

(Jimmy just shrugs.)

You're a bad bastard you are.

JIMMY: Yeah that's right, Tony. I'm a bad bastard. Where has being a good boy ever got you?

TONY: The one night I ever asked yeh not to start anythin'. The one night . . .

JIMMY: Yeah all right Tony. So what do you want me to do now? Get down on me knees and kiss somebody's arse or somethin' just because you're afraid to take a couple of clips in the ear? Look if you don't want to do what I asked you to do, get the fuck out of me sight.

TONY: *(Desperately.)* I'm supposed to be gettin' married in the mornin'.

JIMMY: *(Dismissive.)* Go and fuck off away from me will yeh.

(Jimmy turns away from him. Tony stays where he is. Jimmy turns back and shoves Tony away from him.)

Go on, get out of me sight before yeh make me vomit.

TONY: *(Brushing Jimmy's hand aside.)* Don't push Jimmy.

JIMMY: *(Pushing him again.)* Why?

TONY: I'm warnin' yeh Jimmy, don't start.

(Jimmy shoves Tony yet again. Tony loses his head and goes for him. There is a brawl with the two boys stumbling over the pool table and onto the floor. They punch one another and wrestle until Jimmy gets the better of Tony. He stands over the bleeding boy in a defiant stance.)

JIMMY: Nobody's goin' to wrap me up in a nice neat little parcel. I'm not goin' to make it handy for you to forget about me — not you, not me Ma, nor me Da, not Swan, nobody.

(Jimmy picks up a cue and holds it above his head. Tony cowers away from it. Jimmy turns and storms at the door to the back room and begins kicking it and hunching it with his shoulder. Eventually, as Tony gazes on in awe and disgust, Jimmy manages to break in, falling into the back room. We hear him wrecking the place in there, pulling down cupboards, kicking over chairs, scattering balls and breaking an out-of-sight window. When Jimmy appears in the doorway he has a frenzied look about him.)

Tell them Jimmy Brady done it. The same Jimmy Brady that's scrawled all over this town. Jimmy Brady who bursted that big bully of a bouncer with a headbutt when everyone else was afraid of their livin' lives of him. The same Jimmy Brady that led Detective Garda Swan twice around the houses and back again . . . Yeh see that's the difference between me and Conway. He tiptoes around. I'm screamin'. Me and Stapler are screamin'.

So if you want to join the livin' dead then go ahead and do it by all means Tony but don't expect me to wink at your gravediggers. Conway . . . the big he-man with no bell on his bike. I hates him I'm not coddin' yeh I do.

TONY: *(Tearful.)* It's not Conway's fault you're up to your ears in shit Jimmy. It's not my fault you fell out with your man in the bar. You can't blame Paddy for . . .

JIMMY: All right. It's not Conway's fault, it's not your fault, it's not Paddy's . . . Who's fault is it then Tony? Mine? Tell me who's to blame will yeh til I tear his friggin' head off.

TONY: *(Sighs, stalls, and comes closer to Jimmy, his voice taking on a more tender edge.)* I don't know who's to blame. Maybe it's nobody's fault. Maybe that's just the way it is.

JIMMY: Yeah right, it's nobody's fault. *(Jimmy plonks himself down hopelessly on the bench.)* It's nobody's fault. Everyone's to blame.

(There is a long painful silence. Jimmy lights up a cigarette and drags on it. Tony shuffles nervously across to the back room, eyeing the devastation, heartbroken. Jimmy looks up at him.)

Go ahead in Tony. Go on, be a man.

THE HOSTAGE
by Brendan Behan

Irish: One Male (Cockney) and One Female (Irish)

THE PLAY: Saucy and risqué for its time (originally produced in 1958), *The Hostage* is a play with music that explores the ancient hostilities between the British and the Irish, the Protestants and the Catholics. Set in an Irish bordello/lodging house, a host of bizarre and flamboyant characters pass through the main room of the house regaling the owners with their adventures, both past and present. The normal activity is interrupted with the arrival of the British hostage being held in the hope that the police (British controlled) will release their Irish prisoner who is slated for execution. Mature language and theme.

THE SCENE: One of the local lodgers, Teresa (19), has taken a liking to the hostage, Leslie (19). As the evening wears on, the mismatched pair discuss politics, religion, and the past — coming to the conclusion that, at heart, they have more in common than they think. The strength of their feelings for each other is revealed at the close of this scene.

TIME AND PLACE: Early evening. The main room of an old house in Dublin, Ireland. 1960.

I.R.A. officer and Patrick depart, leaving Teresa alone with Leslie.

LESLIE: You can come out now.

TERESA: No, he might see me.

LESLIE: He's gone, he won't be back for a long time. Come on, sit down and tell me a story — the Irish are great at that, aren't they?

TERESA: Well, not all of them. I'm not. I don't know any stories.

LESLIE: Anything'll do. It doesn't have to be funny. It's just something to pass the time.

TERESA: Yes, you've a long night ahead of you, and so has he.

LESLIE: Who?

TERESA: You know, the boy in Belfast.

LESLIE: What do you have to mention him for?

TERESA: I'm sorry, Leslie.

LESLIE: It's all right, it's just that everybody's been talking about the boy in the Belfast jail.

TERESA: Will I tell you about when I was a girl in the convent?

LESLIE: Yeah, that should be a bit of all right. Go on.

TERESA: Oh, it was the same as any other school, except you didn't go home. You played in a big yard which had a stone floor; you'd break your bones if you fell on it. But there was a big meadow outside the wall, we used to be let out there on our holidays. It was lovely. We were brought swimming a few times, too, that was really terrific, but the nuns were terrible strict, and if they saw a man come within a mile of us, well we . . .

LESLIE: What? . . . Aw, go on, Teresa, we're grown-ups now, aren't we?

TERESA: We were not allowed to take off our clothes at all. You see, Leslie, even when we had our baths on Saturday nights they put shifts on all the girls.

LESLIE: Put what on yer?

TERESA: A sort of sheet, you know.

LESLIE: Oh yeah.

TERESA: Even the little ones four or five years of age.

LESLIE: Oh, we never had anything like that.

TERESA: What did you have?

LESLIE: Oh no, we never had anything like that. I mean, in our place we had all showers and we were sloshing water over each other — and blokes shouting and screeching and making a row — it was smashing! Best night of the week, it was.

TERESA: Our best time was the procession for the Blessed Virgin.

LESLIE: Blessed who?

TERESA: Shame on you, the Blessed Virgin. Anyone would think you were a Protestant.

LESLIE: I am, girl.

TERESA: Oh, I'm sorry.

LESLIE: That's all right. Never think about it myself.

TERESA: Anyway, we had this big feast.

LESLIE: Was the scoff good?

TERESA: The — what?

LESLIE: The grub. The food. You don't understand me half the time, do you?

TERESA: Well, we didn't have food. It was a feast day. We just used to walk around.

LESLIE: You mean they didn't give you nothing at all? Well, blow that for a lark.

TERESA: Well, are you going to listen to me story? Well, are you? Anyway, we had this procession, and I was looking after the mixed infants.

LESLIE: What's a mixed infant?

TERESA: A little boy or girl under five years of age. Because up until that time they were mixed together.

LESLIE: I wish I'd been a mixed infant.

TERESA: Do you want to hear my story? When the boys were six they were sent to the big boys' orphanage.

LESLIE: You're one, too — an orphan? You didn't tell me that.

TERESA: Yes, I did.

LESLIE: We're quits now.

TERESA: I didn't believe your story.

LESLIE: Well, it's true. Anyway, never mind. Tell us about this mixed infant job.

TERESA: There was this little feller, his father was dead, and his mother had run away or something. All the other boys were laughing and shouting, but this one little boy was all on his own and he was crying like the rain. Nothing would stop him. So, do you know what I did, Leslie? I made a crown of daisies and a daisy chain to put round his neck and told him he was King of the May. Do you know he forgot everything except that he was King of the May.

LESLIE: Would you do that for me if I was a mixed infant?

(They have forgotten all about Belfast Jail and the I.R.A. Leslie takes Teresa's hand and she moves away. She goes to the window to cover her shyness.)

TERESA: There's a clock striking somewhere in the city.

LESLIE: I wonder what time it is?

TERESA: I don't know.

LESLIE: Will you give me a picture of yourself, Teresa?

TERESA: What for?

LESLIE: Just to have. I mean, they might take me away in the middle of the night and I might never see you again.

TERESA: I'm not Marilyn Monroe or Jayne Mansfield.

LESLIE: Who wants a picture of them? They're all old.

TERESA: I haven't got one anyway.

(She pulls out a medal which she has round her neck.)

LESLIE: What s that?

TERESA: It's a medal. It's for you, Leslie.

LESLIE: I'm doing all right, ain't I? In the army nine months and I get a medal already.

TERESA: It's not that kind of medal.

LESLIE: Let's have a look . . . looks a bit like you.

TERESA: *(Shocked.)* No Leslie.

LESLIE: Oh, it's that lady of yours.

TERESA: It's God's mother.

LESLIE: Yes, that one.

TERESA: She's the mother of everyone else in the world, too. Will you wear it round your neck?

LESLIE: I will if you put it on.

(She puts it over his head and he tries to kiss her.)

TERESA: Leslie. Don't. Why do you have to go and spoil everything — I'm going.

LESLIE: Don't go! Let's pretend we're on the films, where all I have to say is "let me," and all you have to say is "yes."

TERESA: Oh, all right.

LESLIE: Come on, Kate.

THE LOVERS
by Brian Friel

Irish: One Male and One Female

THE PLAY: Surprising and tragic, Brian Friel's look at the lives of two young lovers seems innocent enough and then takes a surprising twist. Told in two parts, in the first section of the play, the action is taken by the young lovers as we hear the narration of the older lovers. The narration takes an "evening news broadcast" tone, which starkly contrasts with the vibrancy and life of the lovers we watch. The tone proves to be effective in the set-up of the eventual tragedy. The second half of the play reverses the roles as the young lovers become the narrators of the older lovers' story.

THE SCENE: In the middle of the afternoon, Joe and Mag (both 17) have fought, ate, napped, and done very little studying. After some deeply wounding and truthful words to each other, Joe realizes he has a little making up to do.

TIME AND PLACE: A hilltop in Ballymore (a fictional town). County Donegal. Ireland. Early afternoon. June 1966.

JOE: You asleep, Mag?

(Mag neither moves nor opens her eyes.)

MAG: No.

JOE: Nothing wrong with you, is there?

MAG: No.

JOE: Are you in bad form or something?

MAG: No.

JOE: Did I do anything, Mag?

MAG: No.

JOE: As long as those false pains don't come back. *(Going on gaily.)* Pity we hadn't our togs. Be a great day for a swim, wouldn't it? — if we could swim!

MAG: I trapped you into marrying me — that's what you said.

JOE: Huh?

MAG: That's what you said. Put that in your pipe and smoke it — that's what you said.

JOE: Ah, come on, Mag. You're not huffing still.

MAG: And you meant it, too.

JOE: But you ate your lunch and all. You ate more than I did.

MAG: There was hate in your eyes.

JOE: I'm sorry.

MAG: It's no good.

(Pause. Then he decides to win her round by clowning.)

JOE: Mag —

MAG: I'm not looking.

JOE: MAG —

MAG: No.

JOE: Who's this, Mag?

MAG: I'm going asleep.

JOE: *(In mincing voice.)* "Tweeny — Tweeny — Tweeny — Tweeny! Come on, Tweeny girl. Atta girl. Come on. Come on."

MAG: That's not one bit like Mr. O'Hara.

JOE: *(In excessive nasal tones.)* "Good example is something we should all prac- tice, my dear people. Put one bad apple into a barrel of good apples, and all the good apples become corrupt."

MAG: I'm not listening.

JOE: "But put one good apple into a barrel of bad apples, and then — and then — "

MAG: You're not one bit funny.

JOE: " — And then" *(Rapidly.)* "devotions this evening at six o'clock in the name of the father son holy ghost."

MAG: *(In matching tone.)* Ha-men.

JOE: *(East London.)* "So sorry, Joseph, but my Phil 'e's not at 'ome at present."
(Mag suddenly giggles.)
" 'E's out on 'is bi-cycle on one of 'is solitary nature rambles."
(Mag sits up. She laughs out loud.)
"Like 'is poor dad used to. I'll tell 'im you called. Bye-bye."

MAG: "Ta-ta."

JOE: "Ta-ta."

MAG: No. "Ta-ta for now."

JOE: "Ta-ta for now."

MAG: "Call again soon, Joseph."

JOE: "I like my Phil to 'ave chum boys."
(They both howl with spontaneous, helpless laughter. When they try to speak, they cannot finish.)

MAG: Sister Pascal —

JOE: Wha —

MAG: Sister Pascal —

JOE: — is a rascal!

MAG: She says that for every five minutes you laugh, you —

JOE: You what — ?

MAG: — you cry for ten!

(This seems the crowning absurdity. They roll on the ground.)

JOE: Oooooooh . . . !

MAG: God, I'm sore!

JOE: Cruel!

MAG: We'll cry for weeks!

JOE: Nuns — bloody nuns!

MAG: Give me a handkerchief.

(He throws her one. She wipes her eyes. They sober up — and wonder what set them off. She lights a cigarette.)

JOE: What started that?

MAG: I don't know.

JOE: Give me (Handkerchief.). Oh, my God.

MAG: Leave you weak.

JOE: This whole town's nuts.

(Mag is stretched out under the sun again. A wistful mood creeps over them now that the laughter is forgotten.)

MAG: D'you think they'll get married?

JOE: Who?

MAG: Joan and Philip.

JOE: How would I know? They're only seventeen.

MAG: They say they're both going to be architects.

JOE: How long does that take?

MAG: Seven years. Maybe then.

(Joe busies himself with gathering up the remains of the lunch.)

JOE: Maybe then what?

MAG: Maybe then they'll marry, after they qualify.

JOE: Maybe. Who cares.

MAG: I don't.

JOE: Neither do I.

MAG: Why talk about them then?

JOE: You mentioned them first.

MAG: *I* did? You imitated Mr. O'Hara and Phil's mother.

JOE: Maggie, I did not mention Joan O'Hara's name. As a matter of fact, I can't stick the girl.

MAG: Sister Pascal was right.

JOE: What about?

MAG: We *will* cry for twice the length.

JOE: For God's sake, woman!

(He heads off down the far side of the hill to get rid of the old papers he has gathered.)

MAG: *(Quickly.)* Where are you going?

JOE: I am going to dispose of this stuff — if I have your permission.

MAG: You don't have to have my permission for anything. And I don't have to have yours either. 'Cos I'm not married to you yet, Mr. Brennan, in case you have forgotten.

JOE: No, I haven't forgotten.

THE LOVERS
by Brian Friel

Irish: One Male and One Female

THE PLAY: Surprising and tragic, Brian Friel's look at the lives of two young
lovers seems innocent enough, and then takes a surprising twist. Told in
two parts, in the first section of the play, the action is taken by the young
lovers as we hear the narration of the older lovers. The narration takes an
evening news broadcast tone, which starkly contrasts with the vibrancy
and life of the lovers we watch. The tone proves to be effective in the set-
up of the eventual tragedy. The second half of the play reverses the roles
as the young lovers become the narrators of the older lovers' story.

THE SCENE: Joe and Mag (both 17) have spent the warm day sitting on a hill
overlooking Ballymore. They were supposed to be studying for their qual-
ifying exams (GED test). Instead, they while away the hours arguing, teasing, picnicking, napping, and eventually dreaming of their impending
future.

TIME AND PLACE: A hilltop in Ballymore (a fictional town). County Donegal,
Ireland. Late afternoon. June 1966.

*Joe and Mag are now sitting with their arms around one another, looking
down over the town. The boisterousness is all over; the mood is calm, content,
replete. Mag lights a cigarette.*

JOE: This day three weeks.
MAG: Mrs. Joseph Brennan.
JOE: As long as you're not Big Bridie Brogan.
MAG: Who?
JOE: The one who died of pernicious something or other.
MAG: I made that all up.
JOE: Thought you did.
MAG: The flat'll be lovely and cozy at night. But you'll have to stick a bit of
cardboard under the table top to keep it steady. And all the junk'll have to
be thrown into the spare room.
JOE: What junk?

MAG: Your books and things like that.

JOE: The slide rule cost me 37/6d. — it's staying in the kitchen. And you agreed that the dog sleeps inside.

MAG: When do we get him?

JOE: He's not pupped yet. I was only promised him.

MAG: Maybe he'll be a she.

JOE: It's a god I'm promised — the pick of the litter.

MAG: We'll call him . . . Austin!

JOE: For God's sake —

MAG: Austin's his name. Or else he sleeps out.

JOE: Never heard of a bull terrier called that.

MAG: And in the daytime he can sit at the door and guard the pram. Look —

JOE: Where?

MAG: The line of boarders.

JOE: What are they up to now?

MAG: Going to the chapel for a visit.

JOE: *(Counting.)* 14, 16, 18, 20 —

MAG: It seems so remote — so long ago . . .

JOE: — 26, 28, 30, 32 —

MAG: And at home last week, every time I heard the convent bell, I cried: I felt so lost. I would have given anything to be part of them — to be in the middle of them.

JOE: And three nuns.

MAG: We were so safe . . . we had so much fun . . .

JOE: Mm?

MAG: But now I wouldn't go back for the world. I'm a woman at seventeen, and I wouldn't be a schoolgirl again, not for all the world.

JOE: I suppose I'm a man, too.

MAG: Would you go back?

JOE: Where?

MAG: To Saint Kevin's — to being a schoolboy?

JOE: I never think of things like that.

MAG: But if you could — if you had a chance.

JOE: I like studying, Mag.

MAG: Then you'd prefer to go back.

JOE: No. Not there. I'm finished with all that.

MAG: Then you wouldn't want to go back?

JOE: Not to Saint Kevin's. No.

MAG: Good.

JOE: Know something, Mag?

MAG: Mm?

JOE: I think I should forget about studying and London University and all that.

MAG: It that's what you want.

JOE: It's maybe not what I want. But that's the way things have turned out. A married man with a family has more important things to occupy his mind besides bloody books.

(She gives him a brief squeeze. But she has not heard what he has said. Pause.)

JOE: Ballymore.

MAG: Home.

JOE: See the sun glinting on the headstones beside the chapel.

MAG: Some day we'll be buried together.

JOE: You're great company.

MAG: I can't wait for the future, Joe.

JOE: What's that supposed to mean?

(Maggie suddenly leaps to her feet. Her face is animated, her movements quick and vital, her voice ringing.)

MAG: The past's over! And I hate this waiting time! I want the future to happen — I want to be in it — I want to be in it with you!

JOE: You've got sunstroke.

(She throws her belongings into her case.)

MAG: Come on, Joe! Let's begin the future now!

(Not comprehending, but infected by her mood, he gets to his feet.)

JOE: You're nuts.

MAG: Where'll we go? What'll we do? Let's do something crazy!

JOE: Mad as a hatter.

MAG: The lake! We'll dance on every island! We'll stay out all night and sing and shout at the moon!

(Joe does a wolf howl at the sky.)

Come on, Joe! While the sun's still hot!

JOE: O mad hot sun, thou breath of summer's being!

MAG: Away to the farthest island.

JOE: We've no boat.

MAG: We'll take one.

JOE: And get arrested.

MAG: Coward. Then I'll take one.

JOE: I'll visit you in jail.

MAG: Quick! Quick!

(Joe throws his books into his bag.)

JOE: Hold on there.

MAG: Give me your hand. We'll run down the hill.

JOE: You'll get those pains again.

MAG: Your hand.

JOE: You're not going to run down there.

MAG: Come on! Come on! Come on!

JOE: Have sense, Mag —

(She catches his hand and begins to run.)

MAG: We're away!

JOE: Easy — easy —

MAG: Wheeeeeeeee —

JOE: Aaaaaaaaah —

(They run down the hill hand in hand.)

OURSELVES ALONE
by Anne Devlin

Irish: Two Females

THE PLAY: Set in Northern Ireland, the complicated and intrigue-filled lives of a Republican family are given full view as the individuals plot, scheme, betray, and love amidst the constant threat of being found out by British intelligence.

THE SCENE: Josie (25 to 29) is staying with Donna (25 to 30), her brother's wife, to keep an eye on her while her brother serves time in prison. Having grown up together, the two continue to share "sister" moments.

TIME AND PLACE: Donna's flat in Anderstown, West Belfast,. Northern Ireland. Present. Summer. Evening.

Josie is sitting in the dark in a room. Footsteps quickly approach the door. Donna comes in and turns on the light.

DONNA: Josie! What are you doing sitting in the dark? You've let the fire out. *(Josie laughs.)* What's so funny?
JOSIE: My daddy used to say, well close the door quickly and keep it in.
DONNA: Used to say? *(Takes her coat off and sits down.)* You couldn't wait to get away from him.
JOSIE: I know.
DONNA: Is everything all right? You were sleepwalking again last night.
JOSIE: Was I?
DONNA: It's the third time this week. I opened my eyes and there you were. Standing over the cot, looking at Catherine.
JOSIE: Was I?
DONNA: You gave me an awful fright.
JOSIE: I'm sorry.
DONNA: I wouldn't have said anything, but I'm afraid of you waking Catherine. It takes so long to get her to sleep these days.
JOSIE: I think I was dreaming about my mother.
DONNA: Was she quiet for you?
JOSIE: Who?

DONNA: Catherine. Was she quiet while I was out?

JOSIE: Yes.

DONNA: I'll just take a wee look in.

JOSIE: She's asleep! I wish I could sleep like that.

DONNA: What's wrong?

JOSIE: I feel sick all the time now.

DONNA: Is it him?

JOSIE: I can't live like this any more. I sit here night after night wondering will he come tonight.

DONNA: We're all waiting on men, Josie.

JOSIE: If he has to go away for any other reason but her I can stand it.

DONNA: Have you told him this?

JOSIE: No. Of course not. I don't want him to think I care.

DONNA: Aye, but it strikes me that if you were the one with a wife, he might care. Has he ever talked about her?

JOSIE: No.

DONNA: Well I expect she waits too, Josie.

JOSIE: Thanks.

DONNA: At least you have his love.

JOSIE: Love? It's such a silly word. We've never spoken it. It's just that when I'm totally me and he's totally him we swop. Do you know what I mean? *(Pause.)* His arrival is the best time. It's his mouth on my neck, his cool fingers touching me — I make it last right up until he has to leave. And then I row, I fight, I do everything I can to keep him with me and when I hurt him I hurt myself. It's as if we're driven, that bed is like a raft and that room is all the world to us.

DONNA: You're lucky you can feel like that, you might not if you had to live with him.

JOSIE: Live with him? I've dreamt of nothing else.

DONNA: He frightens me Josie — he's not like any man I know.

JOSIE: No he's not.

DONNA: The things I've heard about him. He's a spoiled priest.

JOSIE: Sure I wanted to be a nun once.

DONNA: Aye when you were ten years old. But he's actually been trained as a priest. *(Pause.)* They told him when they blew up the police station near the cemetery that morning that some of our people might get hurt as well. And he asked — how many?

JOSIE: You don't know what you're talking about. Our force is defensive!

DONNA: I'm looking at you but it's him who's talking. I wish I didn't know any of this. I wish I hadn't walked into the room that night and seen you both. I wish you hadn't left the door open.

JOSIE: But you approved of us. You made me come and live with you so it was easier for us to meet. You got me away from my daddy.

DONNA: I was afraid for you if they found out. And because you have Liam's eyes. When I woke last night I thought it was Liam who was standing there, that he'd come back. But when I saw it was you, I knew it was only because I hadn't been with him for so long I was wanting him again.

JOSIE: Don't talk to me about wanting, my body's like armour. The nerve ends are screeching under my skin. I need him back so I can stretch out again.

DONNA: How long since you've seen him?

JOSIE: Five weeks.

DONNA: I wonder does she know. *(Pause.)* Women have a way of knowing these things. I knew with my ex-husband when he was seeing somebody else. I knew the minute he put his hand on me. Once when we were in bed together a woman's name came into my head and I thought, he's not making love to me, he's making love to Margaret — I asked him afterwards, who's Margaret? He froze. He was, you see.

JOSIE: Sometimes when we make love I pretend I'm someone else.

DONNA: Who?

JOSIE: Not someone I know. Someone I make up — from another century. Sometimes I'm not even a woman. Sometimes I'm a man — his warrior lover, fighting side by side to the death. Sometimes we're not even on the same side.

DONNA: That's powerful, Josie! *(Pause.)* What will you do if he doesn't come back?

JOSIE: Why do you say that?

DONNA: The man is still married to someone else. He has known you all these years — but he has never left his wife.

JOSIE: But she's not important to him!

DONNA: Wives are always important.

JOSIE: You only say that because you're so anxious to marry my brother.

DONNA: I must have struck home.

JOSIE: I'm sorry. *(She suddenly stops. Footsteps clattering in the alley towards the door.)* Listen.

DONNA: You've ears like a cat.

JOSIE: It's Frieda. She always walks as if her feet don't belong to her.

DONNA: Here. *(Offers her a hanky.)* Blow your nose. *(The door bursts open. Frieda arrives, breathing deeply. Leans against the closed door.)*

SECTION THREE
RUSSIAN

RUSSIAN INTRODUCTION

The Russian people are long-suffering and incredibly warm and re-silient. Russian history is filled with sorrow. The loss of Russian lives in war and revolutions is unequaled in many Western countries. The many changes of power, the ravage of the beautiful Russian environment by industry and population, and the legendary Russian winters all contribute to the stereotypical image of Russia as a bleak and harsh place filled with bleak and harsh people. Nothing could be further from the truth. If anything, the Russian tribulations have only served to strengthen and fortify the Russian sense of faith. Russians have an amazing ability, even when in the throes of ruin, to continue to hope that things will change for the better, soon.

The Russian culture is colorful and varied. Russian culture has set a stan-dard of excellence in all areas of art. Many nations have attempted to achieve the esteem that the Russian art world holds, and few have ever surpassed its reputation. The Russian Ballet and dancers continue to hold the top spots on lists of "The All-Time Best." Russian music is deep, rich, and filled with the kind of soul that one would expect from a nation so deeply entrenched in sorrow and hardship. Russian authors, poets, playwrights, and teachers are known throughout the world for their pioneering styles and themes. Almost any American actor who has ever studied his or her craft can trace a few of his or her techniques back to the famous Russian acting teacher, Konstantin Stanislavski.

Post–cold war Russia is struggling toward a capitalistic, Westernized so-ciety. Images and essences of Western traditions are slowly creeping into the general Russian culture. The young people like to wear the same trendy clothes that young people worldwide wear. American and British television and films are an ever-present example of the world outside Russia. The young want to know and use Westernized words and phrases.

Just as in the other dialects studied, there exist many different kinds of Russian dialects that vary in strength and sound due to the geography, edu-cation, and experience of the speaker. There are many provinces in the for-mer Soviet Republic, and to be spot on with your character's sound, you may need to do focused and specific research. For our purposes, we will study and play with some basic, overall sound changes prevalent in the Russian lan-guage.

As this is our first consideration of a dialect in which the native language of the speaker is not English, the strength of the accent will be determined by each individual speaker/character. In other words, you can be as fluent in English as you want to be. You can also have fun not being fluent in English. At any rate, your speech patterns will be altered greatly due to the Russian sounds and rhythm of a nonnative English speaker.

- The voice of the Russian comes from deep in the center of the body and "swims around" in the chest and throat region — creating a wonderfully deep rich resonant sound.
- The Russians are very deliberate in the way they speak. They commit to the energy they have at the top of their thought and continue to press on, even when grammatical errors come up.
- The Russian vowel sounds tend to be more guttural and long, perhaps giving them time during the speaking of the vowel to think about the next word in the sentence.
- Remember, this is an accent of a speaker whose native language is not English. This will cause some syntax errors or errors in the stressed syllables of the words.
- The sounds are not vastly different from the sounds we make in American English, but when coupled with the idea that English is not the native language, the delivery of the sounds will reveal the accent.
- Just think of speaking the words as they are spelled, without knowing the American rules for pronunciation (for example *ed* endings in American English come out sounding like *t*, but the Russians would sound out the *ed*).
- When all else fails, swallow your sounds and let the sounds vibrate in your chest.
- There is little mouth movement with the Russian accent; they tend to speak with the mouth mostly closed (another possible reason for the throat and chest resonance).

RUSSIAN FILM, TELEVISION, AND AUDIO REFERENCES

FILM

Rounders	John Malkovic
Air Force One	Gary Oldman (an actor doing a good accent)
The Cutting Edge	The coach
White Knights	Mikhail Baryshnikov, Helen Mirren
Turning Point	Mikhail Baryshnikov
Company Business	Mikhail Baryshnikov
Moscow on the Hudson	Robin Williams (he's pretty good with all dialects)
Anastasia	Disney version, listen to the smaller characters
The Russian House	Klaus Brandauer, Michelle Pfeiffer (she does pretty well)
To Russia with Love	Russian bad guys
Reds	Genuine Russian interviews
Back in the U.S.S.R.	Real Russians
Citizen X	

TELEVISION

"Bullwinkle"	Boris and Natasha

DIALECT TAPES AND BOOKS

Stage Dialects and More Stage Dialects	Jerry Blunt
Dialects for the Stage	Evangeline Machlin
Acting with an Accent/Russian	David Alan Sterns
IDEA website	www.ukans.edu/~idea/index.html

For a more complete and detailed list of films/resources, see Ginny Kopf's book The Dialect Handbook.

RUSSIAN SOUNDS

- Russian accent vowel changes:

ih → ee	his → heez
ee → ih	speech → spihch
er → air (very throaty)	words → vairds
a → ah (or) eh	back → bahk/behk
aw → ow	thought → thowt
(ed endings are sounded out)	looked → lookid

- Russian consonant changes:

[r] trilled before vowels	rate, right, red
[th] → [d]	this, these → dis, dhese
[th] → [t]	thanks, think → tanks, tink
[w] → [v]	with, was, watch → vith, vas, vatch
[v] → [f]	very, movie → fery, moofie
ing + k	singing → singingk
[h] made in throat with a lot of air	house, head
[d] at the end of a word gets an extra [t]	mind → mindt
intrusive [w]	gold, fold → gwold, fwold
intrusive [y]	get, kept, lend → gyet, kyept, lyend

Russian Practice Sentences

[ih] → [ee]:

His trip to Israel was important to him. This is his distant cousin, Leonid.

[ee] → [ih]:

Her speech is neat, what a treat. These are for Cleveland and Sweden. I want meat.

[er] → [air]:

We heard the word that she learned the bird's song. Birds are early risers.

[a] → [ah/eh]:

That was the plan for the man at the stand. She had her hand in the bad man's bag.

[aw] → [ow]:

They thought the cop caught the lout but they thought wrong.

[r]:

Red roses and rhubarb are really remarkable. Ride the river on the raft.

[th] → [d]:

This is the brother of the mother's brother. Is that what they wanted?

[th] → [t]:

Thanks for thinking of things. Throw the ball through the third window.

[d] → [dt]:

Leonid and Ovid were bad men. Worldwide bread is bad for the head.

[v] → [f]:

The glove of the lover was in the cave. Save the wave for the rave.

[ing + k]:

Walking and talking was killing the meeting. With singing, we are playing.

[h]:

Have some homemade hummus. Help the host have the happy hero's holiday.

[w] → [v]:

We are winning the war of the windows. Where is the weather worker?

intrusive [w]:

They told the golden old man the old lonely rope story.

intrusive [y]:

He kept the solemn book. She will get him to lend it.

THE WHITE GUARD
(or The Days of the Turbins)
by Mikhail Afanasyevich Bulgakov

Russian: One Male and One Female

THE PLAY: Set in the time of the Russian Revolution, as the Bolsheviks were clamoring to create a Soviet Union and the Cossacks were marauding, the Ukrainian armed forces stood behind their Hetman (leader/prince). When even he deserted his capital, the people were left to see which side would win out and which government would lead them. The original alliances of the Turbin family are challenged and changed by the end of the play.

THE SCENE: Elena (14) has just said good-bye to her military officer husband who is essentially fleeing the scene of an uncertain future for the capitol city. Her longtime friend and admirer, Leonid Shervinsky (20s) catches her alone for a moment and attempts to lighten her mood.

TIME AND PLACE: Elena's drawing/sitting room. Evening. Winter, 1918. Kiev.

The table is laid for supper.

ELENA: *(At the piano, repeatedly playing the same chord.)* He's gone. How could he . . .

SHERVINSKY: *(Suddenly appearing in the doorway.)* Who's gone?

ELENA: My God! What a fright you gave me, Shervinsky. How did you manage to come in without ringing the bell?

SHERVINSKY: Your front door was wide open. Good evening to you, Yeliena. *(Produces an enormous bouquet from its paper wrapping.)*

ELENA: How many times have I asked you not to do this, Leonid? I don't like you spending money on me.

SHERVINSKY: Money exists to be spent, as Karl Marx said. May I take off my cloak?

ELENA: A typically exaggerated army officer's gesture.

SHERVINSKY: I beg your pardon: a typically exaggerated *guards'* officer's gesture.

(Takes off his cloak in the hall, reappears in his magnificent Circassian tunic.)
I'm so glad to see you again! It's such a long time since I last saw you!

ELENA: If my memory serves me right, you were here yesterday.

SHERVINSKY: Ah, Yeliena, in these terrible times "Yesterday" was an age ago! Well, come on — who's gone away?

ELENA: My husband, Vladimir.

SHERVINSKY: But . . . he was supposed to be coming *back* today!

ELENA: Yes, he did come back and . . . went away again.

SHERVINSKY: Where to?

ELENA: Berlin.

SHERVINSKY: To . . . Berlin? For how long, if you don't mind my asking.

ELENA: About a couple of months.

SHERVINSKY: A couple of months! No! You don't say? . . . Oh dear, how very, very sad! . . . I'm really most upset!

ELENA: Shervinsky, that's the fifth time you've kissed my hand.

SHERVINSKY: It's because I'm so depressed! My God, and everyone's going to be here this evening! Hurrah!

NIKOLKA: *(Offstage.)* Shervinsky!

ELENA: Why are you so delighted?

SHERVINSKY: I'm delighted because . . . Oh really, Yeliena!

ELENA: A well-bred man would know how to hide his feelings better.

SHERVINSKY: Why do you say that? No, I assure you I am extremely well bred. It's just that I'm, well, er overwhelmed . . . So he's gone and you're left behind.

ELENA: As you see. How's your voice?

SHERVINSKY: *(At the piano.)* Ma . . . ma . . . mi, mi, mi . . . He is far, far away . . . far away and will not know . . . Yes . . . I'm in splendid voice tonight. On my way in the cab I thought it had gone off somewhat but as soon as I get here, I find I'm in excellent voice.

ELENA: Did you bring your music with you?

SHERVINSKY: Well, as it happens, I did . . . *(Sings.)* "You are a goddess of the purest degree . . ."

ELENA: The only good thing about you is your voice, and your real calling is to be an opera singer.

SHERVINSKY: I must admit the raw material is there. You know, Yeliena, one day at Zhmerinka I sang the "Epithalamion," and the top note is a "C," as you know — well I sang the "E" above the "C" and held it for nine bars.

ELENA: How many bars?

SHERVINSKY: Seven bars. Don't you believe me? Good God, why, Countess
    Hendrikov was there, and she fell in love with my high "E."
ELENA: And what happened then?
SHERVINSKY: She poisoned herself. With potassium cyanide.
ELENA: Oh Shervinsky, you're so vain, it's like a disease! Gentlemen, Shervinsky's
    here. Come to table!

THE WHITE GUARD
(or The Days of the Turbins)
by Mikhail Afanasyevich Bulgakov

Russian: One Male and One Female

THE PLAY: Set in the time of the Russian Revolution, as the Bolsheviks were clamoring to create a Soviet Union and the Cossacks were marauding, the Ukrainian armed forces stood behind their Hetman (leader/prince). When even he deserted his capital, the people were left to see which side would win out and which government would lead them. The original alliances of the Turbin family are challenged and changed by the end of the play.

THE SCENE: Elena (24) has had a bit too much to drink at dinner, and has let her guard down. Shervinsky (20s), the unflagging admirer, is able to make his move on the emotionally needy lady of the house.

TIME AND PLACE: Elena's drawing/sitting room. Late evening. Winter, 1918. Kiev.

ELENA: I'll go and see what's the matter with him.

SHERVINSKY: *(Blocking the doorway.)* Don't bother, Lena.

ELENA: God, did they have to behave like this? . . . Chaos . . . the rooms thick with cigarette smoke . . . Look, Lariosik's still here!

SHERVINSKY: For heaven's sake, don't wake him up.

ELENA: I'm half drunk myself, thanks to you. Oh, God, I can't even walk straight.

SHERVINSKY: There now, sit down over there. May I sit beside you?

ELENA: Yes, do . . . What's to become of us, Shervinsky? How is all this going to end? Mm? . . . I had a nightmare last night. Everything around us is going from bad to worse.

SHERVINSKY: We'll be all right, Yeliena. You mustn't believe in bad dreams.

ELENA: No, no, my dream was prophetic. I dreamed we were all sailing to America in a ship, sitting in the hold. Then a storm blew up. The wind howled, it was freezing cold, rough sea. And we were in the hold. The water rose up to our feet. We clambered onto some bunks. Suddenly there were rats everywhere — huge, repulsive rats. It was so awful that I woke up.

SHERVINSKY: Do you know something, Yeliena? He's not going to come back.

ELENA: Who?

SHERVINSKY: Your husband.

ELENA: You're not supposed to say that. What business of yours is it whether he comes back or not?

SHERVINSKY: It's very much my business. I love you.

ELENA: Do you expect me to believe you?

SHERVINSKY: It's true, for God's sake — I love you.

ELENA: Well, you can love me in silence.

SHERVINSKY: I won't. It's too boring.

ELENA: Just a moment — what made you start talking about my husband just now?

SHERVINSKY: Because he's like a rat.

ELENA: And you, Leonid, are like a pig! To start with, he doesn't look a bit like a rat.

SHERVINSKY: Oh yes, he does. The pince-nez on that long, sharp nose . . .

ELENA: Charming! Slandering an absent man in front of his wife.

SHERVINSKY: You're completely the wrong person to be his wife.

ELENA: What do you mean by that?

SHERVINSKY: Look at yourself in the mirror. You're beautiful, intelligent — emancipated as they say. Altogether, a magnificent woman. You're a splendid accompanist on the piano. Compared with you, he's nothing but a dummy. A careerist. A General Staff pen pusher.

ELENA: Brave boy — now that his back's turned! *(Closes his mouth.)*

SHERVINSKY: I would say all that to his face. Wanted to for a long time. I'd say it, and challenge him to a duel. You're not happy with him.

ELENA: Is there anyone I *could* be happy with?

SHERVINSKY: With me.

ELENA: No, you won't do.

SHERVINSKY: Why not?

ELENA: What's good about you?

SHERVINSKY: Take a good look, and you'll see.

ELENA: A pair of gaudy aide-de-campe's tassels, a face like a pretty cherub. And a voice. That's all.

SHERVINSKY: I might have known it! Really it's too bad! Everyone says the same thing: either Shervinsky the aide-de-campe or Shervinsky the singer . . . but no one ever sees that Shervinsky's a human being with a soul,

Shervinsky lives like a dog without a kennel. Shervinsky hath no where to lay his head.

ELENA: *(Pushing his head away.)* Ah Casanova — don't think I don't know your tricks! You tell the same sob story to all your women. Including that long, thin one — with the painted mouth . . .

SHERVINSKY: She's not long and thin, she's a mezzo-soprano. I swear to you, Yeliena, I've never said anything of the kind to her and never shall. That was unkind of you, Lena, really unkind.

ELENA: You may *not* call me Lena!

SHERVINSKY: All right — that was unkind of you, Yeliena Vassilievna. You are completely insensitive to my feelings.

ELENA: The trouble is, I happen to like you very much.

SHERVINSKY: Aha! You like me. And you don't love your husband.

ELENA: No, I do love him.

SHERVINSKY: Don't lie, Lena. A woman who loves her husband doesn't have your look in her eyes. I know women's eyes. They tell you everything.

ELENA: I grant you've had plenty of experience.

SHERVINSKY: How could he run away like that?

ELENA: You would have done the same, given the chance.

SHERVINSKY: Me? Never! It's shameful. Admit you don't love him!

ELENA: Very well: I don't love him and I don't respect him. I don't respect him. Satisfied? But that doesn't mean you can jump to conclusions. Take your hands off.

SHERVINSKY: In that case why did you kiss me that time?

ELENA: Liar! I've never kissed you. You're a gold-tasselled liar!

SHERVINSKY: Me — a liar? What about that time at the piano? I was singing "All-powerful God," and we were on our own. I can even tell you the date — it was November the eighth. We were on our own and you kissed me on the lips.

ELENA: I kissed you because I like your voice. Do you see? It was a friendly kiss, because you have a remarkable voice. And that's all.

SHERVINSKY: Is that really all?

ELENA: This is a nightmare, I swear it. All these dirty plates, everyone drunk . . . My husband's left me. And the light's so strong . . .

SHERVINSKY: We'll put that light out. *(Switches off the overhead light.)* That better? Listen, Lena, I love you very much. And I'm not going to let you go. You're going to be my wife.

ELENA: You slide up like a snake . . . like a snake . . .

SHERVINSKY: Why am I like a snake?

ELENA: Because you lead me into temptation. But I warn you — it won't do you any good. You'll get nowhere. Whatever his faults, I'm not going to ruin my life for your sake. You may even turn out to be worse.

SHERVINSKY: Lena, you're so beautiful!

ELENA: Go away! I'm drunk. And *you* got me drunk on purpose. You're notorious. The whole of our life is collapsing. Everything's fallen apart, Leonid.

SHERVINSKY: Don't be afraid, Yeliena. I won't abandon you at a time like this. I'll stay beside you, Lena.

ELENA: Let me go. I'm afraid I might disgrace the name of Talberg.

SHERVINSKY: Lena, leave him altogether and marry me . . . Lena.

(They kiss.)

Will you divorce him?

ELENA: Oh, to hell with everything!

(They kiss.)

HEY, THERE — HELLO!
by Gennadi Mamlin

Russian: One Male and One Female

THE PLAY: Set on the Black Coast seaside, *Hey, There — Hello!* tells the story of two teenage neighbors who have nothing in common but a curious interest in each other at the beginning of the summer and who grow to be close friends by the summer's end.

THE SCENE: Masha (14) has been sent to live with her grandmother for the summer. She is delighted to learn that she has a neighbor right next door who is her age. Valerka (14) is too busy practicing his magic act to be disturbed by inquisitive girls, but his interest is piqued, nonetheless, by this bold, confident young neighbor girl. Masha has broken a board on the fence separating their yards, and has just peeked into Valerka's backyard. This is the first scene and first meeting of the two in the play.

TIME AND PLACE: The present. Summer. A beach area near the Black Sea. Russia. Afternoon. Valerka's backyard.

On the left — extending almost to the proscenium — we see part of a tall board fence. The entire stage from this fence to the right is the backyard of the Dorokhov's house. A low wall built of mixed stones separates the yard from the street. In the yard are a table, chairs, a garden swing. These props are adequate for the scene, but the set designer may use his or her ingenuity in elaborating the decor with objects suggesting a seaside town environment, adding bright touches of southern (Black Sea region) flora.

On the table and chairs are sundry small boxes, rings, and swords — a magician's apparatus. In the center of the yard stands a narrow black chest, the height of a man's neck. A tattered picture poster is pasted to it: a magician in a tailcoat, in garish letters his name — Albert Guido.

It is early morning. Valerka, wearing faded jeans and a blue-and-white striped sailor's jersey, is squatting as he cleans the blade of a sword.

From somewhere in the distance we hear a tune on a trumpet. This melody is the motif for the pantomime scenes. It is therefore important to give it a certain evocative coloring, to distinguish it from all the other offstage sounds in the play, such as the ships' whistles, the popular music played on the beach, etc.

Valerka, dropping the sword, takes a step in the direction from which the trumpet music is heard, but at this instant one of the boards in the fence is moved aside and Masha sticks her head through the opening.

MASHA: *(With the spontaneous friendliness characteristic of simple, good-natured people.)* Hey there — hello! My name is Masha.

VALERKA: *(Looking at Masha unenthusiastically.)* I'll bear that in mind.

MASHA: *(Not aware of his irony.)* I got here Friday. I'm staying with my grandmother.

VALERKA: Taisya?

MASHA: Yes. I lived with her last summer, too, but you weren't here. You were in camp.

VALERKA: It was Mother's idea . . . Why don't you crawl through?

MASHA: *(Coming through the opening.)* I don't have time. I'm doing errands for our roomers . . . What's that in your hand?

VALERKA: A sword.

MASHA: Is it the kind that's swallowed? My grandmother says there's a sword swallower living at your place. *(She reads the poster.)* "Albert Guido." Is he a Spaniard?

VALERKA: Ordinarily he's Semyon Semyonovich Leschinsky, but for the circus it's better to have a name like Guido.

MASHA: You know, when he wears a tailcoat he looks like an orchestra conductor. But in ordinary clothes — he looks like a bookkeeper. I watched him for an hour. He's old! *(Garrulously.)* Yesterday they showed the circus on television. There were clowns. One was very short, the other as tall as a telephone pole. The short one was running away from the tall one, then suddenly he stopped, turned around, and socked the telephone pole with his fist. The pole fell down as if he had been hit by a ton of bricks. *(She laughs heartily.)* Wasn't that funny?

VALERKA: How would *I* know? Maybe it was.

MASHA: *(With conviction.)* It was. Grandmother fell out of her chair laughing. *(She walks across the yard.)* Say, who is that Nikolai who lives with you?

VALERKA: A *homo sapiens*.

MASHA: A who?

VALERKA: A person.

MASHA: He's a strange one. When he fixed our gate Grandma offered him half a ruble. You know, he refused. Then she offered him a whole ruble. Still he refused, saying, "I did it because of your beautiful eyes." What does he do for a living, since he seems to be a millionaire who doesn't need money?

VALERKA: He's a cabinet maker. He happens to be here on vacation, not to earn money.

MASHA: If he's here to rest, then why is he hammering away over there in the shed for the second day now? *(She touches one of the small boxes. The lid pops open and a flower springs up.)* Oh! My God!

VALERKA: Get away from there! And, generally, why don't you get lost!

MASHA: I'm sorry! *(She tries to push the flower back down into the box.)*

VALERKA: I suppose you came to talk. So, talk. But keep your hands to yourself! There's hardly any space to move around in — Guido's stuff is all over the place. They persuaded him to perform at the Seamen's Club. We're repairing his equipment, Nikolai and me. There's a chest in the shed that's used to separate a person's head from his body. If you poke your head into *that,* it'll be curtains for you!

MASHA: *(Peers offstage at a shed, which is not visible to the audience.)* Such goings on! Yesterday Vera, one of our boarders, snuck up to the shed and startled Nikolai with a silly riddle. *(Laughs heartily.)*

VALERKA: So? . . .

MASHA: It was very funny! There he was hammering away, and she springs this silly riddle on him.

VALERKA: Listen, where are you from?

MASHA: Me? I'm from the Voronezh region. Why do you ask?

VALERKA: Anyway, you'd better display your Voronezh sense of humor around here in a whisper. People are still sleeping.

MASHA: Yesterday evening Vera wore boots — I notice that boots are very stylish in the city now, even in summer — and she went down the street with Nikolai, arm in arm. And back home she has a husband! The letter carrier says that he sends her a telegram every other day.

VALERKA: What do you do, run a spying service?

MASHA: All evening yesterday I was peeking through a crack in your fence. Our boarders are uninteresting, not like yours. They come back from the beach, eat their dinner, and then take a nap. After that they play cards or some word game. What a mob has poured in from the city this year! It's horrible! Evenings the sidewalk is so full of them, you'd think it was a demonstration! *(She squats down beside Valerka.)* Can I help?

VALERKA: *(He hands Masha another sword, a rag, and a piece of chalk to clean it with.)* Make sure you don't swallow it!

MASHA: *(Laughs. Valerka looks puzzled. She responds to his look.)* When I hear something witty I laugh, every time! Sometimes even when it's not funny I laugh, just to be polite. But you — you're such a silent one.

VALERKA: No, not silent — just a man of few words. There's a difference.

MASHA: And me — on the contrary, I love to talk. I open my mouth and the words run on like a piece of driftwood in a strong current.

VALERKA: *(Looks at his image reflected in the shining blade of the sword he's been polishing. Suddenly.)* Mashka! Try to imagine what I'll look like ten years from now.

MASHA: How do I do that?

VALERKA: In your mind's eye, silly! Do you have a mind's eye?

MASHA: Of course I have!

VALERKA: Then go ahead and imagine.

MASHA: *(Thinking.)* Should I close my eyes?

VALERKA: All right, close them.

MASHA: *(Closes her eyes and concentrates.)* I can't. I was looking at the sun and all I can see is rings swimming before my eyes. Valerka, where do you eat your dinner?

VALERKA: My mother left money with the cashier at the Oreanda Restaurant. I go there and eat, and she pays for me.

MASHA: Is it true that your mother's now in Madagascar?

VALERKA: *(Nods.)* She's the navigation officer on an ocean liner.

MASHA: And why has your father been in the hospital for so long?

VALERKA: That's not exactly your business. Why don't you just go on with your work?

MASHA: Oh! *(Jumps up and listens.)* I heard a door bang. Grandmother is up and I haven't cut the roses yet. I must run. So long!

VALERKA: Gud-bai. *(Evidently Valerka knows a few English words.)*

MASHA: Are you glad that I came to visit you?

VALERKA: Totally!

MASHA: It was yesterday that I pulled the nails out of the fence board. For a long time now I've been wanting us to become friends.

VALERKA: You're a strange one!

MASHA: What's so strange about me?

VALERKA: I haven't yet given the matter enough thought, but you're strange, for sure!

MASHA: Let's get to be friends first and then you can give me some thought. Those who don't know me might take me for a little fool. To strangers I seem kind of obvious and scatterbrained. Even my own mother criticizes me — says I never keep a single thought to myself. So long!

VALERKA: We've already said gud-bai. Don't let me keep you.

HEY, THERE — HELLO!
by Gennadi Mamlin

Russian: One Male and One Female

THE PLAY: Set on the Black Coast seaside, *Hey, There — Hello!* tells the story of two teenage neighbors who have nothing in common but a curious interest in each other at the beginning of the summer and who grow to be close friends by the summer's end.

THE SCENE: Masha (14) and Valerka (14) have been enjoying antagonizing each other all summer long. Their friendship borders on the passions of young first love but remains brutally honest like old friends or siblings. Masha comes to visit Valerka and brings his attention to his hypocritical nature: most specifically, his claim that he does not charge the boarders ("his friends") at his house. Valerka is truly surprised to hear her accusations.

TIME AND PLACE: The present. Summer. A beach area near the Black Sea. Russia. Afternoon. Valerka's backyard.

The Dorokhov's yard. In the foreground, an easel and a stool, with a box of paints and a brush. It is a hot day. We see Valerka peering through a crack in the fence. Soon Masha's head appears above the fence. He does not see her. She looks at him for a while without smiling then throws a cypress cone at him and disappears. Valerka is startled. He looks around and, seeing no one, resumes looking through the crack into Taisya's yard.

MASHA: *(Crawls through the fence, studies what is painted on the canvas — not looking at Valerka.)* Hello!

VALERKA: *(Abruptly stops looking through the crack, straightens up, then, without turning, draws a line across the fence, steps away from it. After a moment of thought, he draws another line, perpendicular to the first one, admires his handiwork, and slowly turns his head toward Masha.)* Did you rise from the bowels of the earth?

MASHA: Yes. Do you paint?

VALERKA: I create! I'm painting an abstract study of what goes on on the seamy side of this fence.

MASHA: *(Nodding toward the easel.)* Did you paint this, too?

VALERKA: Oh, that? It's a mere jest of genius, a sketch. *(He goes over to the easel.)* War in the Crimea — everything is up in smoke.

MASHA: *(Pointing.)* And what is this? — here?

VALERKA: Not "what" but "who." A boy. In contemporary art what is most important — is to avoid photographic likeness.

MASHA: Do you think you're talented?

VALERKA: Who knows? A fool was once asked: Can you play the violin? He answered: I don't know, I never tried. It's the same with me.

MASHA: *(Continuing to examine the painting.)* And who is this — the boy's grandfather?

VALERKA: What makes you think it's an old man?

MASHA: He's got a beard.

VALERKA: *(Thoughtfully.)* Have it your way — only it happens to be a tree, and not anybody's grandfather. You're looking at an autumn landscape.

MASHA: *(After a pause.)* Go on with your creating. I didn't come to see you anyway. I came to see Nikolai. Your uncle sent me to tell him to come and help carry some fruit to the post office — he's shipping it home. *(She looks penetratingly at Valerka, seems to be about to say something, but controls herself.)* Is Nikolai home?

VALERKA: Take a look. Lately they've all been disappearing first thing in the morning. I wake up — there's no one around. I'm abandoned. They return after dark and fall into bed. If it weren't against the law, they'd probably just live on the beach.

MASHA: What is there for them to do here? Sit around and chew the rag with your uncle?

VALERKA: I suppose it's better to get sunstroke. Or to drown.

MASHA: Where did you get the paints?

VALERKA: Vera gave me her easel and paints and these canvases. She left suddenly, an hour ago, and said I should keep her things so I wouldn't forget her.

MASHA: *(As if stating a simple fact.)* You know, you really are a rat! I mean, a real rat!

VALERKA: What's the matter, Balagayeva? What's eating you?

MASHA: I swore I wouldn't get mixed up in this! That I'd pretend I didn't know anything about it, that it's none of my business. But since hypocrisy has become your second nature . . . I almost believed in your selflessness. Because a person would like to believe that he's surrounded by real people, not crummy ones. You keep carrying on about my grandmother. Her pension is only sixty rubles a month. She doesn't pretend to be a holy-of-holies. You're right, she has nothing but money on her mind. But tell me, how much does your mother earn?

VALERKA: *(Not understanding what she's driving at.)* I don't get it. What *is* eating you?

MASHA: Don't try to evade my question. A navigator on an ocean liner must bring home plenty of pay. And your father's war pension is a lot bigger than what my grandmother gets.

VALERKA: I wouldn't know. We don't talk about money in my family.

MASHA: Why talk about it when you have it? *(Mimicking him.)* "Vera left suddenly." At least if you showed some shame when you lie. But no — you have developed your hypocrisy to a fine art. You lie without blinking an eye. You pretend not to know why Vera packed in such a great hurry, and took off in five minutes flat.

VALERKA: What crazy nonsense you're talking, Masha. What's come over you, anyway?!

MASHA: Go on pretending, acting simple-minded. Your uncle at least lacks your pretenses. Yesterday evening he blurted it all out. He even boasted about it to my grandmother. He says his cousin ought to be grateful to him, that a man is in charge now who's put some sense into her son's head — yours! . . . No, my grandmother doesn't have enough imagination to charge ten kopecks for a free local call made on her telephone. But you planned a dirty scheme like that with your uncle.

VALERKA: *What* ten kopecks?! What are you raving about?

MASHA: Are you trying to tell me you weren't the one who nailed a box beside the telephone for the purpose?

VALERKA: *(With growing bewilderment.)* My father nailed it there — for bills, receipts, papers.

MASHA: It *was* for papers. But now — if your "friends" use the phone they have to put in a coin. "We don't intend to pay for your conversations," your uncle tells them, "and if you've unburdened your heart, talked a long time — put in two coins."

VALERKA: *(Beside himself, roars.)* WHOSE HEART?! WHOSE COINS?!

MASHA: Guido's. Vera's. Anyway, you know better than I do *whose!* It wasn't for *me* that your uncle deposited ten rubles in the savings bank!

VALERKA: *(Now with sad suspicion.)* You say that Vera packed and left — for *what* reason?

MASHA: What an actor you are! *(Mimicking him.)* "It's friends, not boarders, who live in my house!" . . . You know as well as I do that she left because you and your uncle raised the rent for her room — to three rubles a day. He said there was space in that room for *three* cots. But where was she, a student, to get that kind of money?

VALERKA: *(Holding his head.)* Masha! Stop! *(After a pause.)* Do you mean that my uncle has been collecting rent money from Guido, from Nikolai, from Vera?

MASHA: *(Now she is bewildered.)* For a whole week now. A ruble a day. And he's also insisting that they pay up for the past use of the rooms.

VALERKA: What a lowdown rat! The damned extortionist! The Kulak!

MASHA: Did you really not know about all this?

VALERKA: What do you take me for, you bird brain! *(Paces wildly up and down in a state of outrage.)* That's all we need! How low can we sink?! And I kept beating my brains out thinking, why have they been avoiding me — giving me the cold shoulder? . . . He's a rotten swindler!

MASHA: He says he doesn't keep the money for himself, that he deposits it in the bank, in your name.

VALERKA: That doesn't exactly make me feel any better. *(Shouts.)* Just think! Guido barely manages on his pension, but won't charge for his performance! . . . Enough of this!

MASHA: *(Upset.)* Oh, Valerka! I'm not even glad that I told you all this.

VALERKA: Would you be glad if I belonged to the same gang as you and your Taisya? If I did, I'd pray for a storm, throw myself into the sea, and swim till a wave knocked me against a rocky cliff. *(He runs into the house and comes back almost at once with a large suitcase. He throws it onto the table and runs back into the house.)*

MASHA: What are you up to now?

VALERKA: *(Comes out carrying an armful of his uncle's underwear and bedding.)* Put all that into the suitcase.

MASHA: Are you out of your mind? Chasing your own uncle out of the house! A relative!

VALERKA: *(He is now back with a second batch of things.)* Relative? What makes him a relative? "Relative" means being close — in thought, in behavior. Right?

MASHA: But he's your mother's cousin.

VALERKA: So what?! Am I accountable because his cousin gave birth to me? If he claims to be my kin let him first behave so that I won't be ashamed of being related to him! Guido is my kin! Nikolai! Copernicus, who was burned at the stake — he is my kin! But that one is no relative of mine! He's a thief!

(Valerka runs back into the house. Masha, dumfounded, clasps her hands in amazement, then starts to pack the suitcase. Valerka brings out some more of his uncle's things.)

VALERKA: Hurry up! Why are you standing there? Get on with the packing!
(He sits at the table, takes a pencil and paper from his pocket, and starts writing a note. Masha hesitates, then resumes packing. Valerka continues to write.) He's shrewd. He knows Mother is on a voyage and Father is lying sick in the hospital. Neither one of them would have allowed him even to step into our house. They despise money grubbers like him!
(The telephone rings in the house.)

MASHA: The telephone.

VALERKA: Answer it.

MASHA: *(Goes, then calls from offstage.)* It's the hospital. For you.

VALERKA: *(Continuing to write.)* It's on a long cord — bring it out here. *(Pause. Then, realizing what Masha has said, he is frightened.)* The *hospital?!* *(Masha brings out the phone and hands it to him.)* Yes? . . . Yes, Doctor, it's me. *(Dazed.)* When? . . . In a car? What car? *(He drops the receiver and after a brief pause turns to Masha.)* I must hurry! *(Dashes off.)*

THE LOVE-GIRL AND THE INNOCENT
by Alexander Solzhenitsyn

Russian: One Male and One Female

THE PLAY: Set in a co-ed prison in the autumn of 1945, *The Love-Girl and the Innocent* reveals the inner workings and politics behind the paranoid cold war Russian policies. Most of the prisoners had come from the Russian front where they were fighting to save their country in World War II. They then found themselves labeled "enemies of the state" for disagreeing, or not actively agreeing, with the new Soviet system of government.

THE SCENE: Utterly unequipped to handle prison life, Nemov (20s) cowers in a hovel in the prison's foundry. Lyuba (23) finds him and comforts him in her way; she is the love-girl after all.

TIME AND PLACE: Autumn, 1945. A prison work camp. The foundry (iron shop).

The tapping sound inside the cupola stops. Enter Lyuba from the left.

LYUBA: Comrade Gurvich, telephone for you . . . Where is he? He must have dashed out. *(She looks into the room on the right, then comes back. Someone emerges from under the cupola.)* Oy, who's that?
(It is Nemov. He straightens up. His canvas overalls are so torn that in places his skin can be seen through them. His face and his torn cap are covered with gray dust. He is wearing a pair of homemade celluloid spectacles and carrying a chisel and a hammer.)
NEMOV: It's me. Don't you recognize me?
LYUBA: No-oo, it can't be! You look a sight! *(She laughs buoyantly. Nemov lifts his glasses, smiles and scratches his head with his hammer.)* How did you fit in there? There's not room.
NEMOV: Yes, it *was* a bit cramped. But I'm thinner these days. If only there wasn't so much dust . . . Lyuba, that's your name, isn't it?
LYUBA: You've remembered? Such a cold, efficient production chief. You never seemed to notice who anyone was.
NEMOV: Yes, you've got something there. I was still trying to get in with the authorities. A sudden crash and there I was still trying to pull myself back at

the last step. In those days I preferred to bend others than to bend myself. But I feel freer now I'm an ordinary black-faced working man.

LYUBA: There's only one thing wrong with being a black-faced worker — they die.

NEMOV: Well, look at me — chiselling off the slag, singing songs . . .

LYUBA: That's because you're in the foundry. You get good rations in the foundry.

NEMOV: You know something — sometimes I think to myself, are our lives so important? Are they the most valuable thing we have?

LYUBA: *(With great attention.)* What else is there?

NEMOV: It sounds funny talking about it here in the camp, but maybe . . . conscience . . .

LYUBA: *(Gazing at him intently.)* Do you think so?
(Pause.)

NEMOV: How are your hands? I remember you had trouble with them.

LYUBA: My hands? *(She holds them out.)*

NEMOV: But that's impossible! *(He drops the chisel and hammer and takes Lyuba by the hands.)* They're so beautiful and white. It's all gone!

LYUBA: *(Laughs out loud.)* There was never anything there.

NEMOV: What do you mean? I saw it with my own eyes, black blisters all round here . . .

LYUBA: I was swinging the lead!

NEMOV: What does that mean?

LYUBA: I swung the lead, so as not to go on that transport. "Swinging the lead" is what they call it in the camp when you fix it to look ill — like a tumor or a blind eye or a fever.

NEMOV: Can you really do it?

LYUBA: He doesn't believe me! 'Course I can. I fooled you, didn't I?

NEMOV: It's fantastic. How did you fool the warder?

LYUBA: Oh, I think he guessed. But he took pity on me. Wouldn't you have taken pity on me?

NEMOV: . . . Probably not . . .

LYUBA: Have you finished examining my hands? Why don't you let go of them?

NEMOV: I need them . . .

LYUBA: What for? *(Nemov kisses Lyuba's hands.)* You're not going to pretend you like me?

NEMOV: How can you say that?

LYUBA: When they brought us in — I mean the new transport — they made us sit on the ground. You came up to the women, you looked us all over and you chose . . . Granya. Do you remember?

NEMOV: Just a minute . . . what did you think when I chose Granya?

LYUBA: I thought, why didn't he chose me?

NEMOV: It's simple, it was a different criterion.

LYUBA: But your eyes were open, weren't they? How could you have chosen anyone else!

NEMOV: Lyuba, I was looking for a gang leader, someone with drive . . .

LYUBA: I was terribly offended.

NEMOV: Of course I noticed immediately how . . . how pretty you are.

LYUBA: So why did you try to send me out into the forests?

NEMOV: They needed a barber.

LYUBA: Why should I suffer because of that?

NEMOV: No, of course not, there's no reason why you should suffer. A girl like you should wear a fine, white dress, with lilies of the valley pinned here, across the breast. Even in that uniform quilt jacket you look . . . Give me your hands.

LYUBA: What for?

NEMOV: To kiss.

LYUBA: What sort of man kisses like that? On the hands?

NEMOV: It's all I dare.

LYUBA: You're funny. *(Nemov kisses her hands.)* Your hands are all cut.

NEMOV: The slag's sharp. I have to hammer it out with a chisel. Sometimes I miss.

LYUBA: What a life! It's hard for you, isn't it?

NEMOV: It's almost a year now since I was arrested. Since then it's been nothing but gloom and misery. Now for the first time I feel happy.

LYUBA: Happy? On general duties?

NEMOV: Now that you're here . . .

LYUBA: I was here when you were one of the bosses.

NEMOV: It's wonderful not being one of the bosses. If I was I'd think you were trying to get something out of me. But now . . .

LYUBA: Now it's time I went. Let go of me.

NEMOV: Don't go.

LYUBA: Are we just going to stand here, like this? *(Nemov mumbles something.)* Come to the culture room this evening. There's going to be a concert. Come backstage. *(She moves slowly away from him, her back to the door.)*

NEMOV: *(Walking slowly after her.)* Will I see you then, Lyuba? *(Lyuba nods her head and leaves. Nemov stops and stands there gazing after her. The painted curtain falls.)*

MARRIAGE
by Nikolai Gogol

Russian: Two Males

THE PLAY: A Russian farce with humor, quick pacing, and memorable characters, *Marriage* explores the common topic of matchmaking and the "resistant groom."

THE SCENE: Ivan Podkolyosin (mid-20s) is a renowned bachelor who cannot decide whether or not he wants to be married. His friend, Ilya Kochkaryov (mid-20s) will hear no more excuses and decides to arrange a marriage for his friend that very day.

TIME AND PLACE: Podkolyosin's quarters — a bachelor's room. Early evening. St. Petersburg, Russia. 1825.

KOCHKARYOV: Well, brother, we mustn't waste any time. Let's go.

PODKOLYOSIN: Wait — ! Nothing's settled! I've just started to think things over.

KOCHKARYOV: Nonsense, don't be afraid. I'll marry you off so fast you won't even know what's happened. Let's go meet the bride and you'll see how painless it is.

PODKOLYOSIN: You mean — go now?

KOCHKARYOV: Why not? Look, see what comes of not being married? Look at this room: unpolished boots, tobacco all over the table, and you! You lie on the couch like a sloth, turning from side to side.

PODKOLYOSIN: I admit it, Kochkariev, there's no sense of order in my life.

KOCHKARYOV: But once you've got a wife, you'll never recognize the place . . . or yourself. You'll have a nice couch over here, with a cunning lapdog lying on the cushions. Picture yourself on the couch, listening to an adorable little canary in a cage, when suddenly — the lady of the house comes to sit by you, with her soft dainty hands.

PODKOLYOSIN: Soft, dainty hands? Yes . . . yes, they're as soft as milk . . .

KOCHKARYOV: And they don't have just hands, you know, they have . . . God knows what!

PODKOLYOSIN: I'd like it . . . a little lady sitting next to me.

KOCHKARYOV: You've got the picture! We have only to work things out, you needn't worry about a thing — the wedding supper, and so on — I'll take care of everything. Champagne — a dozen bottles won't be enough! And Madiera — half-dozen at least. The bride must have a whole flock of aunts, and they mustn't be served cheap Rhine wine, must they? Now as far as the supper is concerned, I know a caterer — he fills you up! You can't even get out of your chair!

PODKOLYOSIN: Calm down, Kochkariev, you're racing ahead as if we were already at the altar!

KOCHKARYOV: Why retreat now? You agree, don't you?

PODKOLYOSIN: Not exactly. Not yet. No, I haven't agreed at all.

KOCHKARYOV: But you said not one minute ago —

PODKOLYOSIN: — I only said it mightn't be a bad idea.

KOCHKARYOV: But we just worked it out. What's the matter, don't you like the idea of marriage?

PODKOLYOSIN: No, I like the idea, but —

KOCHKARYOV: So? What's wrong with you?

PODKOLYOSIN: Nothing. It's just . . . strange.

KOCHKARYOV: What's strange?

PODKOLYOSIN: It is strange. I was always a bachelor; and then, in a flash, I'm married!

KOCHKARYOV: You ought to be ashamed! I see I'll have to have a heart-to-heart talk with you, father to son. Look at yourself. Closely, like you're looking at me. What do you see? Who are you? No, you don't have the answer, there is no answer. What do you live for? Examine yourself in the mirror. What do you see? The same bored, stupid face, and not much else. But now, imagine yourself: children surrounding you — two, three, maybe half-a-dozen — all exactly like you. Peas in a pod. Right now, you're nothing but an unmarried Court Councilor. But picture yourself at the center of a family of teeny-weeny civil servants, itsy-bitsy court councilors, all pulling on your whiskers. And you'll be barking at them, barking like a dog, bow wow wow! What could be lovelier?

PODKOLYOSIN: But if they turn into little monsters, they'll wreck everything. They'll mix up all my legal papers.

KOCHKARYOV: Let them mix — remember, they look just like you.

PODKOLYOSIN: Damn, it's funny . . . little ones, looking just like me!

KOCHKARYOV: Funny? It's wonderful. Let's go, then.

PODKOLYOSIN: All right, let's go.

KOCHKARYOV: Stepan! Stepan! Help your master! We've got to get him dressed — fast! *(Stepan enters.)*

PODKOLYOSIN: Wait, I think I ought to wear my white vest.

KOCHKARYOV: Don't bother with that now.

PODKOLYOSIN: Damned laundress didn't starch my collar! Again! It won't stand up properly. Tell her, Stepan, tell her if she continues doing my laundry like this I'll find someone new. She carries on with her boyfriend instead of starching my collars.

KOCHKARYOV: All right, all right, but hurry up!

PODKOLYOSIN: One more second. *(He puts on his frock coat, sits down.)* Listen to me, Ilya Fomin Kochkariev, I've got a good idea. You go by yourself.

KOCHKARYOV: By myself — are you out of your mind? Who's getting married, you or me?

PODKOLYOSIN: You're right. But suddenly I don't feel quite like it. Tomorrow will be better.

KOCHKARYOV: The man doesn't have an ounce of brains! Idiot — you're all dressed, and suddenly you "don't feel quite like it"! You're a complete fool.

PODKOLYOSIN: *(He whispers.)* Why are you yelling at me? I haven't done anything to you.

KOCHKARYOV: You're an idiot! Everyone knows it. They all say, "Podkoliosin's an idiot, even though he is a Court Councilor." Why the hell I bother — why, you can't even cross the street by yourself. You're just a damned, lying, lazy bachelor! You're a damned — no, I can't bring myself to use the word that describes you, you . . . damned old woman! Old bedsocks!

PODKOLYOSIN: You're not so appealing yourself. *(He whispers:)* Are you out of your mind, cursing me in front of my servant? You might have done it in private! And such foul language.

KOCHKARYOV: Why shouldn't I swear at you? Who could resist swearing at you? You decide, like any normal human being, to follow my mature advice and get married. And then, out of cowardice, you —

PODKOLYOSIN: All right, I'm coming, I'm coming. Why are you shouting?

KOCHKARYOV: He's coming, he's coming, he's coming! Hey, Stepan! Quick, bring his hat and coat. *(He looks back at Podkoliosin.)* Strange creature. I wouldn't want to play cards with him — he'd keep changing his bid. All right, my dear, it's all over now. I'm not swearing at you any more. *(Exeunt.)*

MARRIAGE
by Nikolai Gogol

Russian: Two Males

THE PLAY: A Russian farce with humor, quick pacing, and memorable characters, *Marriage* explores the common topic of matchmaking and the "resistant groom."

THE SCENE: Ivan Podkolyosin (mid-20s) has just met his match, a beautiful young woman named Agafya. His friend, Ilya Kochkaryov (mid-20s) has left him alone with the young woman in the hopes that he will propose and be ready to whisk her away to the church for the wedding. The meeting between the "lovers" ends sooner than Kochkaryov planned, and his friend seems to be up to his old indecisive tricks again.

TIME AND PLACE: Agafya's house. The parlor. Early evening. St. Petersburg, Russia. 1825.

PODKOLYOSIN: I'm going home now.

KOCHKARYOV: Now? Why?

PODKOLYOSIN: Why should I stay here? I've said everything I had to.

KOCHKARYOV: You poured out your heart to her?

PODKOLYOSIN: Pour? No, well, I didn't exactly pour it out. Yet.

KOCHKARYOV: So why not?

PODKOLYOSIN: You expect me to just walk in and say, "Good afternoon, madam, let's get married?"

KOCHKARYOV: What did you two talk about for half an hour?

PODKOLYOSIN: We chatted about any number of things. I admit it was very pleasant.

KOCHKARYOV: You haven't much time left to settle it. In one hour the church bells will begin to ring for you.

PODKOLYOSIN: Are you crazy? Marry her today — ?

KOCHKARYOV: You gave your word. You swore you'd do it the minute the others were out of the way. So now you're ready to get married.

PODKOLYOSIN: I'm a man of my word. Only . . . not right now. Give me a month to prepare.

KOCHKARYOV: You must be out of your mind.

PODKOLYOSIN: Less than a month's impossible.

KOCHKARYOV: I've ordered the supper from the caterer, you fool. Listen to me, Ivan Kuzmitch — do it!

PODKOLYOSIN: I couldn't, right now.

KOCHKARYOV: Ivan Kuzmitch, I beg you — if not for yourself, do it for my sake.

PODKOLYOSIN: I can't.

KOCHKARYOV: You can, my dear, you will. Don't hesitate.

PODKOLYOSIN: Impossible. The time's not right.

KOCHKARYOV: Why? Why? Look, you're a sensible man, I'm appealing to you, not only as a Court Councilor, but as a friend. My dear, try to look at it rationally.

PODKOLYOSIN: Well . . . perhaps I . . .

KOCHKARYOV: Ivan Kuzmitch, darling! Must I get down on my knees before you? *(He kneels.)*

PODKOLYOSIN: Why would you do that?

KOCHKARYOV: I am on my knees! See? I'll be indebted to you forever, my dearest, only don't be pig-headed.

PODKOLYOSIN: But I can't, I can't *(Kochkriev rises in a rage.)*

KOCHKARYOV: Pig! Pig!

PODKOLYOSIN: Go on, work yourself up.

KOCHKARYOV: The world has never known such stupidity.

PODKOLYOSIN: Go on, go on!

KOCHKARYOV: Why did I go to the trouble? For you! I did it for you! And now I wash my hands of you!

PODKOLYOSIN: Who asked you to go to such trouble in the first place? Please do wash your hands of me.

KOCHKARYOV: Without me you'll never get anywhere. You'll stay an idiot.

PODKOLYOSIN: So what?

KOCHKARYOV: I did it as a mission of mercy, you feeble-minded fool!

PODKOLYOSIN: You needn't have taken the trouble.

KOCHKARYOV: Good, then go to hell.

PODKOLYOSIN: I'm going!

KOCHKARYOV: Bon voyage!

PODKOLYOSIN: Good-bye!

KOCHKARYOV: And may you break both legs on the way. You're a clod, not a Court Councilor. It's all over between us — I hope I never set eyes on you again!

PODKOLYOSIN: You won't. *(He goes.)*

KOCHKARYOV: Good riddance! The world has never seen such stupidity! *(He paces back and forth.)*

THE POWER OF DARKNESS
by Leo Tolstoy

Russian: One Male and One Female

THE PLAY: Almost Greek in its epic proportions of tragedy, *The Power of Darkness* illuminates the consequences of evil choices. Anisya marries an older man with a dumb daughter and has another child by him, but he is old and not passionate enough for her, so she begins to have an affair with their farm boy. As her love for the farm boy (Nikita) grows, she plots to kill her husband and marry Nikita. After she does so, she finds his affections have turned from her to her dumb stepdaughter. To get her out of the house, Anisya plots to marry her off, but there is one hitch—the stepdaughter is pregnant with Nikita's child. Anisya manages to convince Nikita to kill his own child, bury it in the cellar, and come into the house to say the marriage blessing. As he begins to make the blessing, he turns it instead into a confession of his former sins, including the wrongs he did to a young orphan girl before he married Anisya.

THE SCENE: Marina (23), the orphan-girl he wronged, returns to see Nikita (26) give his blessing to his stepdaughter's wedding. At the end of his rope, Nikita begs for understanding and comfort from his former conquest.

TIME AND PLACE: A Russian village. Outside the hut of Nikita. Evening.

Girls go toward the cottage. Songs and the beating of tambourines as they go.

MARINA: *(Assessing the situation.)* I should've gone. I don't want to. I haven't seen him since he rejected me. That's over a year ago now. I'd like to see how he lives with Anisya. People say they don't get on. She's a tough woman. I've heard she's always got to get her own way. I'm sure there have been times when he's thought of me. All he wanted was an easy life. He gave me up for — God help him. I bear him no grudge. It hurt at the time, I'll never again feel such pain. It's worn off now . . . forgotten. I'd like just to see him again. *(Looks toward the cottage and sees him.)* It's him. What's he doing here? Did they tell him I was here? Why's he left the guests? He looks so unhappy. I must go.

(Nikita enters with his head down; swinging his arms from side to side, and muttering incoherently.)

NIKITA: *(Catching sight of Marina.)* Marina! Dear friend! Dearest Marina! What are you doing here?

MARINA: I'm waiting for my husband.

NIKITA: Why don't you come to the wedding. It'll be fun.

MARINA: I'm not in the mood. I'm here to fetch my husband.

NIKITA: Dearest Marina . . . *(He tries to embrace her.)*

MARINA: *(Pushing him off.)* Stop it. That's over. All past. I've come to fetch my husband. He's inside, isn't he?

NIKITA: Come on . . . not even for old time's sake? You don't want to?

MARINA: What's the point. What's past is past!

NIKITA: Just once more?

MARINA: No. Why are you here? Why have you left all your guests?

NIKITA: *(Sits down in the straw.)* You want to know why I'm here? If only you knew. My life's a mess, Marina. It's so bad, I wish I were blind. I left the table. I walked out . . . to get away from all those people. If only I didn't have to see anyone, ever again.

MARINA: *(Coming close.)* Why?

NIKITA: I can't eat, can't drink . . . can't sleep. I'm sick of this life. So sick of it. And what makes me feel worse is to know that I am totally alone. That there's no one to share my pain.

MARINA: Everyone has their own pain. Tears rinse pain away. In the past I've cried and cried.

NIKITA: Your pain belongs to your past. Now it's my turn to suffer.

MARINA: But what's wrong?

NIKITA: I'm fed up with my life. I hate myself. If only you had stayed with me. Now both our lives are ruined. Life isn't worth living.

MARINA: *(Stands by the barn and weeps. She pulls herself together.)* I can't complain, Nikita. God grant everyone as good a life as mine. I mustn't complain. When I got married, I told my husband everything. He forgave me. He doesn't reproach me. He's a humble old man. He's very fond of me. I look after his children and he's very kind to me. I'm happy with my lot. God intended it to happen like this. What's the point in complaining. How could there be anything wrong with your life? You're rich.

NIKITA: My life? If I didn't think it'd spoil the party, I'd get a rope . . . this one here — *(Picks up a rope from the straw.)* I'd chuck it over that beam; tie a noose, walk the beam, put my head in the noose and jump! That's how much I value my life.

MARINA: Don't talk like this. Christ have mercy on you.

NIKITA: You think I'm joking, don't you? You think I'm drunk? I'm not drunk. Drink doesn't affect me any more. I'm thoroughly miserable. The pain is eating me alive. I don't care about anything any more. But Marina, remember . . . Just remember the nights we spent together . . . by the railway . . . See the moon —

MARINA: Don't Nikita! Don't! It still hurts. I'm married, and so are you. My sin has been forgiven. Don't rake up the past.

NIKITA: What am I going to do? Who can I turn to?

MARINA: You know what to do. You've got a wife. Look after her and don't lust after other women. Once upon a time you loved Anisya. Go on loving her.

NIKITA: Not Anisya . . . She's gall and wormwood to me. She's strangling me like rank weeds.

MARINA: She's still your wife. There's no point talking to you. Get back to your guests. Tell my husband I'm waiting for him.

NIKITA: If only you knew the whole story . . . But as you say, there's no point in talking.

[MARINA'S HUSBAND: Marina! Where's my Missis! Marina, where are you?]

NIKITA: He's calling you. Your husband's coming. You'd better go.

MARINA: What about you?

NIKITA: Me? I'll just lie down for a while.

VALENTIN AND VALENTINA
by Mihail Roschin

Russian: One Male and One Female

THE PLAY: Described by the author as a contemporary play, *Valentin and Valentina* explores the issues of love, liberty, and the existence of both in 1970s Russia (the cold war era). Valentin and Valentina are students and happen to be lovers. The attempts of their families to keep them apart only serve to deepen their connection to each other. As their love reaches the point of no return, Valentina begins to have fears and doubts. Love rules in the end.

THE SCENE: After hearing an antilove lecture from her mother, sister, and grandmother, Valentina (18) seeks refuge with Valentin (18) and tries to sort out the meaning of it all.

TIME AND PLACE: A solitary spot in a large city (a bench, a corner in a coffee shop, a library table). 1977. November. Late afternoon, early evening.

Valentina returns to Valentin. She is deep in thought. Valentin is waiting for her. They sit side by side.

VALENTINA: *(Sighing as if after sobbing.)* So Valechka, so that's how it is . . . After all they truly love me, and I love them. I chose mother, when she and father separated. I was a big girl already, eleven. And grandmother has always been my pal, always up-to-date, knew everything . . . And how I dreamed of love, she knew that too. I used to think, when I fall in love, I shall run into the house with flowers, with such an armful, I'll scatter them about. I'll shower mother with them, granny, Zhenia, and I'll shout: my dears, congratulate me, I am in love! And I'll twirl about and sing. All the windows are open, the curtains flutter, like the First of May . . . I shall phone everyone, send father a telegram and they'll be happy too, they'll laugh, embrace me, bake pies, open wine, and I'll play the march from *Aida* . . . *(Sings.)* . . . Tram, tam-ta-ta-tam! Isn't that wonderful?

VALENTIN: *(Seriously.)* Yes.

VALENTINA: Well, and instead what happens . . . I just don't know. Such terrible anger . . . I can't even find the word. It's just something biological . . .

VALENTIN: You're their possession, you're their investment. What they want is to get a decent return from their capital.

VALENTINA: My Marxist! No, it's just that people torment most, those whom they love most.

VALENTIN: That I don't understand. Don't you think I've grown to love them? If for nothing else — that they're yours: I could shower them with flowers too and say: my dears, what a daughter you have! And they say, "Hello, hello, come in, have some jam, what a well-read, nice boy, such a pleasure . . ." And instead, they are so . . . two-faced! They'll ruin everything for us! It's like some witch's spell.

VALENTINA: Don't! Valia! . . . Val . . .

VALENTIN: Yes, of course . . . Never mind! Never mind! After all, legally we are of age, and legally we could . . .

VALENTINA: Legally, it seems to me, I'm frozen.

VALENTIN: Frozen? Oh, come here! *(Flings wide his coat, embraces her in it.)*

VALENTINA: Valechka, my dearest . . .

VALENTIN: Alechka . . . Do you love me?

VALENTINA: Yes. Very much . . . Wait, and what happened in your home? Wait . . .

VALENTIN: Later . . . let go . . . you see how frozen my hand is . . . let go!

VALENTINA: Stop it!

VALENTIN: I won't stop, let go!

VALENTINA: Come on, I'm ticklish! *(They laugh.)*

VALENTIN: You silly, let go!

VALENTINA: Go away! *(They laugh, kiss. Valentina breaks away.)*

VALENTIN: Val!

VALENTINA: Go away.

VALENTIN: Al!

VALENTINA: What?

VALENTIN: Will you come to my house?

VALENTINA: Yes.

VALENTIN: Definitely.

VALENTINA: Yes.

VALENTIN: Definitely — definitely?

VALENTINA: You are mad.

VALENTIN: Yes, I am mad.

VALENTINA: *(Laughing, lovingly.)* You are a mad, dizzy, silly boy! And they're right when they say . . . how can anyone build a home with you? All you'll do is kiss.

VALENTIN: And why build a home? To make soup in?

VALENTINA: Not soup. It's the nucleus of society, the foundation of the state.

VALENTIN: *(Mischievously.)* Down with family and private property! Will you come?

VALENTINA: Yes, I'll come, my goodness! You better tell me what happened with you.

VALENTIN: Yeah, well!

VALENTINA: "Yeah, well, yeah, well!" I've picked up this "yeah, well" from you!

VALENTIN: And I got this from you! *(Repeats a characteristic gesture of hers.)*

VALENTINA: And I from you like so! *(Copies one of his movements. Both laugh.)* We are after all awfully silly!

VALENTIN: Children!

VALENTINA: We are surrounded by dangers, and we . . .

VALENTIN: And we kiss! *(Finds a chance to kiss her.)*

VALENTINA: Tell me, I'm asking you.

VALENTIN: *(Obediently.)* All right!

VALENTIN AND VALENTINA
by Mihail Roschin

Russian: One Male and One Female

THE PLAY: Described by the author as a contemporary play, *Valentin and Valentina* explores the issues of love, liberty, and the existence of both in 1970s Russia (the cold war era). Valentin and Valentina are students and happen to be lovers. The attempts of their families to keep them apart only serve to deepen their connection to each other. As their love reaches the point of no return, Valentina begins to have fears and doubts. Love rules in the end.

THE SCENE: Valentina (18) has come to visit Valentin (18) at his home while his mother is away for a few days. As the potential for deeper intimacy arises, so do Valentina's suspicions about the depth of Valentin's love for her.

TIME AND PLACE: Valentin's apartment living room. Early evening. November. 1977.

VALENTIN: *(Calling after Masha.)* Afterward straight home! *(He moves toward Valentina.)*

VALENTINA: Wait! Wait a minute! *(About Masha.)* Doesn't she guess?

VALENTIN: What do you mean? She's a child!

VALENTINA: Some child! People think that about us, that we are children . . . wait, I am just so tired.

VALENTIN: Do you want to lay down?

VALENTINA: *(Corrects his grammar.)* Not lay, lie . . .wait, Val . . .

VALENTIN: Why are you like this? Tonight is . . . I missed you so. It seems as if I haven't seen you in a hundred years . . . You know, I understood: love is when not seeing each other is impossible, the agony just eats you up. It seems, without seeing her one more day you won't be able to breathe . . . yes? For you, too? And another thing I noticed: the only time that I don't think of you is when I am with you. Otherwise — all the time, every minute.

VALENTINA: I fall asleep, I wake up — only you . . . I walk, eat, sit at lectures . . . for a long time I haven't heard a thing at lectures.

VALENTIN: Exactly, exactly . . . It's so fantastic that we met. Actually I always imagined . . . although like all the guys I used to laugh, what's all this love, nonsense! But that's how it is! That's it! It is!

VALENTINA: Wait, Valechka. It is so . . . it terrifies me.

VALENTIN: Do you remember how I couldn't even touch you?

VALENTINA: And I wished every minute that you'd at least take me by the hand . . . and it was I who started it?

VALENTIN: Of course, at the movies, remember? Actually, I had nothing to do with it!

VALENTINA: Aha, granny is right. She says: men have become like women, and women like men.

VALENTIN: Now, now, and who gave you the apple first? I'll never forget it! Remember that morning? You kept walking slower and slower, swinging your little . . . bookbag, looking back at me.

VALENTINA: And you came up and said, "Miss, would you like an apple?" Just like the Serpent.

VALENTIN: No, dumbbell . . . Like Paris.

VALENTINA: See, we already have a long history! We've recalled that first meeting a hundred times.

VALENTIN: And it's never boring.

VALENTINA: Aha, someone said: lovers never bore each other, because they speak only of themselves.

VALENTIN: La Rochefoucauld said it. What an edition of his works has just come out! Where do you get money for books? What a library Sergei Sergeevich has!

VALENTINA: You become a professor, you will too.

VALENTIN: I want to be everybody: a welder, a baker, a poet, a physicist, a trolley driver, a shoemaker.

VALENTINA: You're like a little boy!

VALENTIN: And a professor also! Alechka!

VALENTINA: Just a minute, wait . . . And have you always met girls that way?

VALENTIN: I? Actually, I never met any.

VALENTINA: Oh! Swear that you never had any other romance!

VALENTIN: I've sworn already, what's the matter with you?

VALENTINA: Swear again! Some Lenochka, in that tourist camp, this Katiusha, your neighbor! Well?

VALENTIN: Katiusha? That's a laugh!

VALENTINA: And that beauty Dina from your class?

VALENTIN: Well Dina! — Dina is like one of the family, what's wrong with you?

VALENTINA: No, no, look me in the eye! You libertine, you're nothing but a Don Juan, don't laugh . . . If I hear any more about this Dina, I don't know what I'll do!

VALENTIN: Oh, Alia, stop it! What Dina, what Katiusha? Actually, I don't see anyone. All the girls have disappeared from the city, there's no one, except you.

VALENTINA: Don't, wait.

VALENTIN: Alia!

VALENTINA: Wait dear . . .

VALENTIN: Well, Alia . . .

VALENTINA: You only think of one thing.

VALENTIN: Yeah, well?

VALENTINA: And what if something happens?

VALENTIN: *(Carefree, boyishly.)* So we'll have a boy, so what!

VALENTINA: You — nut.

VALENTIN: We'll buy him a railroad.

VALENTINA: I'd rather jump off a bridge.

VALENTIN: Alia!

VALENTINA: And college?

VALENTIN: *(Same carefree tone.)* To hell with college!

VALENTINA: We have nothing.

VALENTIN: I'll go to work.

VALENTINA: I can't allow you because of me to . . .

VALENTIN: *(Seriously now.)* Listen, Alia, I'll die for you, if I have to! Don't you understand?

VALENTINA: You really love me?

VALENTIN: Oh, I don't know how to say it . . .

VALENTINA: And what if it all ends? You know, according to Freud, love lasts about four years.

VALENTIN: Freud, who? To hell with him.

VALENTINA: First love always ends badly.

VALENTIN: First love does not end ever . . . Alia, Alia . . .

(Lights dim, blue lights of the gas range can be seen. They kiss and move to the bed. Doorbell rings. Confusion. Masha flies in. She pretends not to look at them.)

VALENTIN AND VALENTINA
by Mihail Roschin

Russian: One Male and One Female

THE PLAY: Described by the author as a contemporary play, *Valentin and Valentina* explores the issues of love, liberty, and the existence of both in 1970s Russia (the cold war era). Valentin and Valentina are students and happen to be lovers. The attempts of their families to keep them apart only serve to deepen their connection to each other. As their love reaches the point of no return, Valentina begins to have fears and doubts. Love rules out in the end.

THE SCENE: The question of having other people in their lives has challenged Valentin (18) and Valentina (18) to examine their souls and the depth of their connection to each other. As Valentina is seeing Navy men off at the pier, Valentin accepts a classmate's invitation to come home with her and visit. Here he sits with Dina (18) and endures her overtures, still thinking only of Valentina.

TIME AND PLACE: Dina's room. November 1977. Late afternoon, early evening.

Gousev kisses Zhenia on the cheek, grabs Valentina by the hand and runs off with her. Valentina stops for a second, she sees Valentin half-lying on the floor of Dina's room. Low lights. A record player is playing.

VALENTIN: It's funny, one remembers the way we were in high school, or even half a year ago, and it seems donkey's years away. We thought: we are already grown-ups! We read poetry, we smoked, drank . . .
DINA: Kissed. *(She kisses him.)*
VALENTIN: Yes. Analyzed, argued.
DINA: Always about politics.
VALENTIN: Yes, it's funny.
DINA: Listen, do you need blue jeans? I know a guy who can get them.
VALENTIN: I'll do without. *(Continuing.)* Children play at war, but it's not war. Little girls play dolls and mothers . . . and we played grown-ups. But it was not for real.

DINA: And now it's for real for you?

VALENTIN: I don't know. In any case, the pain is real.

DINA: What a pessimist you've become. I've signed up for a tour to Bulgaria in June. Imagine, eighteen days! Golden sands, Varna. And not expensive. Exciting? Four of us signed up. Two gals from surgery and two from therapy.

VALENTIN: *(Thinking aloud.)* "All of us in our youth are a bit of the pessimist," said Gorky. "Because we want so much and can do so little." Excellently said!

DINA: There's the sea, bars, dancing all night! One word — South!

VALENTIN: I've always envied the fellows who are already doing something, working, responsible for something, needed by someone. But we: the gang, fooling around . . .

DINA: You've become so serious — it's terrible. We're only young once, Valia! Let's stay that way for awhile.

VALENTIN: The game has ended, life has begun. Because one must be responsible. At least for one person.

DINA: Life, life! It's good because it's life! You say it as if some — hard labor has started. Take me, I work in the hospital, carry bed pans, give enemas, and that's not the Celebrity Club, and it's not a month in the country, so what? Sometimes it's disgusting, too much. But life is gorgeous! I have everything: I can dress, go anywhere, eat whatever I want! *And* in the South!

VALENTIN: I want to understand: am I ready or not?

DINA: For life you mean? *(Laughs.)* As if it will wait for you. I look at you: and I get scared. I want to fall in love, too, very much, but if this is how it all is, pardon me! I'll take something simpler. You know, you fall head over heels for a guy and then: *(Sings, from* Eugene Onegin.) "I write to you with apprehension. What more is there for me to say?" Maybe you have to get married, but what for? To wash diapers? In a year I've heard and seen enough in the hospital, lord, a hospital is like an encyclopedia, you learn everything. I feel sorry for you! And we the frivolous ones, we shall overcome! *(Dances.)* Dina is not a monster, Dina is not an old hag, we are in fashion now, understand?

VALENTIN: Yes, you'll overcome.

DINA: Don't get nervous! We have a young surgeon, Arkadyi Ivanovich, he swoons when I walk down the hall. "Dina" he says, "Sandro Botticelli!"

VALENTIN: *(Laughs.)* Do you know at least who Botticelli is?

DINA: Don't worry, I bought a little book . . . Nowadays everybody knows everything. Here is Nefertiti. *(Points to the walls and shelves.)* Here's Botticelli for you. Yessenin — five volumes, Marcello, Alain Delon.

VALENTIN: Ah, you have changed a bit. Which grade was it in that you could-
n't point out Africa on the map? The eighth?

DINA: No, the ninth, but that's not important, while you are here pointing it
out, I'll go there.

VALENTIN: I wouldn't be surprised.

DINA: Just you wait, they'll send Arkadyi Ivanovich there — we've already had
four transferred — and good-bye!

VALENTIN: All right already, Botticellia, I'm going.

DINA: Stay, what's wrong with you! *(She kisses him.)*

VALENTIN: Thanks.

DINA: *(Suddenly.)* If someone would love me so, I don't know what I would do!
I'd go to the ends of the world! You think: Dina is a fool, Dina is giddy,
squeaked by in school and still just squeaks by . . . Eh! . . .

VALENTIN: What's wrong with you?

DINA: Oh, nothing! And you, you should rejoice. Why are you so . . .

VALENTIN: *(With a dry chuckle.)* I'm rejoicing.

DINA: I see . . . All right, arrivederci, tomorrow I'm on at seven . . .

VALENTIN: Good luck. Bring a rose from Bulgaria, their roses are famous. *(He
leaves the room.)*

DINA: South! That's the word!! *(She leaves.)*

(Valentin and Valentina run to each other. They embrace fiercely.)

THE WOOD DEMON
by Anton Chekhov

Russian: Two Females

THE PLAY: As Chekhov's earlier rendition of *Uncle Vanya,* the *Wood Demon* is quite similar in story line and theme, with the bonus of more humor and fun. The plotline remains basically the same as Chekhov's more well known classic.

THE SCENE: Sonya (20) has been resistant to accepting her beautiful step-mother, Yelena (27), but as her life presents her with challenges in the area only another woman could understand, Sonya seeks out the counsel and friendship of her new mother.

TIME AND PLACE: Sonya's dining room. After 1 AM.

Yelena Andreyevna enters. She opens the windows.

YELENA ANDREYEVNA: The storm is over! How fresh the air is!
    (Pause.)
    Where is Wood Demon?
SONYA: He's gone.
    (Pause.)
YELENA ANDREYEVNA: Sophie?
SONYA: What?
YELENA ANDREYEVNA: How long are you going to keep this up? We haven't done each other any wrong — why should we be enemies? Enough, now.
SONYA: Oh, yes, I myself . . . *(She embraces her.)* Dearest!
YELENA ANDREYEVNA: Isn't this better? . . . *(Both are moved.)*
SONYA: Did papa lie down?
YELENA ANDREYEVNA: No, he's in the living room, sitting up. Sometimes you and I go a whole month without saying a word to each other. God knows why. Now, we'll . . . *(She looks at the table.)* What's this?
SONYA: For Wood Demon.
YELENA ANDREYEVNA: And there's wine, too . . . Let's drink to friendship! *Brüderschaft.*
SONYA: Yes, let's!

YELENA ANDREYEVNA: From the same glass . . . *(She pours.)* This is much better. Well, then — friends?

SONYA: Yes, friends! *(They drink and kiss.)* I've wanted to make up with you for a long time, but I was shy . . . *(She cries.)*

YELENA ANDREYEVNA: Why are you crying?

SONYA: It's nothing, nothing at all.

YELENA ANDREYEVNA: Oh, now, that's enough . . . *(She cries.)* You silly thing, now you've made me cry! *(Pause.)* You've been angry with me because you thought I married your father for selfish reasons. If you believe in solemn vows, then I swear to you that I married him for love. I was fascinated by him, by his learning, his fame. It was not real love, it was make-believe, but at the time I thought it was real. It's not my fault. And from the day that we were married, you have been tormenting me with your sly, suspicious looks . . .

SONYA: No, peace, peace! That's all over. This is the second time today I've been called sly and suspicious.

YELENA ANDREYEVNA: Don't be suspicious! It's not becoming. You must trust people or life is impossible.

SONYA: You know what they say: "A frightened crow is even afraid of a bush." I've been disappointed so many times!

YELENA ANDREYEVNA: By whom? Your father is a good, honest man, a hard worker. You taunted him today for being happy. If that were ever true, he was too busy to notice it. As for me, I never intended any harm to your father or to you. Your Uncle Zhorzh is kind and good, but unhappy, unfulfilled . . . So who is it that disappoints you?

(Pause.)

SONYA: Tell me something, as friend to friend . . . Are you happy?

YELENA ANDREYEVNA: No.

SONYA: I knew it. One more question. Tell me honestly, wouldn't you like a young husband?

YELENA ANDREYEVNA: What a child you are! . . . Of course, I would! *(She laughs.)* Well, ask me something else. Go ahead . . .

SONYA: Do you like Wood Demon?

YELENA ANDREYEVNA: Yes, very much.

SONYA: *(Laughing.)* Oh, I'm so silly, aren't I? . . .He's gone, and I can still hear his voice and his footsteps, and whenever I look at a window — I seem to see his face . . . I want to tell you everything . . . but not here, I'm too shy! Let's go to my room, we can talk there. You think I'm silly, don't you? Admit it . . . He's a good man, isn't he?

YELENA ANDREYEVNA: Very. Very . . .

SONYA: But his forests, his peat . . . all that seems strange to me. I don't understand . . .

YELENA ANDREYEVNA: Forests are not the point. What matters, my dear, is that he has talent. Do you know what that means? Courage, clarity, generosity of spirit . . . When he plants a little tree or digs up a load of peat, he's already making plans a thousand years ahead, dreaming about the happiness of mankind. Such men are rare and must be loved. May God be with you! You are both pure, brave and honest. He has a wild, extravagant nature — but you are sensible and practical . . . You're so right for each other . . . *(She rises.)* While I am a boring, unimportant passerby. As a matter of fact, Sonya, if you really think about it, I am probably very, very unhappy. *(She walks around in agitation.)* There is no happiness in this world for me! None! Why are you laughing?

SONYA: *(Laughing and covering her face.)* I am so happy! How happy I am!

YELENA ANDREYEVNA: It's true, I'm so unhappy!

SONYA: I am happy! . . . Happy!

YELENA ANDREYEVNA: I feel like playing! I'd like to play something . . .

SONYA: Yes, play! *(She embraces her.)* I don't want to go to bed . . . Play!

YELENA ANDREYEVNA: I will. Your father is not asleep, but when he doesn't feel well, he doesn't like music. Go ask him. If it's all right with him, I'll play . . . Go . . .

SONYA: I will. *(She exits. From the garden, the sound of the night watchman, tapping.)*

YELENA ANDREYEVNA: I haven't played my piano in a long time. I'll play, and cry like a baby. *(Out the window.)* Is that you tapping, Yefim?

[THE VOICE OF THE WATCHMAN: Eh-heh!]

YELENA ANDREYEVNA: Don't tap. The master is not well.

[THE VOICE OF THE WATCHMAN: I'm going. *(He whistles.)* Zhuchka! Trezor! Zhuchka!]

(Pause.)

SONYA: *(Returning.)* No.

SECTION FOUR

AMERICAN

(New York)

AMERICAN (NEW YORK)
INTRODUCTION

In dialects class, the accent that brings out the most energy, enthusiasm, and bold character choices from the actors is the New York accent. Although some may argue that there is no New York dialect any more, there are definite region-specific patterns and sound changes that color the speech of the lifelong New York area resident. These speech qualities, coupled with the physical character and energy of the New York native, make for wonderfully new, typically assertive, good choices in acting classes. Quiet people find a reason to be loud, physically restrained people find an excuse to be more expressive, and people who tend to go for the easiest, stereotypical choice are encouraged to move beyond that into a less common, deeper option. Students love playing with a New York accent!

As with most major metropolitan areas, New York City is home to an eclectic group of accents and speech patterns. When playing a character from a tough, bustling American city, the most frequently used accent is a general New York accent, most closely equated to the borough of Brooklyn. For our purposes, scenes in this section represent the various districts of New York, Long Island, and New Jersey.

New York, traditionally, is and has been home to many different ethnic groups and social classes. Because of its proximity to Ellis Island, the population of New York in the early days was a broad mix of new arrivals. Neighborhoods formed where people clustered in groups based on a shared language, history, and culture. This same segregation still exists today; one can find a neighborhood for every culture and ethnicity.

The accents of New Yorkers, therefore, are not necessarily uniform to all New York inhabitants. The actor who is undertaking a Brooklyn accent must research the nationality and upbringing of his or her character to figure out which flavor of the Brooklyn accent will be most appropriate. Although there are some consistent sound changes, each ethnic/borough group will offer its own unique pronunciation or inflection pattern. Simply put, an Italian Brooklyn accent sounds different from a Jewish Brooklyn accent, which sounds different from an Italian Bronx accent and so forth.

It is important to remember that the New York accents evolved from a culture of working-class, recently immigrated, usually undereducated, expressive people. Although the corporate world of today tends to breed a general, common American speech, and it is more difficult to find a thick New York accent in the population of the upwardly mobile working class, the New York accent in all its variations does still exist.

To remain truthful and nonstereotypical, the actor must keep it simple when applying the New York accent to the character at hand. For the New York sounds/patterns, less is more.

- Owing in part to the tradition of being a blue-collar laboring community, there is a toughness or roughness in the delivery of the New York accent . . . completely bold.
- The native languages of the speaker and his or her relatives will determine the exact sound of the New York accent.
- Stereotypical, but still quite prevalent, is the inordinate amount of swearing among New Yorkers. The swearing, however, is not as loaded as it is for people in other regions. Swearing to a New Yorker is almost like a verbal pause of thought (much the way Californians say "like" all the time.) Of course, the actor will only swear if the script says to swear, and it may not be necessary to make the swear word the operative of the line—it may not be important.
- New Yorkers, due to the rushed pace of city living and overcrowding, speak quickly with little room for anyone to interrupt them.
- People from New York deliver their words without fear — they are totally unafraid to voice their opinions. A friend from Brooklyn reports that you always know who your enemies and who your friends are in Brooklyn — no one puts on the false pretense of being kind to your face and then talks bad about you when you're gone. They tell you to your face if they don't like you or what you said, and if you've got a problem with it, well, "that's *your* problem!"
- The volume of the accent tends to be slightly higher than average.
- Without sacrificing the intelligibility of your words for the audience, the dialect can be less articulate and a little mumbly.
- The dialect tends to resonate (depending on the ethnicity of the speaker) in the sinuses, throat, and/or chest.
- New Yorkers are unapologetic in their carriage and speech.

New York Film, Television, and Audio References

Television
"All in the Family" (Bronx)
"Laverne and Shirley"
"The Nanny"
"Seinfeld"

"Taxi"
"Welcome Back Kotter"
"Who's the Boss"

Dialect Tapes and Books
Stage Dialects
Dialects for the Stage
Acting with an Accent — NYC

Jerry Blunt
Evangeline Machlin
David Alan Stern

NEW YORK SOUNDS

- Keep in mind that the following vowel changes represent a general New York sound; some characters may require a more specifically placed sound.

a → a/eyuh (nasalized)	Al, sand, can → eyuhl, seyuhnd, ceyuhn
ah → oowa (rounder)	all, daughters → oowall, doowatuhz
oo → uhoo	two, new shoe → tuhoo, nuhoo, shuhoo
ow → aoh (sharper)	how, cow, now → haoh, caoh, naoh

- The question of *r* — the *r* sound is dropped at the ends of words and before consonants. If the *r* appears at the end of a word and the next word starts with a vowel, you would say the *r* sound (car and driver).

ear → ee uh	here, near, we're → hee uh, nee uh, wee uh
air → ehyuh	pears, there, where → pehyuhz, thehyuh, whehyuh
oor → oo wuh	sure, pure, poor → shoo wuh, pyoo wuh, poo wuh
are → ah	cart, far, large → caht, fah, lahge

- Other consonant changes:

  [t] [d] → [tₕ] [dₕ]   top, don't, tan → tₕop, dₕon't, tₕan
  (air splashes off these as you make them against your top teeth)
  [h] → [y]   huge, humid, human → yuge, yumid, yuman
  (dropped at the beginnings of words)
  [t] → [d]   better, butter, put it over → bedduh, budduh, pud id ovuh
  (between vowels)

- Other consonant changes:

  [g]   going, coming → goin', comin'
  (dropped on -ing endings)
  [ing] + [g]   singer, Long Island, ringing → sing guh, lawng gisland, ring gin
  (with some speakers)
  [th] → [d]   this, them, those → dhis, dhem, dhose
  [th] → [t]   with, think, thanks → wit, tink, tanks

New York Practice Sentences

a → a or eyuh:
Angela and Andrew can't stand Candace. Can Anne dance with half the band?

ow → aoh:
How does the cow go around the clown? The crown fell on the brown ground.

ah → oowa:
My daughter Dawn loves to talk to dogs about coffee and wall-to-wall carpet.

oo → uhoo:
Two youths in the pool. The glue is for Blue Tooth, the goon.

ear → ee uh:
Get over here! I have no fear of the deer. Here is near the Lear jet.

air → ehyuh:
Where was the care for the bare bear on the stairs? I dare you to stare there.

oor → oo wuh:
The poor pure loser was sure new to the sewer. The poor doer was newer than the boor.

are → ah:
The car is far from the park. Dark is hard to part from stark.

[t] [d] → [t$_h$] [d$_h$]:
Don't tell Darcy about Tony and Terri. Take that doughnut down to Dawn.

[h] → [y]:
Huge humid clouds settled down on the humans.

[t] → [d]:

    The better the butter, the better the batter. The pretty little petal was metal.

[ing + g]:

    I was singing and thinking that I could sing all day. Long Island is ringing

.

[th] → [d]:

    Without these things, this would not get done.

[th] → [t]:

    Think about it, thanks aren't thoughtful unless they're thankful.

DOES A TIGER WEAR A NECKTIE?
by Don Petersen

American (New York): One Male and One Female

THE PLAY: Set in the 1960s in a rehabilitation center for young addicts, the characters of Don Petersen's play range from the hopeless to the hopeful and all types in-between. The stakes are high as the youth in the island rehab center try to find refuge from their pasts, their habits, and the chains that keep them tied to their addictions. Personal relationships between teachers and students, junkies and shrinks and classmates are revealed in heightened emotional moments and dramatic confrontations. Mature, dated language and theme.

THE SCENE: Against her better judgment and all efforts to the contrary, Linda (18) has fallen in love with Conrad (20). On his release day, his enthusiasm and optimism for the future is shot down by the frightened Linda.

TIME AND PLACE: 1960s. A rehabilitation center . . . located on an island in a river bordering a large industrial city. The school auditorium. A few days before Christmas, around 8:00 PM.

Offstage, we hear Conrad call out.

CONRAD: Linda! Hey, honey, where are ya? *(He enters left, wearing a coat, suit and hat, and carrying a suitcase.)* Hi. Hi, baby.

LINDA: *(Distantly.)* Hi, yourself.

CONRAD: *(Puts down suitcase, takes off coat, and approaches her at table.)* How come you didn't go down there? You hear what happened?

LINDA: *(Clearing table.)* Yeah, I heard. Bickham tried to walk on the water.

CONRAD: *(Shivering.)* That ain't water, baby, that's liquid ice. That sonofabitch is frozen fish food by now.

LINDA: *(Drops a fork into the basket.)* One less junkie . . . Irish bastard at that.

CONRAD: *(Sits at table.)* Oh, God, sometimes you shock me, girl, the way you come on.

LINDA: I *shock* you. *(Laughs.)* Then you's in the wrong place.

CONRAD: *(Pointedly.)* Yeah. And that's why I'm leaving here tonight . . . for good.

LINDA: *(Mockingly.)* Round five . . . Killer Conrad. Well, while it lasts, you're lookin' pretty splibby.

CONRAD: *(Stands up and shows off his clothes.)* Thanks. New suit and coat . . . my sister sent 'em to me.

LINDA: *(Casually. Rises, goes back to work.)* When's the next boat?

CONRAD: Who knows? They ain't gonna send none out till they drag near the landing. Fraid the body will get all chomped up.

LINDA: *(She stares for a moment . . . then moves back to work at table.)* Where you goin' out there in that *real* world? You got a place to hole up?

CONRAD: Yeah. I got me a place. My sister's crib.

LINDA: Oh. *(A long nervous pause.)* Well, I got to put this stuff away.

CONRAD: *(Rises.)* Oh? You want me to give you a hand?

LINDA: Sure, if you want to. *(Holds out tablecloth.)* Here, let's fold this. *(Each takes an end. As two ends meet, he comes close to her.)*

CONRAD: Hello . . . hello, Linda.

LINDA: *(Pause. An impasse.)* What she do? This sister you're gonna crib with?

CONRAD: *(Evasively.)* Oh, this and that. She makes it best she can.

LINDA: She got a habit?

CONRAD: Yeah . . . she's shootin'.

LINDA: How she feed it? Hustlin'? *(Conrad nods.)* Who's pullin' in the tricks for her?

CONRAD: Some stud called Charlie One Leg. He ain't a bad old cat. — Cripple. He got shot up in some war back a ways.

LINDA: And you're movin' in with *them,* huh? A junkie sister and a one-legged pimp. *(Disgustedly.)* Sheeit!

CONRAD: I'm just stayin till I get a job and a crib, and then I'm goin' to night school.

LINDA: *(Goes back up to table.)* Oooooh, he's gonna get a *job!* Pimpin', pushin? or numbers?

CONRAD: *(Follows her.)* No, dig it! Somethin' legit!

LINDA: Yeah? Like *what?*

CONRAD: *(Earnestly.)* Gas jockey, garment district . . . I don't care what it is.

LINDA: *(Throwing props into boxes.)* Ooooh, this stud's got *big* ideas. Garment district . . . night school. High school deeeeeploma.

CONRAD: That's right, lady! You wait and see.

LINDA: Oh, I'll *wait,* all right! Listen, how long you gonna take that "district" jazz? "Boy! Hurry up, boy! Run them dresses to ACME! And, *boy,* sweep that floor when you're through!" *(Laughs.)* Sheeet!

CONRAD: *(Defensively.)* I can take anything till I finish school!

LINDA: Yeah? Then what ya got? With that deeploma, and *your skin,* buster, you might make a shippin' clerk.

CONRAD: *(Pursuing her.)* That's a *start,* Miss Talker. You don't know *where* I'd go from there.

LINDA: *(Cruelly.)* Oooooh! Dig this boy! Rockefeller in technicolor!

CONRAD: You better believe that, too!

LINDA: *(Extends her hand.)* Well, good luck from the Queen Mother. *(Walks around him.)* Now, if you'll excuse me, I got work to do.

CONRAD: *(Disgusted, he moves down right to bench.)* I'll *excuse* you, all right.

LINDA: *(Pulls away.)* Let loose, I got work to do.

CONRAD: This ain't no way to say good-bye.

LINDA: I'm like Popeye. I am what I am.

CONRAD: You don't think I can make it. You don't even care what happens to me.

LINDA: If I did, what could I do about it?

CONRAD: *(Softly.)* You could be nice, cause I'm leavin' tonight.

LINDA: *(Angrily.)* I ain't your mama! I'm a two-dollar whore. Now get the hell out of here, will ya? You don't need me any more.

CONRAD: *(Moves to her.)* Maybe I do. Maybe I *do* need you.

LINDA: What for? What you gonna do with me in the White House? Or will they paint it black?

CONRAD: *(Slaps his forehead and moves away.)* Aw, squash it! Dig it or not . . . this world is changin'!

LINDA: *(Flippantly.)* Yeah, it's gettin' *worse.*

CONRAD: Take a look at this island! We got black doctors, black social workers . . . black everything!

LINDA: Sheeit! When you gotta say black in *front,* it ain't gettin' no better!

CONRAD: *(Moves to suitcase left and puts on overcoat.)* Okay! I'm goin'! But *dig* the South! Dig *America!*

LINDA: America?? You know where you can stick *that!*

CONRAD: *(Slams on his hat.)* And *dig* Africa!

LINDA: *(Slamming the dishes into the basket.)* Give it to Tarzan!

CONRAD: And dig *yourself.* Stay a junkie! But black is on the move, baby, and I'm goin' with it. *(Grabs his suitcase.)*

LINDA: *(Mockingly.)* Don't forget your white wash!

CONRAD: *(Drops suitcase and throws coat on the floor . . . moves to her . . . pokes a finger at her.)* Oooooooooh, bitch! I got *your* number. Over at phycology they call that . . . *Projectin'.* Flashin' out your *own* fear on someone else. *You're* the one who's scared!

LINDA: *(Pulls away from him.)* Are you through *psycholo*gizin'?

CONRAD: *(Stalks back to coat and suitcase.)* Yeah. Yeah! YEAH!! I'm through!

LINDA: *(Points off left.)* Then hoof it for the ferry, and if it ain't there, KEEP GOIN' TILL YOUR HAT FLOATS!!

(In the distance, the night is pierced by the sounds of sirens. Linda freezes at the table. . . Conrad halts down left, near his suitcase.)

CONRAD: *(In a sharp whisper.)* Listen!! *(In a hush.)* Harbor cops. *(Sirens fading. Solemnly.)* They musta snagged onto Bickham.

LINDA: *(Turns away.)* Poor bastard . . . he don't know how lucky he is.

CONRAD: Shut up, girl. You're gettin' down wrong. That boy's dead out there . . . with a belly full of mud.

LINDA: *(Softly.)* He ain't dead . . . he's got it *made*.

CONRAD: *(Stands solemnly down left with his coat and suitcase in hand.)* Okay, okay I give up on you. You're hopeless. You want the river, too, but you ain't got the guts. You hang on to your misery, baby, cause that's *all* you got. You was cradled in a wastebasket, and you're still lookin' for it. But you'll need junk to swallow it, and you'd even hustle God to get it.

LINDA: *(At the table.)* Gowan! Get out! We'll see who needs it.

CONRAD: I'm goin', and you can eat my dust. My name is *Conrad*, see, and I'm gonna start listenin' to him.

LINDA: *(As he turns to go.)* You *listen* to him! In two months you'll have tracks all over your ass.

CONRAD: *(Turns and starts to go off left.)* Rub it on your chest, bitch. You make me sick.

LINDA: *(Screams cruelly.)* I'll meet ya comin' back . . . when I'm goin' out!

CONRAD: *(Moving off.)* Not here or no place else, baby.

GOLDEN BOY
by Clifford Odets

American (New York): One Male and One Female

THE PLAY: Ultimately tragic, this is the story of Joe, the youngest son of an Italian immigrant father who wants only the best for his talented son. Joe had been an award-winning violinist, and his father hoped he would pursue a career in music, but Joe's need to assert his independence resulted in his becoming a prizefighter. Along the way, he broke his hands and essentially ended his music career. He also fell in love with his manager's mistress, which led to his ultimate unhappiness and destruction.

THE SCENE: In this first private scene between Joe (21) and Lorna (20s), we see the beginning of a promising friendship. Lorna has been sent to woo Joe into fighting for Moody and to ask him to give it all he can.

TIME AND PLACE: Tuesday night. A bench in Central Park, New York City Mid-1930s.

Joe and Lorna sit on a bench in the park. It is night. There is carousel music in the distance. Cars ride by in front of them in the late spring night. Out of sight a traffic light changes from red to green and back again throughout the scene and casts its colors on their faces.

LORNA: Success and fame! Or just a lousy living. You're lucky you won't have to worry about those things . . .

JOE: Won't I?

LORNA: Unless Tom Moody's a liar.

JOE: You like him, don't you?

LORNA: *(After a pause.)* I like him.

JOE: I like how you dress. The girls look nice in the summer time. Did you ever stand at the Fifth Avenue library and watch those girls go by?

LORNA: No, I never did. *(Switching the subject.)* That's the carousel, that music. Did you ever ride on one of those?

JOE: That's for kids.

LORNA: Weren't you ever a kid, for God's sake?

JOE: Not a happy kid.

LORNA: Why?

JOE: Well, I always felt different. Even my name was special — Bonaparte — and my eyes . . .

LORNA: I wouldn't have taken that too serious . . . *(There is a silent pause. Joe looks straight ahead.)*

JOE: Gee, all those cars . . .

LORNA: Lots of horses trot around here. The rich know how to live. You'll be rich . . .

JOE: My brother Frank is an organizer for the C.I.O.

LORNA: What's that?

JOE: If you worked in a factory you'd know. Did you ever work?

LORNA: *(With a smile.)* No, when I came out of the cocoon I was a butterfly and butterflies don't work.

JOE: All those cars . . . whizz, whizz. *(Now turning less casual.)* Where's Mr. Moody tonight?

LORNA: He goes up to see his kid on Tuesday nights. It's a sick kid, a girl. His wife leaves it at her mother's house.

JOE: That leaves you free, don't it?

LORNA: What are you hinting at?

JOE: I'm thinking about you and Mr. Moody.

LORNA: Why think about it? I don't. Why should you?

JOE: If you belonged to me I wouldn't think about it.

LORNA: Haven't you got a girl?

JOE: No.

LORNA: Why not?

JOE: *(Evasively.)* Oh . . .

LORNA: Tokio says you're going far in the fighting game.

JOE: Music means more to me. May I tell you something?

LORNA: Of course.

JOE: If you laugh I'll never speak to you again.

LORNA: I'm not the laughing type.

JOE: With music I'm never alone when I'm alone — Playing music . . . that's like saying, "I am man. I belong here. How do you do, World — good evening!" When I play music nothing is closed to me. I'm not afraid of people and what they say. There's no war in music. It's not like the streets. Does this sound funny?

LORNA: No.

JOE: But when you leave your room . . . down in the street . . . it's war! Music can't help me there. Understand?

LORNA: Yes.

JOE: People have hurt my feelings for years. I never forget. You can't get even with people by playing the fiddle. If music shot bullets I'd like it better — artists and people like that are freaks today. The world moves fast and they sit around like forgotten dopes.

LORNA: You're loaded with fireworks. Why don't you fight?

JOE: You have to be what you are — !

LORNA: Fight! see what happens —

JOE: Or end up in the bughouse!

LORNA: God's teeth! Who says you have to be one thing?

JOE: My nature isn't fighting!

LORNA: Don't Tokio know what he's talking about? Don't Tom? Joe, listen: be a fighter! Show the world! If you made your fame and fortune — and you can — you'd be anything you want. Do it! Bang your way to the light-weight crown. Get a bank account. Hire a great doctor with a beard — get your eyes fixed —

JOE: What's the matter with my eyes?

LORNA: Excuse me, I stand corrected. *(After a pause.)* You get mad all the time.

JOE: That's from thinking about myself.

LORNA: How old are you, Joe?

JOE: Twenty-one and a half, and the months are going fast.

LORNA: You're very smart for twenty-one and a half "and the months are going fast."

JOE: Why not? I read every page of the Encyclopaedia Britannica. My father's friend, Mr. Carp, has it. A shrimp with glasses had to do something.

LORNA: I'd like to meet your father. Your mother dead?

JOE: Yes.

LORNA: So is mine.

JOE: Where do you come from? The city is full of girls who look as if they never had parents.

LORNA: I'm a girl from over the river. My father is still alive — shucking oysters and bumming drinks somewhere in the wilds of Jersey. I'll tell you a secret: I don't like you.

JOE: *(Surprised.)* Why?

LORNA: You're too sufficient by yourself . . . too inside yourself.

JOE: You like it or you don't.

LORNA: You're on an island —

JOE: Robinson Crusoe . . .

LORNA: That's right — "me, myself and I." Why not come out and see the world?

JOE: Does it seem that way?

LORNA: Can't you see yourself?

JOE: No . . .

LORNA: Take a bird's-eye view; you don't know what's right or wrong. You don't know what to pick, but you won't admit it.

JOE: Do you?

LORNA: Leave me out. This is the anatomy of Joe Bonaparte.

JOE: You're dancing on my nose, huh?

LORNA: Shall I stop?

JOE: No.

LORNA: You're a miserable creature. You want your arm in gelt up to the elbow. You'll take fame so people won't laugh or scorn your face. You'd give your soul for those things. But every time you turn your back your little soul kicks you in the teeth. It don't give in so easy.

JOE: And what does your soul do in its personal vanity case?

LORNA: Forget about me.

JOE: Don't you want — ?

LORNA: *(Suddenly nasty.)* I told you to forget it!

JOE: *(Quietly.)* Moody sent you after me — a decoy? You made a mistake, Lorna, for two reasons. I make up my own mind to fight. Point two, he doesn't know you don't love him —

LORNA: You're a fresh kid.

JOE: In fact he doesn't know anything about you at all.

LORNA: *(Challengingly.)* But you do?

JOE: This is the anatomy of Lorna Moon: She's a lost baby. She doesn't know what's right or wrong. She's a miserable creature who never knew what to pick. But she'd never admit it. And I'll tell you why you picked Moody!

LORNA: You don't know what you're talking about.

JOE: Go home, Lorna. If you stay, I'll know something about you . . .

LORNA: You don't know anything.

JOE: Now's your chance — go home!

LORNA: Tom loves me.

JOE: *(After a long silence, looking ahead.)* I'm going to buy a car.

LORNA: They make wonderful cars today. Even the lizzies —

JOE: Gary Cooper's got the kind I want. I saw it in the paper, but it costs too much — fourteen thousand. If I found one secondhand —

LORNA: And if you had the cash —

JOE: I'll get it —

LORNA: Sure, if you'd go in and really fight!

JOE: *(In a sudden burst.)* Tell your Mr. Moody I'll dazzle the eyes out of his head!

LORNA: You mean it?

JOE: *(Looking out ahead.)* Those cars are poison in my blood. When you sit in a car and speed you're looking down at the world. Speed, speed, everything is speed — nobody gets me!

LORNA: You mean in the ring?

JOE: In or out, nobody gets me! Gee, I like to stroke that gas!

LORNA: You sound like Jack the Ripper.

JOE: *(Standing up suddenly.)* I'll walk you back to your house — your hotel, I mean. *(Lorna stands. Joe continues.)* Do you have the same room?

LORNA: *(With sneaking admiration.)* You're a fresh kid!

JOE: When you're lying in his arms tonight, tell him, for me, that the next World's Champ is feeding in his stable.

LORNA: Did you really read those Britannia books?

JOE: From A to Z.

LORNA: And you're only twenty-one?

JOE: And a half.

LORNA: Something's wrong somewhere.

JOE: I know . . . *(The slowly walk out as . . . fadeout.)*

GOLDEN BOY
by Clifford Odets

American (New York): One Male and One Female

THE PLAY: Ultimately tragic, this is the story of Joe, the youngest son of an Italian immigrant father who wants only the best for his talented son. Joe had been an award-winning violinist, and his father hoped he would pursue a career in music, but Joe's need to assert his independence resulted in his becoming a prizefighter. Along the way, he broke his hands and essentially ended his music career. He also fell in love with his manager's mistress, which led to his ultimate unhappiness and destruction.

THE SCENE: It's been a year since he started fighting for Moody, and Joe (22) has come to fall in love with Lorna (20s.) At their regular Tuesday night meeting, Joe tries to get Lorna to leave Moody.

TIME AND PLACE: Tuesday night. A bench in Central Park, New York City Mid-1930s.

Lorna and Joe sit on the same park bench.

JOE: Some nights I wake up — my heart's beating a mile a minute! Before I open my eyes I know what it is — the feeling that someone's standing at my bed. Then I open my eyes . . . it's gone — ran away!

LORNA: Maybe it's that old fiddle of yours.

JOE: Lorna, maybe it's you . . .

LORNA: Don't you ever think of it any more — music?

JOE: What're you trying to remind me of? A kid with a Buster Brown collar and a violin case tucked under his arm? Does that sound appetizing to you?

LORNA: Not when you say it that way. You said it different once . . .

JOE: What's on your mind, Lorna?

LORNA: What's on yours?

JOE: *(Simply.)* You . . . You're real for me — the way music was real.

LORNA: You've got your car, your career — what do you want with me?

JOE: I develop the ability to knock down anyone my weight. But what point have I made? Don't you think I know that? I went off to the wars 'cause someone called me a name — because I wanted to be two other guys. Now it's happening . . . I'm not sure I like it.

LORNA: Moody's against that car of yours.

JOE: I'm against Moody, so we're even.

LORNA: Why don't you like him?

JOE: He's a manager! He treats me like a possession! I'm just a little silver mine for him — he bangs me around with a shovel!

LORNA: He's helped you —

JOE: No, Tokio's helped me. Why don't you give him up? It's terrible to have just a Tuesday-night girl. Why don't you belong to me every night in the week? Why don't you teach me love? . . . Or am I being a fool?

LORNA: You're not a fool, Joe.

JOE: I want you to be my family, my life — Why don't you do it, Lorna, why?

LORNA: He loves me.

JOE: I love you!

LORNA: *(Treading delicately.)* Well . . . Anyway, the early bird got the worm. Anyway, I can't give him anguish. I . . . I know what it's like. You shouldn't kick Moody around. He's poor compared to you. You're alive, you've got yourself — I can't feel sorry for you!

JOE: But you don't love him!

LORNA: I'm not interested in myself. But the thing I like best about you . . . you still feel like a flop. It's mysterious, Joe. It makes me put my hand out. *(She gives him her hand and he grasps it.)*

JOE: I feel very close to you, Lorna.

LORNA: I know . . .

JOE: And you feel close to me. But you're afraid —

LORNA: Of what?

JOE: To take a chance! Lorna, darling, you won't let me take you up! I feel it all the time — you're half dead, and you don't know it!

LORNA: *(Half smiling.)* Maybe I do . . .

JOE: Don't smile — don't be hard-boiled!

LORNA: *(Sincerely.)* I'm not.

JOE: Don't you trust me?

LORNA: *(Evasively.)* Why start what we can't finish?

JOE: *(Fiercely.)* Oh, Lorna, deep as my voice will reach — *listen!!* Why can't you leave him? Why?

LORNA: Don't pull my dress off — I hear you.

JOE: Why?

LORNA: Because he needs me and you don't —

JOE: That's not true!

LORNA: Because he's a desperate guy who always starts out with two strikes against him. Because he's a kid at forty-two and you're a man at twenty-two.

JOE: You're sorry for him?

LORNA: What's wrong with that?

JOE: But what do *you* get?

LORNA: I told you before I don't care.

JOE: I don't believe it!

LORNA: I can't help that!

JOE: What did he ever do for you?

LORNA: *(With sudden verve.)* Would you like to know? He loved me in a world of enemies, of stags and bulls! . . . and I loved him for that. He picked me up at Friskin's hotel on Thirty-ninth Street. I was nine weeks behind in rent. I hadn't hit the gutter yet, but I was near. He washed my face and combed my hair. He stiffened the space between my shoulder blades. Misery reached out to misery —

JOE: And now you're dead.

LORNA: *(Lashing out.)* I don't know what the hell you're talking about!

JOE: Yes, you do . . .

LORNA: *(Withdrawing.)* Ho hum . . . *(There is silence. The soft park music plays in the distance. The traffic lights change. Lorna is trying to appear impassive. Joe begins to whistle softly. Finally Lorna picks up his last note and continues; he stops. He picks up her note, and after he whistles a few phrases she picks him up again. This whistling duet continues for almost a minute. Then the traffic lights change again.)*

LORNA: *(Beginning in a low voice.)* You make me feel too human, Joe. All I want is peace and quiet, not love. I'm a tired old lady, Joe, and I don't mind being what you call "half dead." In fact it's what I like. *(Her voice mounting higher.)* The twice I was in love I took an awful beating and I don't want it again! *(Now half crying.)* I want you to stop it! Don't devil me, Joe. I beg you, don't devil me . . . let me alone . . .

(She cries softly. Joe reaches out and takes her hand; he gives her a handkerchief, which she uses.)

LORNA: *(Finally.)* That's the third time I cried in my life . . .

JOE: Now I know you love me.

LORNA: *(Bitterly.)* Well . . .

JOE: I'll tell Moody.

LORNA: Not yet. Maybe he'd kill you if he knew.

JOE: Maybe.

LORNA: Then Fuseli'd kill him . . . I guess I'd be left to kill myself. I'll tell him . . .

JOE: When?

LORNA: Not tonight.

JOE: Swiftly, do it swiftly —

LORNA: Not tonight.

JOE: Everything's easy if you do it swiftly.

LORNA: He went up there tonight with six hundred bucks to bribe her into divorce.

JOE: Oh . . .

LORNA: *(Sadly.)* He's a good guy, neat all over — sweet. I'll tell him tomorrow. I'd like a drink.

JOE: Let's drive over the Washington Bridge.

LORNA: *(Standing.)* No, I'd like a drink.

JOE: *(Standing and facing her.)* Lorna, when I talk to you . . . something moves in my heart. Gee, it's the beginning of a wonderful life! A man and his girl! A warm living girl who shares your room . . .

LORNA: Take me home with you.

JOE: Yes.

LORNA: But how do I know you love me?

JOE: Lorna . . .

LORNA: How do I know it's true? You'll get to be the champ. They'll all want you, all the girls! But I don't care! I've been undersea a long time! When they'd put their hands on me I used to say, "This isn't it! This isn't what I mean!" It's been a mysterious world for me! But, Joe, I think you're it! I don't know why, I think you're it! Take me home with you.

JOE: Lorna!

LORNA: Poor Tom . . .

JOE: Poor Lorna! *(The rest is embrace and kiss and clutching each other. Slow fadeout.)*

THE HOUSE OF RAMON IGLESIA
by Jose Rivera

American (New York): Two Males

THE PLAY: Ramon Iglesia is the proud patriarch of a Puerto Rican immigrant family trying to make it work in New York. The house they have lived in for the past twenty years is technically theirs, but they need the signatures of the original owner and her daughters to sell the house and move back to Puerto Rico. Their three sons have divergent views on life in America. Javier, the oldest, hates everything Puerto Rican, and does his best to assimilate into American culture, to the point of ignoring his relationship to his family. Julio, the middle son, is the beast of the family; tough, strong-willed, and proud of himself, his heritage, and his country (he was the first born in America). Charlie, the youngest, is the closest in personality to his mother. He yearns to return to Puerto Rico. Through the help of Javier, and the dramatic circumstances that bring about his decision to help, the Iglesias are able to finally return to Puerto Rico.

THE SCENE: Julio (19) has enlisted in the Marines, and Javier (22) has taken him to the enlistment center, where he will say good-bye to his younger, somewhat stronger, brother.

TIME AND PLACE: 4:00 AM Marine Corps Recruiting Office in Holtsville, New York. Very cold. February 1980.

Outside in front of the Marine Corps Recruiting Office in Holtsville, New York. It's 4:00 AM. It's very cold. Julio and Javier enter, carrying bags.

JAVIER: God, Julio.
JULIO: This is it.
JAVIER: God, Julio.
JULIO: Stop being a pussy.
JAVIER: *God*, Julio.
JULIO: Go stay in the car if you're so cold.
JAVIER: You had to pick the coldest damn night of the millennium, didn't you?
JULIO: Go back in the car if you're so cold.
JAVIER: I don't want to sit in there by myself —

JULIO: I don't want to miss anybody —

JAVIER: No one's stupid enough to be out here this early, in this freezing weather . . .

JULIO: Well, you wanted to come out with me —

JAVIER: I thought you would have the good sense to stay in the *car.*

JULIO: A Marine's got to get used to the cold, wimp!

JAVIER: Oh, Mother of God, spare me. *(Julio puts his bags down and looks around. He checks his watch.)*

JULIO: Nobody.

JAVIER: Who's supposed to come?

JULIO: Sergeant Overbaby.

JAVIER: Who?

JULIO: Overbaby.

JAVIER: You're giving your future to a man named *Overbaby?*

JULIO: *(Looking into the office.)* It's not quite four; I'm early . . .

JAVIER: He's probably in a snowbank doing pushups in the nude . . .

JULIO: I think he told me he has to come in from Hempstead.

JAVIER: "I sing of Olaf, glad and big." Do you know that poem?

JULIO: Maybe I should give him a call . . .

JAVIER: "I sing of Olaf, glad and big."

JULIO: Who's Olaf, your boyfriend?

JAVIER: He was a Swede, a pacifist, and got the life kicked out of him in a poem because he would not kiss your fucking flag.

JULIO: *(Looking at Javier.)* Sometimes I think you have the basic mentality of a handball.

JAVIER: I'm going to give your recruiting officer a copy of it . . .

JULIO: Great. They'll have me shot for having a flake for an older brother. Why don't you stop living in the sixties? Be like me! Adjust to the times! Be a beast!

JAVIER: I'd rather be in bed thank you. *(Javier walks over to the recruiting office window and looks inside the window.)* That's interesting. Hmmmmmmm. That's very, *very* interesting. Wow.

JULIO: What is it?

JAVIER: Well. Up against the wall. In there. Are all these little boxes . . .

JULIO: I sense something profoundly stupid coming on.

JAVIER: . . . *and* above each of the little boxes is a name, rank and serial number . . . and inside each of the little boxes — let me make sure — *(He looks into the window.)* Yep! Inside each of the little boxes is a pair . . . of human testicles . . . little Marine testicles.

JULIO: Har. Har. Har. Yuck. Yuck.

JAVIER: Isn't that part of the Deal? You give Uncle Sam your balls, and what's left of your nervous system, and they zap you and turn you into a grunt!

JULIO: I'm not going to be a grunt — I'm going to be a technician, asshole, a hydraulics *technician.*

JAVIER: Right. Exactly like the ads. "High school dropout? Can't read English or do long division? Join the Marines and become a neutron physicist!" Ha!

JULIO: It's not like that, Bolshevik!

JAVIER: "Learn bio-warfare and global defoliation!"

JULIO: Hey, at least I didn't waste four years in some obscure little college, learning political science, just so I can come home and hang my brain on the loading dock of a warehouse! *That's* good! That's real progress!

JAVIER: Leave me alone.

JULIO: I, howsoever, am getting my brain together in a big way, with a future, and a job, out in the world where the real power is.

JAVIER: *Nuts!*

JULIO: True!

JAVIER: The real world? You're going right from Mommy's bosom to Uncle Sam's! Fed, clothed and told what to do. *And* you might get killed in the process. Might get mistaken for a Southeast Asian and blown to bits —

JULIO: Javier, for Chrissakes, it's 1980, it's *peacetime!*

JAVIER: Accidents can happen in peacetime!

JULIO: Accidents *don't* happen in peacetime! Not to Marines!

JAVIER: And promise me you won't develop a drug habit, or go to Iran.

JULIO: Promise me you'll never run for public office! You're so hopeless! What a mother hen! I can't believe you! Javier, you're such an old nurse . . .

JAVIER: I am not.

JULIO: You are. You're an old nurse. You're a den mother.

JAVIER: I am *not.*

JULIO: I know the real Javier. Nonviolent, nonalcoholic, boring, abnormal . . .

JAVIER: Listen, have a great military career. I'll see you later.

JULIO: Javier the Saint. The unhappy Javier.

JAVIER: Leave me alone.

JULIO: Awwwww, I know one of the things he's unhappy about. I know why he broods. What does Caroline want from your ass this time? What is the evil woman doing to our hero now?

JAVIER: Nothing. She's . . . been looking for furniture that's all. *(Beat.)* Do you think Overbaby will let me join the Corps?

JULIO: The Corps don't take the mentally ill . . . the castrated . . . or the pussy-whipped, and you, dear bro, show signs of becoming all three. *(Julio walks away from Javier.)*

JAVIER: *(Lost in thought.)* Don't call me bro. *(Looking at Julio.)* Do you remember *Patton? (Takes Julio's arm, imitates George C. Scott.)* "When you put your hand into a mess of goo that ten seconds ago was your best friend's face, you'll know what to do!"

JULIO: *(Smiling.)* And the line from *Apocalypse Now?*

TOGETHER: *(Imitating Robert Duvall.)* "I love the smell of napalm in the morning. It smells like victory!"
(They laugh.)

JULIO: *(Beat.)* So. What are you going to do about Dad?

JAVIER: I don't know. He told me he wants to start a restaurant down in Arecibo — but he hasn't even found a place to live yet. He hasn't even sold the house.

JULIO: Listen, don't fuck with his dreams. When I'm gone you have to keep that house together. That's the only thing I can tell you. It's your *job.*

JAVIER: I don't want that job. I want to solve my problems — not Dad's, not Mom's, not Caroline's; mine. I always used you to protect myself —. *(A car can be heard pulling up.)* Wait; listen —. *(Julio looks out into the distance.)* Yep. The Marines have landed.

JULIO: Already? Really? *(Getting his stuff together.)* This is it, my friend.

JAVIER: Dammit. I had — so many things I wanted to tell you. Ideas and advice — all sorts of things.

JULIO: Well unless you can say them in ten words or less you better just say good-bye. I can feel myself turning into government property even as we speak.

JAVIER: I'm going to miss you.

JULIO: I'm going to miss you too. Hey, the truth — doesn't that Overbaby look like a grim guy?

JAVIER: Terrifying. Awesome.

JULIO: You take care of everybody — and make sure they write — and keep Mom from getting too excited — and for Godsakes, why don't you make it big already? I mean, doesn't that Overbaby look like a *really grim guy? (Julio salutes Javier and exits. Javier waves to Julio. Julio re-enters the stage and embraces Javier. Blackout.)*

THE INDIAN WANTS THE BRONX
by Israel Horowitz

American (New York): Two Males

THE PLAY: Horowitz's stark presentation of two tough New York hoodlums challenges today's politically correct and sensitive audiences with its overt harshness and cruelty. However, beyond the surface of violence that the young men exhibit lie the souls of lost youth who have run out of hope.

THE SCENE: In the middle of the one-act play, the boys' true personalities start to show as they reveal their different perceptions of the truth of their pasts. Joey (20 to 22) is starting to reveal a kindness and purity while Murph (20 to 22) continues to revel in his callous disdain for anything good and kind. The boys are tormenting a third person in the scene, an old man from India who is lost and frightened by the unfamiliar New York City surroundings.

TIME AND PLACE: A bus stop on upper Fifth Avenue, New York City. A chilly evening. September. The present.

MURPH: *(Does a "take." Flatly.)* This Turkie's a real pain in the ass.

JOEY: Naw. I think he's pretty interesting. I never saw an Indian before.

MURPH: *(Crosses to Joey and slaps the back of Joey's head.)* Oh. It's fascinating. It's marvelous. This city's a regular melting pot. Turkies. Kikes like you. *(Pause.)* I even had me a French lady once.

JOEY: A French lady, huh?

MURPH: Yep. A real French broad.

JOEY: You been at your mother again?

MURPH: *(Hits him on the arm.)* Wiseass. Just what nobody likes. A wiseass.

JOEY: Where'd you have this French lady, huh?

MURPH: I found her in the park over there. *(Points.)* Just sitting on a bench. She was great. *(Boasts.)* A real *talent*.

JOEY: Yeah, sure thing. *(Calls into the park.)* Hello, talent. Hello, talent! *(Pauses.)* I had a French girl, too. *(Turns to avoid Murph's eyes, caught in a lie.)* Where the hell's that bus?

MURPH: Sure you did. Like the time you had a mermaid?

JOEY: You better believe I did. She wasn't really French. She just lived there a long time. I went to first grade with her. Geraldine. She was my first girl-friend. *(Talks very quickly.)* Her old man was in the army or something, 'cause they moved to France. She came back when we were in high school.

MURPH: Then what happened?

JOEY: Nothin'. She just came back, that's all.

MURPH: I thought you said you *had* her?

JOEY: No, she was just my girlfriend.

MURPH: In high school?

JOEY: No, ya' stoop. In the first grade. I just told you.

MURPH: You had her in the first grade?

JOEY: Jesus, you're stupid. She was my girlfriend. That's all.

MURPH: *(Feigns excitement.)* Hey . . . that's a *sweet little story.* *(Flatly.)* What the hell's wrong with you?

JOEY: What do ya' mean?

MURPH: What do you mean, "what do you mean?" First you say you had a French girl, then you say you had a girlfriend in first grade, who went to France. What the hell kind of story's that?

JOEY: It's a true one, that's all. Yours is full of crap.

MURPH: What's full of crap?

JOEY: About the French lady in the park. You never had any French lady unless you been at your own old lady again. Or maybe you've been at Pussyface?

MURPH: Jesus, you're lookin' for it, aren't you?

JOEY: I mean, if you gotta' tell lies to your best buddy, you're in bad shape, that's all.

MURPH: *(Gives Joey a high sign.)* Best buddy? You? *(Noogie gesture to Joey. The noogie sign to The Indian. He returns the obscene gesture, thinking it an American sign of welcome.)*

JOEY: Turkie! Is that how it is in Ceylon, sir?

MURPH: Say-lon? What the hell is say-long?

JOEY: See, ya jerk. Ceylon's part of India. That's where they grow tea.

MURPH: No kiddin? Boy it's terrific what you can learn just standin' on a cor-ner with a schmuck like you. Tea, huh? *(To The Indian, he screams:)* Hey! *(Looks for bus, crosses to Indian. The Indian turns around, startled, but catches Murphy at the game and smiles. Murph returns the smile and asks:)* How's your teabags? *(No response.)* No? *(To Joey.)* Guess you're wrong again. He don't know teabags.

JOEY: Look at the bags under his eyes.

MURPH: Turkie looks like he's getting bored.

JOEY: Poor old Indian. Maybe he wants to play a game.

MURPH: You know any poor old Indian games?

JOEY: We could burn him at the stake. *(He laughs.)* That ain't such a terrible idea, you know. Maybe make an Indian stew.

MURPH: Naw, we couldn't burn a nice fellow like Turkie. That's nasty.

JOEY: We got to play a game. Pussyface always tells us to play games. *(To the apartment.)* Ain't that right, Pussyface? You always want us to play games.

MURPH: *(Screams.)* Hey! *(The Indian jumps, startled again.)* Hey! I know a game. *(Makes false jump at Indian.)* "Indian — Indian — Where's the Indian?"

JOEY: That's a sweet game. I haven't played that for years.

MURPH: *(Steps toward Joey.)* Wiseass. You want to play a game, don't you?

JOEY: Indian-Indian. Where's the Indian?

MURPH: Sure. It's just like Ring-a-leave-eo. Only with a spin.

JOEY: That sounds terrific.

MURPH: *(Crosses to Joey.)* Look. I spin the hell out of you until you're dizzy. Then you run across the street and get Pussyface. I'll grab the Indian and hide him. Then Pussyface and you come over here and try to find us.

JOEY: We're going to spin, huh?

MURPH: Sure.

JOEY: Who's going to clean up after you? Remember the ferris wheel, big shot? All those happy faces staring up at you?

MURPH: I ain't the spinner. You're the spinner. I'll hide the Chief. Go on. Spin.

JOEY: How about if we set the rules as we go along? *(To the Indian.)* How does that grab you, Chief?

[INDIAN: I'm sorry, but I can't understand your language.]

MURPH: He's talking Indiana again. He don't understand. Go on. Spin. I'll grab the Chief while you're spinning . . . count to ten . . . hide the Chief, while you're after Pussyface. Go on. Spin.

JOEY: I ain't going to spin. I get sick.

MURPH: Ain't you going to play?

JOEY: I'll play. But I don't spin any better than you can. I get sick. You know that. How about if you spin and I hide the Chief. You can get Pussyface. She likes you better than me, anyhow.

MURPH: Pussyface ain't home. You know that. She's in New Jersey.

JOEY: Then what the hell's the point of this game, anyway?

MURPH: It's just a game. We can pretend.

JOEY: You can play marbles for all I care. I just ain't going to spin, that's all. And neither are you. So let's forget the whole game.

MURPH: *(Fiercely.)* Spin! Spin!

JOEY: You spin.

MURPH: *(Slaps Joey on the arm.)* Hey. I told you to spin. *(Murph squares off against Joey, menacingly. Joey looks Murph straight in the eye for a moment and then says:)*

JOEY: Okay. Big deal. So I'll spin. Then I get Pussyface, right? You ready to get the Chief?

MURPH: Will you stop talking and start spinning?

JOEY: All right. All right. Here I go. *(Joey spins himself meekly, as Murph grabs the Indian and runs for the trash can. Joey giggles as he spins ever so slowly. Murph glances at Joey as Joey pretends. Murphy is confused.)* There. I spun. Is that okay?

MURPH: That's a spin?

JOEY: Well, it wasn't a fox trot.

MURPH: I told you to spin! Any slob knows that ain't no spin! Now spin, God damn it! Spin!

JOEY: *(Crosses to Murph.)* This is stupid. You want to play games. You want a decent spin. *(Strikes at Murph.)* You spin. *(He walks straight to Murph — a challenge. Joey slaps Murph. They freeze.)*

MURPH: *(Circles Joey as if to hit him. He squares off, viciously. Raises his arms. Looks at Joey cruelly and orders.)* Spin me.
(Joey brings Murph's arms behind Murph's back and holds Murph's wrists firmly, so Murph is helpless. Joey spins him three times. Slowly at first. Then faster. Faster. Joey's hostility is released. Joey laughs.)

JOEY: You wanted to spin. Spin. Spin. *(Joey spins Murph frantically. The Indian watches in total horror, not knowing what to do. The Indian cuddles next to the Bus Stop sign: his island of safety. Murph screams.)*

MURPH: Enough, you little bastard!

JOEY: *(Continues to spin him.)* Now YOU get Pussyface. Go on. *(He spins Murph all the faster as in a grotesque dance gone berserk.)* I'LL hide the Chief. This is your game! This is your game. YOU get Pussyface. I'll hide the Chief. Go on, Murphy. You want some more spin. *(Joey has stopped spinning now as Murph is obviously ill.)* You want to spin some more?

MURPH: Stop it, Joey. I'm sick.

JOEY: *(Spins Murph once more around.)* You want to spin some more or are you going to get Pussyface and come find the Chief and me?

MURPH: You little bastard.

JOEY: *(Spins Murph once again, still holding Murph helpless with his arms behind his back.)* I'LL hide the Chief. YOU get Pussyface and find us Okay? Okay? Okay?

MURPH: *(Stumbling to upstage right.)* Okay. You bastard. Okay.

JOEY: *(Spins Murph once more.)* Here's one more for good luck. *(Joey spins Murph three more times, fiercely, then shoves him offstage. Murphy can be heard retching, about to vomit, during the final spins. Joey first pushes Murph offstage, then grabs the Indian, who pulls back in terror. Murph stumbles off as Joey grabs the Indian, pushes him behind litter baskets.)*

LIFE AND LIMB
by Keith Reddin

American (New York): One Male and One Female

THE PLAY: Set in the pre– and post–Korean war era, this disturbing tale follows the lives of a young newlywed New Jersey couple and the havoc that war wreaks on their lives. Using elements of fantasy and gritty realism in a seriocomic play, Keith Reddin paints a grim and ultimately rewarding picture of love, war, and death. Mature language and theme.

THE SCENE: In the first scene of the play, we are introduced to the newlywed couple, Franklin and Effie (both 20 to 22) as Franklin prepares to go away to the war.

TIME AND PLACE: Summer 1952. A bench on a boardwalk. (Atlantic City? Coney Island?) Early evening.

A bench downstage. Summer 1952. Franklin in uniform, Effie in print dress. Both face forward, sitting on bench. Early evening.

EFFIE: Keep your eyes closed. *(Feeds him a spoonful of frozen custard.)* Guess what flavor.

FRANKLIN: Pistachio Fudge.

EFFIE: Be serious.

FRANKLIN: I'm serious. I'm very serious. *(He tastes a spoonful of custard.)* It was vanilla. You want another frozen custard?

EFFIE: No thanks.

FRANKLIN: How's about cotton candy?

EFFIE: You gonna make me sick, Franklin.

FRANKLIN: Go on.

EFFIE: I don't feel so good.

FRANKLIN: Gimme a kiss. *(They kiss.)* You don't use your tongue no more?

EFFIE: I told you I don't feel so good.

FRANKLIN: Always used to slip the tongue. I didn't grow up doing this.

EFFIE: Too many people around, Franklin. They looking at us.

FRANKLIN: I remember things like that.

EFFIE: It's the salt air too, makes me feel dizzy.

FRANKLIN: I got that surprise for you.

EFFIE: Was that where you were this afternoon?

FRANKLIN: You were with Doina. Going swimming, so I thought.

EFFIE: She thought you were mad at me. She figured you going off to Korea you wanted to be by yourself and walk around. I tell her, Doina, he's just going out on the boardwalk he says he's looking for a going-away present. Doina, she says, it's you should be buying Franklin the going-away gift, she says this, he's the one going away. He's the one going to fight. Mom wasn't too crazy about you joining up either. She telling me to go to dances at the armory. Mi rumpi i gambi i primu chi vaio la.

FRANKLIN: How many times I have to tell you, I don't want you talking in Italian.

EFFIE: Sorry, Franklin.

FRANKLIN: You know I hate that.

EFFIE: Yeah.

FRANKLIN: Your mother, cursing at me in Italian, she knows I don't know what she's talking about.

EFFIE: She loves you, Franklin.

FRANKLIN: Effie.

EFFIE: Well, sometimes she's afraid of you.

FRANKLIN: Gimme a break. What's she want from me? I married you. I work hard. I feed you. I buy you presents.

EFFIE: I know.

FRANKLIN: I bring you flowers. It's not your birthday or anything, but I bring you home things. We go to Atlantic City. I even took you on the Staten Island Ferry, but does she understand this? Never again. I don't want to go back there.

EFFIE: Now stop.

FRANKLIN: Your brother the fireman. He makes me barf. Wearing his firehat at the dinner table. Carrying around that axe, who is he kidding?

EFFIE: He likes the fire department.

FRANKLIN: I care? Your whole family cracks me up. Him and Marie, eating food all over the apartment, stubbing out his cigarettes into the dining room table, what zoo do these people come from?

EFFIE: They're in love.

FRANKLIN: That kid, Paulie, playing with himself at the table.

EFFIE: He never done that.

FRANKLIN: You think I don't see that, huh? Pulling himself off at the dinner table, then running off saying he's gotta do business.

EFFIE: He's just a boy, Franklin.

FRANKLIN: A sick person, that's what he is. An eight-year-old kid doing that. Your mother, she sees. Runs into the kitchen and makes all this coffee. Nobody wants any coffee but she runs into the kitchen. You know why? 'Cause she's ashamed of her own son.

EFFIE: Why you so mean, Franklin?

FRANKLIN: Sometimes I'm glad I don't have to go back there. Sometimes I'm glad I'm going to Korea.

EFFIE: You come home a big hero. *(Pause.)*

FRANKLIN: I'm really tired, Effie, let's go home.

EFFIE: They're going to turn on all the lights soon. You promised.

FRANKLIN: I know.

EFFIE: You said we could stay till the arcade was all lit up, you told me.

FRANKLIN: I thought you didn't feel well.

EFFIE: But you know we make this big trip on the bus, we should stay till they turn on the lights. *(Pause.)* So what you get me?

FRANKLIN: When?

EFFIE: You. You told me you got me something.

FRANKLIN: It's stupid now.

EFFIE: Let me see. *(Franklin rolls up his right sleeve.)*

FRANKLIN: Here, look.

EFFIE: That's your arm, ain't it?

FRANKLIN: On my arm.

EFFIE: You got a tattoo.

FRANKLIN: Yea, I got a tattoo.

EFFIE: Why'd you do that?

FRANKLIN: I thought you'd like it. See it's got a heart with your name on it. I figured I'd wear your name with me when I go to Korea, then see, I'd be thinking about you and the other guys would see how much we're in love. *(Pause.)*

EFFIE: That's nice, Franklin. That's a very nice present. *(They kiss.)*

FRANKLIN: I think we should go home. *(Pause.)* When I get back, Effie, boy are we gonna do things. See, then we can have a car. A big car, we don't have to ride the bus ever again. We fix up our kitchen, people they come to our place for dinner. You fix a nice dinner in your new kitchen, and then see, people they sit down at our table, they put real napkins in their laps. We finish dinner, we go to the living room, we sit on a new couch, I buy. This is a new couch, not some used job from your uncle in the furniture business, this is a new couch I buy. Then we all watch something on television.

EFFIE: We gonna get a television?

FRANKLIN: Why not? I come home from work, we have dinner, we watch television.

EFFIE: When are we getting a television?

FRANKLIN: This is after I get back.

EFFIE: Oh. Okay.

FRANKLIN: I'm gonna do all these things for you, Effie. *(Pause, kisses her. Looking around.)* Let's go home now.

EFFIE: We should find Doina.

FRANKLIN: Doina'll find her own way home. Let's go. Don't look at me like that, Effie, huh?

EFFIE: What? What I do now?

FRANKLIN: Just please don't look at me like that.

EFFIE: What you got against Doina?

FRANKLIN: Doina, her whole world is sitting in the five and ten, having a coffee, eating some shitty macaroni and cheese. She don't read a newspaper, she don't add numbers, we can do better than that, huh? We are gonna do things. Lots of things. You see, I get back, we do things. You want a Cracker Jack for the bus?

EFFIE: You shouldn't call her stupid. She's my best friend, Franklin. She's the first one in her family to finish school.

FRANKLIN: So what? What do you know about the world? You gotta know things about the world. I'm going off to fight. Look, I'll get your Cracker Jack and we'll go home. *(Walking off.)* Christ, what do you even know about Korea?

EFFIE: I know plenty about Korea.

LIFE AND LIMB
by Keith Reddin

American (New York): One Male and One Female

THE PLAY: Set in the pre– and post–Korean war era, this disturbing tale follows the lives of a young newlywed New Jersey couple and the havoc that war wreaks on their lives. Using elements of fantasy and gritty realism in a seriocomic play, Keith Reddin paints a grim and ultimately rewarding picture of love, war, and death. Mature language and theme.

THE SCENE: Just back from Korea, Franklin (20 to 22) steps off the plane for a reunion with his wife, Effie (20 to 22). A far cry from the hopeful and excited young soldier/husband he was before losing his arm in the battle at Pork Chop Hill, Franklin finds himself unable to understand the lightness of Effie's conversation. Things are just not the same as they were before.

TIME AND PLACE: Fort Dix military air field. Fall 1953. Dark evening.

Fort Dix military airfield. Fall 1953. A section of chain-link fence and a sign indicating a military airfield. In the darkness we hear the sound of a propeller transport plane. It is very loud. The lights fade up on Franklin in uniform, his sleeve pinned to his jacket. Effie stands holding a box of candy. She wears a stylish dress.

EFFIE: Hi Franklin!
FRANKLIN: Hi Effie!
EFFIE: You look good, Franklin.
FRANKLIN: Thanks. *(Pause.)*
EFFIE: I brought you some salt water taffy.
FRANKLIN: From Atlantic City?
EFFIE: You bet.
FRANKLIN: Nice. *(Pause.)*
EFFIE: They feed you enough in the hospital?
FRANKLIN: Why do you ask?
EFFIE: You look a little thin.
FRANKLIN: I lost some weight. The arm.

EFFIE: Stop.

FRANKLIN: That's probably why I look different.

EFFIE: I'm used to it already.

FRANKLIN: Hey, it's okay. *(Pause.)* They tell you it takes time. To adjust. You lose a limb, this takes time to adjust. I talked to some people.

EFFIE: Were they nice people?

FRANKLIN: They were okay. Mostly other guys who were missing things, arms, legs, fingers. Some guys got it much worse than me, you know.

EFFIE: Uh huh.

FRANKLIN: Some guys they're missing their . . . you know what.

EFFIE: I'm sorry.

FRANKLIN: You step on a mine, blammo, it's gone.

EFFIE: I . . .

FRANKLIN: You can't ever get it back. *(Pause.)* Yeah, I talked to a lot of people.

EFFIE: You started combing your hair different.

FRANKLIN: I read in a magazine this is the new style.

EFFIE: I ain't seen that style yet.

FRANKLIN: Oh.

EFFIE: But I don't read magazines about combing hair.

FRANKLIN: Yeah, well this is how they do it now.

EFFIE: It's different.

FRANKLIN: You look the same.

EFFIE: You look older, Franklin.

FRANKLIN: I'm . . . you know my gums are acting up.

EFFIE: Your gums.

FRANKLIN: Something got . . . uh . . . messed up with, something you know happened to my gums over in Korea, and my teeth are loose and they hurt once in a while.

EFFIE: Doina and me, we seen this picture last week.

FRANKLIN: Really.

EFFIE: You're not gonna believe this, Franklin, this is something maybe you have not heard about, but this picture, it's exciting . . .

FRANKLIN: What?

EFFIE: This movie, it was in 3-D.

FRANKLIN: Huh?

EFFIE: This picture, it was like specially designed for three-dimensional projection.

FRANKLIN: So?

EFFIE: So? So, well you watch this movie, see, and things they pop out at you, right out of the screen, they sorta come out at you, like real life, but it's a movie.

FRANKLIN: You and Doina seen this?

EFFIE: It was very wonderful and exciting, and we went twice in one week, over at the Plaza theater.

FRANKLIN: Twice.

EFFIE: This picture was called *Bwana Devil* and it starred Robert Stack and there was Barbara Britton and Nigel Bruce. You have to wear these special glasses. I brought one back for you. Here. *(She gives the glasses to Franklin. He tries them on.)*

FRANKLIN: You look kinda green, Effie.

EFFIE: Oh, Franklin, jeez, this was something special. We're in deepest Africa, see, and these lions are killing all these guys working on the railroad. 'Til Robert Stack, see, he goes after them, and hunts them down; they had lions jumping out at you and everything.

FRANKLIN: Maybe we should go now. *(Pause.)*

EFFIE: Sure —

FRANKLIN: I feel like lying down for a while.

EFFIE: Okay. I'm sorry.

FRANKLIN: No.

EFFIE: You turn around and hundreds of people are wearing these cardboard glasses like you were on another planet, only it was the plain old Plaza theater.

FRANKLIN: Shut up.

EFFIE: I thought you'd want to know.

FRANKLIN: Stop talking.

EFFIE: I'm sorry, what did I do now?

FRANKLIN: Stop talking so stupid all the time, you truly embarrass me.

EFFIE: Franklin . . .

FRANKLIN: Just got off the fucking plane and you're talking about some pissant movie and why am I still wearing these stupid glasses? *(He tears them off.)* What am I supposed to do now?

EFFIE: About what?

FRANKLIN: About working, getting a job, supporting us, making a goddam living.

EFFIE: You still okay, Franklin.

FRANKLIN: I'm not okay, I'm not, shit my mouth hurts. You make me mad . . . *(He starts to cry.)* and I yell at you and my mouth hurts. I don't

want to lose my teeth too, please Effie, don't let them pull my teeth. I've
had these teeth since I was a kid. I need them, and my gums messed . . .

EFFIE: It's okay, sssh . . .

FRANKLIN: But.

EFFIE: Sssssssssh.

FRANKLIN: I can't eat the salt water taffy, don't you understand?

EFFIE: It's fine, Franklin, it's real good to have you back.

FRANKLIN: I'm fucking falling apart here.

EFFIE: You look good Franklin. You still got all your good parts. You're not
missing any of that. *(Pause.)*

FRANKLIN: No.

EFFIE: Then it's okay. A lotta guys, hey, they're missing everything, many
guys, they're dead, they have nothing.

FRANKLIN: That's right.

EFFIE: We're going home now, okay?

FRANKLIN: *(Wiping his eyes.)* Yeah.

EFFIE: Some people are over at the apartment want to say hello to you. Will
you do that?

FRANKLIN: I don't want to see anybody.

EFFIE: They've been waiting all day to see you, why don't you say hello, have
a few beers, you feel better.

FRANKLIN: Okay. A few beers.

EFFIE: Good.

FRANKLIN: We have a few beers, and they go. Then we can be alone. *(They
start to walk off.)*

EFFIE: Sure. *(Lights fade.)*

THE MINEOLA TWINS
by Paula Vogel

American (New York): One Male and One Female

THE PLAY: Described by the author as "a comedy in seven scenes, four dreams and five wigs," *The Mineola Twins* follows the life paths of identical twins from age 17 to 47. The twins could not be any more opposite, much to their consternation, and their sons seem to have been born to the wrong mother (Myra's son is more like Myrna and vice versa). The historical time periods serve as both a backdrop and an inspiration for the attitudes and actions of the main characters.

THE SCENE: At the beginning of the play, the "good twin" Myrna has been bemoaning the effect her sister's bad reputation may have on her life. Her fiancé, Jim (22), lends a sympathetic ear. After some heavy making out, Myrna makes Jim leave so as to protect her virginity until their marriage. Jim leaves to go have a talk with Myra (17) and ask her to control her loose behavior. The talk doesn't go exactly the way he planned.

TIME AND PLACE: A cheap motel in Mineola, Long Island. Late evening. 1959.

Later that evening.
We see the interior of a cheap motel used for trysts of GI's on leave from Mitchell Air Force Base. The blinking neon of "MOTEL" flashes throughout the scene. At the start of the scene, Myra sits up in bed, agitated. She wears a push-up Maidenform and a panty girdle. Myra manages to smoke, furiously, in between cracking her gum. There is a heap in the bed beside her, curled under the cheap chintz spread, completely covered, and hogging the entire bedspread. Occasionally, we hear muffled sobs.

MYRA: "I Like Ike. I Like Ike." I mean, is that cornball or what? Can you believe how way-in this country is? They like some bald, golfing dude whose idea of a hot time is having Mamie stroke his clubs! They voted for that square twice! "I Like Ike —" I mean, that is yo-yo's-ville. *(She stops, pops her gum. Listens to the heap.)* Hey, man. Hey, daddy, I'm dishing politics, man, I'm trying to connect. *(She nudges the heap.)* Hey. Hey. You gonna come out sometime this decade?

(The heap covers itself with some insistence.)

MYRA: Hey. Suit yourself, daddy-o. No skin offa my pearly whites. I've had cats cry before the Act, and I've had lotsa cats wail during. You're the first one to boo-hoo after. *(She waits for a response. Tries again.)* Hey, I gotta idea. You got any bread? Any wheels? We could just spook in your bomb and get some burgers. Or We go peel on outta here and spin into the Village. It's crazy down there, any night of the week. We go take in the Vanguard — do you dig that scene? It's the most, the meanest . . . we could do a set, and then blow the joint and just walk around the streets. There's this one guy, Ace, who walks around with a *parrot* on his shoulder. It's crazy. He's so hip — you pay him a dime, and he gives you a poem, on the spot. He poetizes on a dime. And these poems — they don't rhyme or anything. They're deep. They don't *mean,* they just *are.* It's far-out!

(Jim, in a fury, pops up.)

JIM: Speak English, can't you! If you want to talk to me, speak English! English!

MYRA: Wow.

(Pause. Jim huddles, still clutching the spread around him. Myra does her best Julie Andrews.)

MYRA: "The Rain in Spain Stays Mainly in the Plain . . ." Is that better?

JIM: Jesus. You've watched too many James Dean movies.

MYRA: *(Stung.)* He only made *three.* And then he *died.*

(Myra is moved. Jim is surprised.)

JIM: Hey, look, I wasn't making fun of him or anything.

MYRA: He was important to a lot of people. He lived fast, died young . . . and really messed up his face.

JIM: I'm sure he was important to impressionable young women. But that doesn't mean he could act. Couldn't drive, either.

MYRA: Oh, he could drive. It was the yo-yo on the other side of the yellow line he didn't count on. I'll bet he was going over a hundred in that Spyder, the top down, he was flying, he was putting something down! Some asshole yo-yo in a *Ford,* for God's sake!

(Jim clears his throat.)

JIM: The Ford Motor Company happens to be one of my clients.

MYRA: Oh. That's nice. What do you do for them?

JIM: Well, I advise them on strategies for younger buyers, as a representative of a new and growing market in this country — consumers under twenty-five. We're devising a new model that's going to sweep aside the competition.

MYRA: So where is this company of yours you work at devising and marketing and sweeping?

JIM: Madison Avenue.

MYRA: Manhattan? Midtown Manhattan?

JIM: Last time I looked, that's where Madison Avenue was.

MYRA: You work in Manhattan? And you don't live there?

JIM: I like more air and more space and more *green.*

MYRA: Oh, man. You're free, white, over twenty-one, and you get to get up every morning, and take the L-I-double R into Manhattan. If I were you, I'd cash in the return ticket to Mineola and find a pad like — *(Snap.)* that.

JIM: You'll get your chance.

MYRA: Not soon enough. You think if you get a wife and one of those cornball aprons and tongs and barbecue hamburgers in Mineola on the weekends, your bosses will promote you faster?

JIM: There's nothing wrong with Mineola.

MYRA: "There's no shineola in Mineola, there's just shit —"

JIM: *(Shocked.)* You shouldn't say words like that.

MYRA: Like shineola? What is there to do in Mineola? Go to bingo, go to the PTA, fight over whether or not *Catcher in the Rye* should be allowed in our libraries! Mineola's so dull, there wasn't even a Red scare here! No self-respecting communist would even try to infiltrate the school system! In Mineola, people keep their blinds up because *nothing happens* on a Saturday night.

JIM: You are full of hate.

MYRA: I'm restless! Don't you sometimes feel like you're gonna jump out of your skin if you don't do something, go somewhere?

JIM: Well, sometimes.

MYRA: Yeah? And then what do you do?

JIM: I go for a nice, brisk walk around the block.

MYRA: How old are you?

JIM: *(In his deepest chest voice.)* I'm . . . twenty-two. Going on twenty-three.

MYRA: Oh, man. I've gone with juvenile delinquents older than you.

JIM: I'll bet you have.

(Pause. They shift in the bed.)

JIM: So — this fellow with the parrot — Ace?

MYRA: Yeah, Ace.

JIM: What is his poetry like?

MYRA: It's hard to describe in words. It's like jazz riffs without the music. It's just a torrent of feeling and colors and *truth*.

JIM: No rhyme?

MYRA: Rhyme is out. Square. Dead.

JIM: Tell that to Robert Frost.

MYRA: What, we're talking aesthetics here? Aesthetics after sex?

JIM: Look, I'm trying to "connect," okay?

MYRA: You think poetry's gotta be Barbara Frietchie? "Shoot If You Must This Old Gray Head"?

JIM: Look, I've read *On the Road*.

MYRA: You have?

JIM: Yes. In hardcover.

MYRA: Jeez. I've never done it with anyone else who's read Kerouac.
    (This pleases Jim.)

JIM: So I'm your first?

MYRA: Yeah. In that way, you are. Nobody reads Kerouac in Mineola.

JIM: Well, I have.

MYRA: So, what did you think?

JIM: Of Kerouac? It was kind of long.

MYRA: Yeah. Dull.
    (They smile at the small island of agreement.)

MYRA: You're okay for a man who wears ties.

JIM: You're okay, too. You're nothing like your sister —
    (It strikes Jim.)

JIM: Oh, my God! Your sister! Oh, God, Oh, God —

MYRA: Look, don't clutch on me, Jim . . . Hang loose, okay? Just breathe. It's gonna be all right.

JIM: Oh, man, what am I going to do? What am I going to tell her?

MYRA: We'll keep it a secret. Okay? I would sincerely like to keep something secret from little Miss Tom Peep.

JIM: Oh, God. She'll find out.

MYRA: She's pried into everything I own. She knows how far down my throat every guy's tongue has probed . . . I tried to keep a diary, but I gave up on it. I got tired of her saliva strains smudging the ink.

JIM: She'll look into my eyes. She'll know.

MYRA: What, you think your eyes are gonna look different now? Oh, boy. Where did you get your information? Health classes at Mineola High?

Although I'll bet you are going to walk in a different way. You know what they call it when they lower the front end of a car to streamline it? So it's real fast for dragging? They call it raking. And that's you, daddy-o. You've been raked.

JIM: I've got to think. You've got to help me think.

(Pause. Myra snaps her gum.)

JIM: Could you maybe not pop your gum?

(Myra, with great ceremony, removes her gum and places it on the head-board.)

MYRA: Okay? Now we can think great thoughts. Okay. This changes nothing, okay? You don't tell her, she doesn't ask. Don't ask, don't tell. The formula for modern marriages.

JIM: You sound like an expert. When are you getting married?

MYRA: Hardehar-har. There's never been a movie made that's even close to how I'm gonna live. I'm making it up from scratch. No marriage. No laundry, no cooking. No children. Just freedom.

JIM: But you're a girl! You can't do that!

MYRA: I am going to spend my life doing everything people tell me I can't do.

JIM: Maybe I should think over this marriage thing. No sense in rushing everything.

MYRA: Look, Jim — you oughta marry my sister. She's been collecting recipes until she has dinner completely *planned* for the first year.

JIM: Are you hot? There's no air in here —

MYRA: And she's been practicing her signature, "Mrs. James Tracy. Mrs. James Tracy." And sometimes just initials "MRT."

JIM: How do you know that?

MYRA: I read her dumb-shit diary, too.

JIM: I can't marry Myrna.

MYRA: You're kidding.

JIM: No. I'm seeing things differently now. I've been raked.

MYRA: Oh shit. She's gonna blame me.

JIM: This has nothing to do with you.

MYRA: That doesn't matter. Everything's my fault. If she doesn't make Homemaker of America, it's 'cause her sister's a slut.

JIM: No, see, Myrna was right.

MYRA: Now this I gotta hear.

JIM: It's the domino theory. Okay, let's say nobody notices anything different about me, right? I look the same, talk the same, almost walk the same. Like if I had a twin myself, but completely different on the inside.

Tomorrow morning, I go into work, nobody notices. A year from now, I walk down the aisle with my intended, your sister, and she doesn't know the difference. The priest gives us the sacrament, and there's no lightning bolts striking me dead.

MYRA: I'm with you so far.

JIM: So virginity is not only *not* just a state of mind. It's a figment of imagination.

MYRA: That's what I was trying to tell you a while back when you were boo-hooing.

JIM: So don't you see? The domino theory? There goes virginity, there goes my promotion, my work ethic, monogamy, mortgages, raising 2.5 children, truth in advertising, belief in a deity, living in the suburbs, caring for my aging parents and saluting the flag.

MYRA: Wow. Heavy.

(Jim and Myra sit next to each other in bed. Contemplate.)

MYRA: Wanna cigarette? *(She offers her pack.)*

JIM: Sure.

(They puff.)

MYRA: My brain hurts. That usually never happens *after* sex.

JIM: Yeah. I guess.

MYRA: So this was your first time.

JIM: Yes . . . Myra? Was I — could you tell me — was I —

MYRA: You were wonderful, Jimmy. You know, I've never known anyone like you, Jim Tracey. You're the kind of guy a girl could dream about.

JIM: Thanks . . . Myra? How "many" guys have you —

MYRA: Gone all the way with? To Home Plate?

JIM: Yes. Do you mind my asking?

MYRA: Well, there are all the guys on the first-string — and I'm working on the second-string who have their letters —

JIM: Whoa! So it's really true about you. You really are a Whore of Babylon!

MYRA: Hey! Wait a minute! First of all, I happen to really like football. Second of all, we just jammed on a philosophical thing here, like a neutrality of moral consequence, so where do you get off calling me that? Putting that down?

JIM: I was talking about me. Men are defined by what they do — their actions in the world. It's different for you — you're a girl. There are . . . absolutes in the world for girls. Girls don't do, they just are.

(Furious, Myra gets out of bed and starts dressing. She tries not to cry.)

MYRA: Why — why did you have to do this? I thought . . . for a minute — I thought you were different. I thought you understood.

JIM: Why are you getting all steamed up? I'm just another notch on your belt, right?

MYRA: I hope my next decade is better than this one.

JIM: I mean, girls are born the way they are. Men *become*.

MYRA: I can't believe I fall for it every time.

JIM: Myrna was born "good." You were born . . . "nice."

MYRA: I'm cool to the guys, thinking, dip that I am, that they're gonna be cool back. That this time is gonna be different. I don't get it, I really don't. I'm nice to you, right? I made you feel good, I went all the way, I gave you what you wanted, no questions asked, no demands — why then do you guys always do this?

(Jim is oblivious to the tirade.)

JIM: So the bottom line is — you did sleep with the football team.

(Myra reaches the door, disheveled but dressed. She turns, goes back for her gum on the headboard.)

MYRA: Well, lucky for us one of us had some experience.

THE MONOGAMIST
by Christopher Kyle

American (New York): One Male and One Female

THE PLAY: After years of work, Dennis finally produces a volume of poetry suitable for publishing that earns him some acclaim. The theme? Monogamy. Inspired by his own writing, he finally marries his longtime lover, Susan, a professor of feminist literature. Soon, she is taken under the spell of one of her more charming male students, Tim, and she finds herself cheating on Dennis; what's more *Dennis* finds her cheating on Dennis. This leads Dennis to reciprocate with an equally young partner, Sky. As Dennis is forced to face the success of his book, the failure of his marriage, and the mentoring he must do with his new young lover, he begins to acknowledge the holes in his once strongly held, sixties-era philosophies.

THE SCENE: In one of the more bizarre twists of the play, Sky (18 to 20), Dennis's lover, is alone in a room with Tim (18 to 20), Susan's lover. Amidst their differences in principles, they manage to find common ground in passions.

TIME AND PLACE: September 1991. Dennis's studio. Daytime.

The studio. Sky is playing "Stairway to Heaven" on the guitar. Badly. A knock. She goes to the door and opens it. Tim enters.

SKY: Oh. Hi. Who are you?

TIM: I guess you're the coed. Is Dennis here?

SKY: I don't know where he is. Who are you?

TIM: I'm the guy who broke up his marriage. Tim.

SKY: Okay. I'm Sky. How're you doing?
   (They shake hands.)

TIM: Fine, fine. Do you know when he'll be back?

SKY: No idea. Do you, uh, want a beer?

TIM: Okay, sure. All right.

SKY: Sit down.

(She exits. He looks over Dennis's array of video cassettes. Sky returns with two beers.)

TIM: Thanks. I came to apologize.

SKY: About his wife? I don't really think —

TIM: About reading his diary.

SKY: Wow. You read his diary?

TIM: Some of it.

SKY: Cool.

TIM: He doesn't think so.

SKY: So, like, what did it say?

TIM: It's mostly a bunch of sentimental stuff about when he first met Susan. He was different then.

SKY: Different?

TIM: Yeah. Younger. More alive. He's kind of obsessive now, don't you think? I mean obsessive in the unhealthy sense.

SKY: Yeah.

TIM: I'm sorry. I don't mean to criticize him to you.

SKY: It's all right. You've got a point about obsessiveness.

TIM: I only want to be friends with him. We have a lot of things in common.

SKY: Do you think Dennis is a pervert?

TIM: Hey, well, I wouldn't know.

SKY: I think he's kind of perverted, really. At first I thought he was just more open to talking about sex, you know? But now I think it's something perverted. Something major. It's kinda like he'd rather think about it than do it. We haven't had sex for over a week. You think maybe it's a generation thing?

TIM: You know, I got this community service job at a nursing home — I like old people — and some of them are, you know, *randy.* It surprised me.

SKY: Yeah?

TIM: Yeah. And these people are, like, way older than Dennis.

SKY: Right.

TIM: So I don't think it's an age thing. It's Dennis.

SKY: It's cool you're helping out old people and all.

TIM: It's part of my sentence.

(Beat.)

SKY: Okay.

TIM: I had this professor last year. And I got caught breaking into her house because she wouldn't see me anymore. I'm not proud of it.

SKY: Okay.

TIM: I broke a couple of things, sure. I lost my temper. But I like things to have a resolution, you know? That's why I need to talk to Dennis. To get him to understand. Otherwise, it won't rest with me.

SKY: I remember now. You were in the *Princetonian*.

TIM: Yeah.

SKY: Okay. Cool. *(Beat.)* I was wondering, like, how you feel about blotter acid. I have some.

TIM: I don't usually do drugs.

SKY: You got principles or something?

TIM: My father did a lot of drugs.

SKY: Mine too. But he gave it up to become a lawyer.

TIM: Yeah?

SKY: I've actually been thinking about giving it up, too. Once I get through this sheet. I mean, I really don't think it's my gig anymore, you know? It's so retro.

TIM: Yeah.

SKY: I mean, fuck the sixties. Hippies. It's bogus. Right? We're new. We're cool. Twenty-something. Generation X. I don't need this retro shit.

TIM: Yeah, I don't really understand why so many people are trying to — I don't know — escape their generation or something. It's hypocritical. I'm sure everything was just as boring in the sixties. And they didn't have VCRs or cable or home computers.

SKY: Hypocritical. Exactly.

TIM: But then, I like a tie-dye shirt as much as the next guy.

SKY: Thanks, Tim.

TIM: It's nothing. It's a nice shirt.

SKY: She dumped you, didn't she?

TIM: Yeah.

SKY: I'm sorry.

TIM: It's all right. I'm used to it now.

SKY: Did you break into her house?

TIM: No, I'm way past that stage. I used to be really stupid.

SKY: No — I admire you for it. You stood up to her. That baby boomer bitch. She took advantage of your youth and you spit it back in her face. And you totally got away with it, too. That was so excellent, Tim.

TIM: I didn't exactly get away with it.

SKY: Community service.

TIM: It's worse that it sounds. But I don't regret what I did. I needed the resolution.

SKY: How do you feel about abortion, Tim?

TIM: I'm pro-choice.

SKY: Excellent.

TIM: It's one issue I really care about, you know? I'm going into advertising because I think that's where I can make a difference. Advertising can really change people's minds on these issues.

SKY: You know, Tim, you make a lot of sense. I think we see things the same way.

TIM: We do *(Beat.)* What was your name again?

SKY: Sky. *(Beat.)* You wanna fuck?

TIM: Wow. I wasn't expecting that.

SKY: Sorry.

TIM: I don't usually get along this well with women in my age group.

SKY: Say the word and we'll forget I ever mentioned it.

TIM: No. Let's not do that. Does this couch open into a bed?

SKY: Yeah.

TIM: Cool.

(The open the sofa bed.)

TIM: Sky?

SKY: Yeah?

TIM: Is it too late for me to change my mind about that blotter acid?

(She produces a sheet of blotter acid as the lights fade.)

WELCOME TO THE MOON
(and other plays): THE RED COAT
by John Patrick Shanley

American (New York): One Male and One Female

THE PLAY/SCENE: A one-act/one-scene portion of a series of short scenes that compose the *Welcome to the Moon* play, *The Red Coat* is the first episode dealing with love, passion, and the moon. The scenes in the collection are loosely tied together by the recurring themes of love and the moon but are otherwise completely unrelated. In this scene, John (17) has been waiting for Mary (16) to arrive at the party he's just left. The effect of the wine, the moonlight, and his building passion for Mary overcomes John and he reveals himself to her at last.

TIME AND PLACE: The present. Late night. The front stoop of a city apartment building.

Night time on a side street. A street light shines down on some steps through a green tree. Moonlight mixes in the shadows. A seventeen-year-old boy sits on the steps in a white shirt with a loosened skinny tie, black dress pants, and black shoes. He is staring off. His eyes are shining. A sixteen-year-old girl enters, in neighborhood party clothes: short skirt, blouse, penny loafers.

JOHN: Hi, Mary.

MARY: Oh! I didn't see you there. You're hiding.

JOHN: Not from you, Mary.

MARY: Who from?

JOHN: Oh, nobody. I was up at Susan's party.

MARY: That's where I'm going.

JOHN: Oh.

MARY: Why did you leave?

JOHN: No reason.

MARY: You just gonna sit here?

JOHN: For awhile.

MARY: Well, I'm going in.

JOHN: Oh. Okay . . . Oh! I'm not going in . . . I mean came out because . . . Oh, go in!

MARY: What's wrong with you, John?

JOHN: I left the party because you weren't there. That's why I left the party.

MARY: Why'd ya leave the party 'cause I wasn't there?

JOHN: I dunno.

MARY: I'm going in.

JOHN: I left the party 'cause I felt like everything I wanted was outside the party . . . out here. There's a breeze out here, and the moon . . . look at the way the moon is . . . and I knew you were outside somewhere, too! So I came out and sat on the steps here and I thought that maybe you'd come and I would be here . . . outside the party, on the steps, in the moonlight . . . and those other people . . . the ones at the party . . . wouldn't be here . . . but the night would be here . . . and you and me would be talking on the steps in the night in the moonlight and I could tell you . . .

MARY: Tell me what?

JOHN: How I feel!

MARY: How you feel about what?

JOHN: I don't know. I was looking out the window at the party . . . and I drank some wine . . . and I was looking out the window at the moon and I thought of you . . . and I could feel my heart . . . breaking.

MARY: Joh . . .

JOHN: I felt that wine and the moon and your face all pushing in my heart and I left the party and I came out here.

MARY: Your eyes are all shiny.

JOHN: I know. And I came out here looking for the moon and I saw that street light shining down through the leaves of that tree.

MARY: Hey yeah! It does look pretty.

JOHN: It's beautiful. I didn't know a street light could be beautiful. I've always thought of them as being cold and blue, you know? But this one's yellow . . . and it comes down through the leaves and the leaves are so green! Mary, I love you!

MARY: Oh!

JOHN: I shouldn't've said it. I shouldn't've said it.

MARY: No, no. That's all right.

JOHN: My heart's breaking. You must think I'm so stupid . . . but I can feel it breaking. I wish I could stop talking. I can't. I can't.

MARY: I never heard you talking like this before.

JOHN: That's 'cause this is outside the party and it's night and there's a moon up there . . . and a street light that's more beautiful than the sun! My

God, the sidewalk's beautiful. Those bits of shiny stuff in the concrete . . . look how they're sparkling up the light!

MARY: You're crying! You're crying over the sidewalk!

JOHN: I love you, Mary!

MARY: That's all right. But don't cry over the sidewalk. You're usually so quiet.

JOHN: Okay. Okay.

(*A pause. Then John grabs Mary and kisses her.*)

MARY: Oh . . . you used your tongue. (*He kisses her again.*) You . . . should we go into the party?

JOHN: No.

MARY: I got all dressed . . . I tasted the wine on your . . . mouth. You were waiting for me out here? I wasn't even going to come. I don't like Susan so much. I was going to stay home and watch a movie. What would you have done?

JOHN: I don't know.

(*Kisses her again. She kisses him back.*)

MARY: You go to St. Nicholas of Tolentine, don't you?

JOHN: Yeah.

MARY: I see you on the platform on a hundred and forty-ninth street sometimes.

JOHN: I see you, too! Sometimes I just let the trains go by until the last minute, hoping to see you.

MARY: Really?

JOHN: Yeah.

MARY: I take a look around for you but I always get on my train. What would you have done if I hadn't come?

JOHN: I don't know. Walked around. I walk around a lot.

MARY: Walk around where?

JOHN: I walk around your block a lot. Sometimes I run into you.

MARY: You mean that was *planned?* Wow! I always thought you were coming from somewhere.

JOHN: I love you, Mary. I can't believe I'm saying it . . . to you . . . out loud. I love you.

MARY: Kiss me again.

(*They kiss.*)

JOHN: I've loved you for a long time.

MARY: How long?

JOHN: Months. Remember that big snowball fight?

MARY: In the park?

JOHN: Yeah. That's when it was. That's when I fell in love with you. You were wearing a red coat.

MARY: Oh, that coat! I've had it for ages and ages. I've had it since the sixth grade.

JOHN: Really?

MARY: I have really special feelings for that coat. I feel like it's part of me . . . like it stands for something . . . my childhood . . . something like that.

JOHN: You look nice in that coat. I think I sensed something about it . . . the coat . . . it's special to me, too. It's so good to be able to talk to you like this.

MARY: Yeah, this is nice. That's funny how you felt that about my coat. The red one. No one knows how I feel about that coat.

JOHN: I think I do, Mary.

MARY: Do you? If you understood about my red coat . . . that red coat is like all the good things about when I was a kid . . . it's like I still have the good kid things when I'm in that red coat . . . it's like being grown up and having your childhood, too. You know what it's like? It's like being in one of those movies where you're safe, even when you're in an adventure. Do you know what I mean? Sometimes, in a movie the hero's doin' all this stuff that's dangerous, but you know, because the kind of movie it is, that he's not gonna get hurt. Bein' in that red coat is like that . . . like bein' safe in an adventure.

JOHN: And that's the way you were in that snowball fight! It was like you knew that nothing could go wrong!

MARY: That's right! That's right! That's the way it feels! Oh, you do understand! It seems silly but I've always wanted someone to understand some things and that was one of them . . . the red coat.

JOHN: I do understand! I do!

MARY: I don't know. I don't know. I don't know about tomorrow but . . . right this minute I . . . love you!

JOHN: Oh, Mary!

MARY: Oh, kiss me, John. Please!

JOHN: You're crying!

MARY: I didn't know. I didn't know two people could understand some things . . . share some things.

(*They kiss.*)

JOHN: It must be terrible not to.

MARY: What?

JOHN: Be able to share things.

MARY: It is! It is! But don't you remember? Only a few minutes ago you were alone. I feel like I could tell you anything. Isn't that crazy?

JOHN: Do you want to go for a walk?

MARY: No, no. Let's stay right here. Between the streetlight and the moon. Under the tree. Tell me that you love me.

JOHN: I love you.

MARY: I love you, too. You're good-looking, did you know that? Does your mother tell you that?

JOHN: Yeah, she does.

MARY: Your eyes are shining.

JOHN: I know. I can feel them shining.

(The lights go down slowly.)

SECTION FIVE
AMERICAN
(Southern)

AMERICAN (SOUTHERN) INTRODUCTION

Most Americans find it relatively simple to imitate a Southern accent. We are exposed to it in many different arenas — films, television shows, and the evening news. The South is a place of history, mystery, and ideals and is compelling in its stories and personalities.

American actors, at some point in their careers, will have to do a Southern accent. It is practically unavoidable. So many great plays have been written both *about* the South and *by* Southern authors that one would have to make a conscious effort to avoid them to never do a Southern accent!

Traditionally, when one first attempts a Southern accent, it is with a sense of the ridiculous. We put on a Southern accent when we want to sound dumb or when we imitate an intense preacher. These two insulting stereotypes have pervaded the American consciousness so deeply, that it becomes a challenge to change our way of thinking about the Southern accent. Indeed, as a Dialect Coach, I have found that my Southern friends who serve as primary sources for the sound changes I use, are very suspicious of anyone else attempting to do a Southern accent. They feel that it will always come out sounding stereotypical, "hick," and not true.

To resist the urge to do a stereotypical accent, it is up to the actor to research the history and sociology of his or her character thoroughly. The actor must know what his or her character's educational level is, what his or her influences were growing up, where he or she is from, and what that means to the language of the people around that character.

The Southern accents vary greatly depending on where you are in the South. Places east of the Mississippi River tend to have a bit more drawl and slightly softer *r*'s than places west of the Mississippi. The original settlers of the land have an influence on the evolution of the dialect; for example, when the Welsh settlers arrived in western North Carolina, they kept moving farther and farther inland toward the mountains that reminded them of home. The very specific Appalachian Mountain dialect can possibly be traced back to those original Welsh settlers and their unique Welsh dialect! Likewise, the original British inhabitants of Georgia may have had a lasting impact on the very proper, British-sounding, Georgia dialect.

For the most part, a general, well-done Texas dialect will serve you as the most common Southern dialect used in scene study classes or on stage. As with each dialect you study, you must read the entire play and character descriptions to accurately place your accent. What follow are some general sound substitutions that should give you a wide representation of the sounds of the South.

- The Southern drawl is achieved by saying a slight *uh* sound before or after you say a pure vowel sound (like the sound *ay* may become *uhay*). It is not separate from the pure vowel, but is done almost at the same time as the vowel, very quickly and subtly. The vowel sound moves around a bit.
- Depending on where you are, the pace of the Southern dialect can vary from the extremes of incredibly quick and piercing to slow and syrupy. Different paces of speech lie between those two extremes.
- Southern dialects are spoken with the lips and tongue relaxed. This will give you a feeling of total throat and facial relaxation. This does not suggest a lack of energy, but rather an ease in the speech and rhythm of the dialect/character. This dialect can feel relaxing and comfortable.
- If you overdo the drawl or the relaxation element of the dialect, your character will seem stereotypical and caricatured. Be careful.
- Subtlety works well in this dialect. You may not need to change much in your own speech pattern to achieve this dialect. In fact, adopting only a few of the suggested changes may give you enough of a southern sound to lend your character some credibility.
- Warm up your facial muscles and do some jaw-releasing exercises before working on this dialect; the more free and relaxed your face is, the more relaxed and free your sounds will become.

SOUTHERN FILM, TELEVISION, AND AUDIO REFERENCES

FILM

Texas:
The Apostle
A Time to Kill
Contact
Places in the Heart
Raising Arizona
Broadcast News
Perfect Harmony
Trip to Bountiful
1918
Courtship
*Come Back to the Five and Dime,
    Jimmy Dean, Jimmy Dean*

Alabama/Mississippi:
Double Jeopardy
Forrest Gump
Steel Magnolias
Ghosts of Mississippi
Mississippi Burning
Cat on a Hot Tin Roof
Fried Green Tomatoes
To Kill a Mockingbird

Georgia/Deep South/Plantation:
The Gift
Midnight in the Garden of Good and Evil
Beloved
Passion Fish
Deliverance
The Color Purple
Gone With the Wind
Driving Miss Daisy

Tennessee/Arkansas:
Sling Blade
Nine to Five
Best Little Whorehouse in Texas
Rhinestone
The River Rat

TELEVISION

"Beverly Hillbillies"
"Designing Women"
"Empty Nest"

"Golden Girls"
"Grace Under Fire"
"In the Heat of the Night"

Dialect Tapes and Sources

American Southern Dialects	Gillian Lane-Plescia
American Southern Dialects (2)	Gillian Lane-Plescia
Stage Dialects	Jerry Blunt
More Stage Dialects	Jerry Blunt
Dialects for the Stage	Evangeline Machlin
Acting with an Accent — American South	David Alan Stern
IDEA website	www.ukans.edu/~idea/index.html

For a more complete and detailed list of films/resources, see Ginny Kopf's book The Dialect Handbook.

SOUTHERN SOUNDS

Southern vowel changes:

ih	→ eeuh	this, his	→ theeyus, heeyuz
a	→ a or ayuh	man, can	→ mayuhn, cayuhn
ow	→ a	how, now	→ ha,na
oh	→ uhoh	goes, show	→ guhohz, shuhoh
aw	→ ah	all, tall	→ ahl, tahl
uh	→ uh (relaxed)	of, dove	→ uhv, duhv
eh	→ ih	ten, men	→ tin, min
eye	→ ah	night, right	→ naht, raht
ay	→ uhay	paper, day	→ puhaypuh, duhay
oo	→ uhoo	routes, news	→ ruhoots, nuhooz

The *r* dipthongs:

ear	→ eer or eeuh	here, dear	→ heeyuh, deeyuh
or	→ ohr or owuh	your, more	→ yowuh, mowuh
air	→ ehyuh or air	there, where	→ theyuh, whehyuh
are	→ ah or are	cart, large	→ caht, lahge

Southern consonant changes:

[r]	dropped in some regions, hardened in others
[ing] → [in]	bikin', hikin', farmin'

Some special word pronunciations in the South:

Sir = suh
can't = kaint
-day (of the week) = dih

SOUTHERN PRACTICE SENTENCES

[ih] → [eeuh]:
   This is his distant cousin Isabelle. His fist hit the tip of his brim.

[a] → [a or ayuh]:
   The man's plan was hard to understand. Can Stan give the land to Nan?

[ow] → [a]:
   How do the cows know how to plow? Around town, I wear a crown.

[oh] → [uhoh]:
   Oh, Joe, you know how it goes. Don't go to the road show . . . it's slow.

[aw] → [ah]:
   All the lawyers are tall and may fall. Crawl through the hall.

[uh] → [uh (relaxed)]:
   The Doves of Love are from Lubbock. With my gloves, I scrubbed my
   tub clean.

[eh] → [ih]:
   Ten of the seventeen men were from Tennessee. Get the pen from the
   pen center.

[eye] → [ah]:
   The night was white with the light from the sky. Moonlight is right for
   flight.

[ay] → [uhay]:
   Take the paper from the Mayor to the Lady of the Lake. The day is going
   away.

[oo] → [uhoo]:
   The two of you are blue in the tooth. I grew two foot in two weeks!

[or] → [ohr or ohuh]:
   Your four-year-old broke the store horsey. Go ye forth and multiply!

[ear] → [eer or eeuh]:
   Here is your beer, Dear. The deer is afeared of the rearview mirror.

AM I BLUE
by Beth Henley

American (Southern): One Male and One Female

THE PLAY: Set in New Orleans, in the fall of 1968, this fun one-act play explores the coming-of-age for a Southern farm boy and his accidental encounter with a free-spirited Southern girl on a rainy night, hours before his eighteenth birthday.

THE SCENE: Ashbe (16) has invited John Polk (17) back to her place after getting them both kicked out of a bar for being underage. Initially resistant to the idea of going home with a complete stranger, John Polk agrees and spends the final few hours of his seventeenth year in the crazy, honest world of his new friend.

TIME AND PLACE: Ashbe's run-down apartment in New Orleans. 11:45 PM. A fall evening. 1968.

JOHN POLK: *(He has heard the conversation and is taking off his coat.)* Hey, Ashbe — *(She looks at him blankly, her mind far away.)* You want to talk?

ASHBE: No. *(Slight pause.)* Why don't you look at my shell collection? I have this special shell collection. *(She shows him collection.)*

JOHN POLK: They're beautiful, I've never seen colors like this. *(Ashbe is silent, he continues to himself.)* I used to go to Biloxi a lot when I was a kid . . . one time my brother and I, we camped out on the beach. The sky was purple. I remember it was really purple. We ate pork and beans out of a can. I'd always kinda wanted to do that. Every night for about a week after I got home, I dreamt about these waves foaming over my head and face. It was funny. Did you find these shells or buy them?

ASHBE: Some I found, some I bought. I've been trying to decipher their meaning. Here, listen, do you hear that?

JOHN POLK: Yes.

ASHBE: That's the soul of the sea. *(She listens.)* I'm pretty sure it's the soul of the sea. Just imagine when I decipher the language. I'll know all the secrets of the world.

JOHN POLK: Yeah, probably you will. *(Looking into the shell.)* You know, you were right.

ASHBE: What do you mean?

JOHN POLK: About me, you were right. I am a sheep, a normal one. I've been trying to get out of it, but now I'm as big a sheep as ever.

ASHBE: Oh, it doesn't matter. You're company. It was rude of me to say.

JOHN POLK: No, because it was true. I really didn't want to go into a fraternity, I didn't even want to go to college, and I sure as hell don't want to go back to Hollybluff and work the soybean farm till I'm eighty.

ASHBE: I still say you could work on a ranch.

JOHN POLK: I don't know. I wanted to be a minister or something good, but I don't even know if I believe in God.

ASHBE: Yeah.

JOHN POLK: I never used to worry about being a failure. Now I think about it all the time. It's just I need to do something that's — fulfilling.

ASHBE: Fulfilling, yes, I see what you mean. Well, how about college? Isn't it fulfilling? I mean, you take all those wonderful classes, and you have all your very good friends.

JOHN POLK: Friends, yeah, I have some friends.

ASHBE: What do you mean?

JOHN POLK: Nothing — well I do mean something. What the hell, let me try to explain. You see it was my "friends," the fraternity guys that set me up with G.G., excuse me Myrtle, as a gift for my eighteenth birthday.

ASHBE: You mean, you didn't want the appointment?

JOHN POLK: No, I didn't want it. Hey, ah, where did my blue drink go?

ASHBE: *(As she hands him the drink.)* They probably thought you really wanted to go.

JOHN POLK: Yeah, I'm sure they gave a damn what I wanted. They never even asked me. Hell, I would have told them a handkerchief, a pair of argyle socks, but, no, they have to get me a whore just because it's the cool thing to do. They make me sick. I couldn't even stay at the party they gave. All the sweaty T-shirts, and moron sex stories — I just couldn't take it.

ASHBE: Is that why you were at the Blue Angel so early?

JOHN POLK: Yeah, I needed to get drunk but not with them. They're such creeps.

ASHBE: Gosh, so you really don't want to go to Myrtle's?

JOHN POLK: No, I guess not.

ASHBE: Then are you going?

JOHN POLK: *(Pause.)* Yes.

ASHBE: That's wrong. You shouldn't go just to please them.

JOHN POLK: Oh, that's not the point anymore, maybe at first it was, but it's not anymore. Now I have to go for myself — to prove to myself that I'm not afraid.

ASHBE: Afraid? *(Slowly, as she begins to grasp his meaning.)* You mean, you've never slept with a girl before?

JOHN POLK: Well, I've never been in love.

ASHBE: *(In amazement.)* You're a virgin?

JOHN POLK: Oh, God.

ASHBE: No, don't feel bad, I am too.

JOHN POLK: I thought I should be in love —

ASHBE: Well, you're certainly not in love with Myrtle. I mean, you haven't even met her.

JOHN POLK: I know, but, God, I thought maybe I'd never fall in love. What then? You should experience every thing — shouldn't you? Oh, what's it matter, everything's so screwed.

ASHBE: Screwed? Yeah, I guess it is. I mean, I always thought it would be fun to have a lot of friends who gave parties and go to dances all dressed up. Like the dance tonight — it might have been fun.

JOHN POLK: Well, why didn't you go?

ASHBE: I don't know. I'm not sure it would have been fun. Anyway, you can't go — alone.

JOHN POLK: Oh, you need a date?

ASHBE: Yeah, or something.

JOHN POLK: Say, Ashbe, ya wanna dance here?

ASHBE: No, I think we'd better discuss your dilemma.

JOHN POLK: What dilemma?

ASHBE: Myrtle. It doesn't seem right you should —

JOHN POLK: Let's forget Myrtle for now. I've got a while yet. Here have some more of this blue-moon drink.

ASHBE: You're only trying to escape through artificial means.

JOHN POLK: Yeah, you got it. Now come on. Would you like to dance? Hey, you said you liked to dance.

ASHBE: You're being ridiculous.

JOHN POLK: *(Winking at her.)* Dance?

ASHBE: John Polk, I just thought —

JOHN POLK: Hmm?

ASHBE: How to solve your problem —

JOHN POLK: Well —

ASHBE: Make love to me!

JOHN POLK: What?!

ASHBE: It all seems logical to me. It would prove you weren't scared and you wouldn't be doing it just to impress others.

JOHN POLK: Look, I — I mean I hardly know you —

ASHBE: But we've talked. It's better this way, really. I won't be so apt to point out your mistakes.

JOHN POLK: I'd feel great stripping a twelve-year-old of her virginity.

ASHBE: I'm sixteen! Anyway, I'd be stripping you of yours just as well. I'll go put on some Tiger Claw perfume. *(She runs out.)*

JOHN POLK: Hey, come back! Tiger Claw perfume, Christ.

ASHBE: *(Entering.)* I think one should have different scents for different moods.

JOHN POLK: Hey, stop spraying that! You know I'm not going to — well, you'd get neurotic, or pregnant, or some damn thing. Stop spraying, will you?

ASHBE: Pregnant? You really think I could get pregnant?

JOHN POLK: Sure, it'd be a delightful possibility.

ASHBE: It really wouldn't be bad. Maybe I would get to go to Tokyo for an abortion. I've never been to the Orient.

JOHN POLK: Sure getting cut on is always a real treat.

ASHBE: Anyway, I might just want to have my dear baby. I could move to Atlanta with Mama and Madeline. It'd be wonderful fun. Why I could take him to the supermarket, put him in one of those baby seats to stroll him about. I'd buy peach baby food and feed it to him with a tiny golden spoon. Why I could take colored pictures of him and send them to you through the mail. Come on — *(Starts putting pillows onto the couch.)* Well, I guess you should kiss me for a start. It's only etiquette, everyone begins with it.

JOHN POLK: I don't think I could even kiss you with a clear conscience. I mean, you're so small with those little cat eye glasses and curly hair — I couldn't even kiss you.

ASHBE: You couldn't even kiss me? I can't help it if I have to wear glasses. I got the prettiest ones I could find.

JOHN POLK: Your glasses are fine. Let's forget it, okay?

ASHBE: I know, my lips are too purple, but if I eat carrots, the dye'll come off and they'll be orange.

JOHN POLK: I didn't say anything about your lips being too purple.

ASHBE: Well, what is it? You're just plain chicken I suppose —

JOHN POLK: Sure, right, I'm chicken, totally chicken. Let's forget it. I don't know how, but, somehow, this is probably all my fault.

ASHBE: You're darn right it's all your fault! I want to have my dear baby or at least get to Japan. I'm so sick of school I could smash every marshmallow in sight! *(She starts smashing.)* Go on to your skinny pimply whore. I hope the skinny whore laughs in your face which she probably will because you have an easy face to laugh in.

JOHN POLK: You're absolutely right, she'll probably hoot and howl her damn fizzle red head off. Maybe you can wait outside the door and hear her, give you lots of pleasure, you sadistic little thief.

ASHBE: Thief — was Robin Hood — oh, what's wrong with this world? I just wasn't made for it is all. I've probably been put in the wrong world, I can see that now.

JOHN POLK: You're fine in this world.

ASHBE: Sure, everyone just views me as an undesirable lump.

JOHN POLK: Who?

ASHBE: You for one.

JOHN POLK: *(Pause.)* You mean because I wouldn't make love to you?

ASHBE: It seems clear to me.

JOHN POLK: But you're wrong, you know.

ASHBE: *(To self, softly.)* Don't pity me.

JOHN POLK: The reason I wouldn't wasn't that — it's just that — well, I like you too much to.

ASHBE: You like me?

JOHN POLK: Undesirable lump, Jesus.

COME BACK TO THE FIVE AND DIME, JIMMY DEAN, JIMMY DEAN
by Ed Graczyk

American (Southern): Two Females

THE PLAY: Using flashbacks and real time, the story of the "Disciples of James Dean" is told. We see the young beginnings of the adults they become as old friends gather for a reunion at their childhood club.

THE SCENE: A flashback scene (but real and in the present for the actors playing it). Mona (17) has been away for a while because of her health and Sissy (27) has been holding their rituals together. Now, as new twists play into their innocent, youthful dreams and games, the stage is set for major life changes.

TIME AND PLACE: Mid-September. 1955. A rural town in Texas, somewhere near Marfa, where the movie *Giant* was made. The local five and dime store.

Sissy (then) followed by Mona, enters from the back room of the store. She has the same gigantic boobs forcing her thin sweater to its limit. She also wears a short skating skirt. Mona (then) is helping her carry boxes of cosmetics that they will hang from the display rack.

SISSY (THEN): *(Entering.)* Me an' Joe was gonna get Stella May to take your place doin' the McGuire Sisters, but she wouldn't have been as good as you.

MONA (THEN): I don't thing we should do that act anymore because of all that's happened. Juanita says it was that thing at the senior dance with Lester T. Callahan that started all the trouble.

SISSY (THEN): I thought it was a riot, a real riot. They all thought he was my cousin from Oklahoma City . . . especially Lester T.

MONA (THEN): He really does make a very pretty girl, doesn't he?

SISSY (THEN): Lester T. sure thought so, didn't he? . . . thought he was the cutest thing he'd ever seen. I would have given anythin' to see the expression on his face when he got Joe in the backseat of his car, reached in his dress, squeezed them balloons and strawberry jello exploded all over his rented white tuxedo. *(Laughs.)* Serves the bastard right for two-timin' me right in front of my face.

MONA (THEN): Joe should never have carried the joke so far. You think Lester T. will ever get even with him like he said?

SISSY (THEN): Shoot, I wouldn't put it past that goon-head.

MONA (THEN): It's been nearly three months. Maybe he's forgot.

SISSY (THEN): He ain't forgot . . . hell, it's the only thing outta twelve years of school he's remembered. *(Looks out the window.)* Thank God, that rain's finally gonna stop. I got me a date over at the graveyard tonight.

MONA (THEN): We've got a meetin' of the Disciples, did you forget?

SISSY (THEN): The meetin' ain't gonna last all night, is it? I just can't get over your bein' back . . . seems like I'm dreamin' or somethin'.

MONA (THEN): *(Excited.)* Oh, me too. *(They hug.)* I missed you so very much.

SISSY (THEN): And me, you.

MONA (THEN): I was so afraid for this summer to be over. Now, it can stay summer forever, can't it?

SISSY (THEN): Shoot, I hope not. The heat's been so hot I think it's beginnin' to shrink my bazooms. *(Throws out her chest.)* They look like they've shrunk any to you?

MONA (THEN): *(Inspecting.)* They both look the same to me.

SISSY (THEN): You think they might be as big as Marilyn Monroe's?

MONA (THEN): I think they might be bigger.

SISSY (THEN): *(Thrilled.)* You really mean it? Sidney said they were, but you know him.

MONA (THEN): He told you that?

SISSY (THEN): He's such a card . . . always pinchin' my bottom behin' one of the counters. Not where Juanita can see him though. She thinks he's as prim an' proper as a preacher. Boy, does he pull the wool over her eyes.

MONA (THEN): Where is he today, anyhow? . . . hung over again?

SISSY (THEN): Had some kinda meetin' over in Waco. *(She takes a lipstick, eyebrow pencil, etc. from the rack and applies them.)*

MONA (THEN): I'll never forgive him for firin' Joe.

SISSY (THEN): Well, whattaya expect from the buttholes in this town?

MONA (THEN): I'm afraid he might leave town now he's got no job.

SISSY (THEN): Hey, you got a thing for him maybe?

MONA (THEN): No!

SISSY (THEN): You do! That's why you really came back, isn't it?

MONA (THEN): *(Quickly.)* It was my asthma . . . my asthma . . . we're friends, that's all . . . just like you an' me.

SISSY (THEN): Okay . . . okay . . . Jeez, I was only kiddin' . . . Here try some of this new cheek blush that just come in. *(Starts to apply it on her.)* Hey, ain't you just bustin' for that movie to come out so's you can see yourself up there on the movie screen with James Dean? *(A squeal and a shiver.)* Ooh! He can drag me off to the graveyard any ol' night he wants . . . rainin' or not.

MONA (THEN): *(Nervous.)* Did you ever dream about what it would be like? You know, to make love to somebody real famous like him?

SISSY (THEN): All the time . . . but you really should experiment with some "nobody" before you tackle someone as important as him. That's all I'm doin' . . . sort of like homework for the big test later on. I just can't get over somebody your age haven' never been over to the graveyard with anyone before.

MONA (THEN): It's . . . it's too spooky.

SISSY (THEN): Oh, you get used to it after awhile. Some of the guys get scared an' have trouble gettin' goin', but they're mainly after my bazooms anyhow. They all gotta squeeze an' feel aroun' . . . most of 'em get their kicks just doin' that.

MONA (THEN): Aren't you afraid you'll get caught?

SISSY (THEN): Shoot, nobody goes over to that ol' graveyard no more. It's all grown over with stickers an' tall grass, an' the gravestones have all been pushed over to use for layin' places. I always do it on top of Colonel Jaspar P. Ramslan' the second . . . soun's dreamy, don't he?

MONA (THEN): Wouldn't it be terrible to be left alone like that with nobody to pick the weeds off your body.

SISSY (THEN): Mona, how creepy!

MONA (THEN): I don't know anybody who's ever died, an' I hope I never do. I'm so afraid I might never remember them anymore.

SISSY (THEN): *(Laughs.)* What the hell's that supposed to mean?

MONA (THEN): *(Laughs also.)* I don't know. I'm always sayin' stuff like that I can't explain.

SISSY (THEN): I can get in enough trouble sayin' stuff I *can* explain. *(Gets moving.)* I better get the rest of them boxes unpacked before Juanita gets back . . . c'mon an' help me.

MONA (THEN): Sissy, I feel somethin' so deep inside me about James Dean that I can't get words to come out about it.

SISSY (THEN): You mean love?

MONA (THEN): No, it's somethin' more.

SISSY (THEN):   More than love? There's nothin' more than love . . . love's the end.

MONA (THEN): No, Sissy, you're wrong. There's somethin' beyond the end. *(The lights start to cross-fade.)* As soon as I can save up enough money, I'm gonna buy Reata . . . an' you an' me an' Joe will move there an' live forever an' ever . . . Wouldn't that be wonderful.

SISSY (THEN):   But it's only the front, silly . . . it's not a real house . . . c'mon. *(She exits. Mona [then] rushes after her.)*

MONA (THEN): It could be, Sissy . . .

[MONA: *(To herself.)* It's just "deceivin' to the eye," that's all.]

CYRA AND ROCKY
by Cherie Bennett

American (Southern): Two Females

THE PLAY: A contemporary version of the story of Cyrano de Bergerac, *Cyra and Rocky* is a reversed-role interpretation of the famous tale of deception and love. Forced to write to each other because of an English assignment, Chrissy and Rocky begin, begrudgingly, to exchange letters (she lives in Nashville, he lives in Michigan). When they reach high school, and the assignment continues and includes sending a photo of themselves along with the next letter, their interest in each other grows as each discovers how attractive the other is. That is when Chrissy enlists the help of Cyra, her best friend and a far more poetic and articulate writer. Rocky begins to fall in love with Chrissy's (actually Cyra's) letters and plans to meet Chrissy in person. In typical Cyrano fashion, there is deception, true friendship, and the discovery of the real heart behind the words that Rocky hears.

THE SCENE: Rocky has just sent another letter to Chrissy (14) and has admitted that he admires her writing . . . only the trouble is, it was Cyra's (14) writing that he liked. Chrissy tries to get Cyra to continue the charade.

TIME AND PLACE: Present. Chrissy's bedroom. Nashville, Tennessee.

Lights down on Rocky's room, up on Chrissy's. Loud Grateful Dead music — the same song Rocky had on, blares from a tape deck. Chrissy's best friend, Cyra, does skateboard tricks, as Chrissy reads out loud from Rocky's latest letter.

CHRISSY: Oh, my gosh, Cyra, listen to this! *(Reading.)* "Your letter was so beautiful, as beautiful as you are. It's so amazing to connect this deeply with someone you've never even met, and I can't help but wonder what you look like naked — your naked soul that is. Be brave enough to send me all the unedited words that are your naked soul, and I shall do the same. Yours, Rocky."

CYRA: *(As if narrating a skateboard tournament.)* Yes! Cyra Berger executes a perfect layback grind, folks, which puts her in first place! And the crowd goes wild! *(Cyra makes crowd cheering noises with her mouth and cupped hands.)*

CHRISSY: Cyra —

CYRA: *(As if she's an MTV veejay.)* MTV music news update: Unknown but soon-to-be-superstar Cyra Berger has just been hired to replace Jerry Garcia for the Grateful Dead's national tour — let's go to videotape —

CHRISSY: Cyra — you're not listening to me! Turn off that awful music! *(Chrissy marches over and turns off the tape deck.)*

CYRA: That "awful music" just happens to be the Grateful Dead, which just happens to be some of the best music on the planet.

CHRISSY: About my pen pal. He —

CYRA: — wants to see you naked.

CHRISSY: My naked *soul*, he says!

CYRA: I'm so sure.

CHRISSY: But he's not like that! He's really deep! Like you! I wish I had your brains, Cyra . . .

CYRA: Yeah, well, I wish I had your body.

CHRISSY: You're beautiful.

CYRA: No. Guys see me, they see . . . you know. *You're* beautiful.

CHRISSY: But Rocky fell in love with my *inner* beauty, because of my last letter. And we both know *I* didn't write my last letter. *You* did.

CYRA: I especially liked that "only shallow people define others by how they look or by the silly activities they try on and discard like cheap clothes at the mall." And notice how I got in that you look great in a miniskirt and made you sound deep at the same time. Guys love that.

CHRISSY: It was brilliant.

CYRA: True.

CHRISSY: *You're* brilliant.

CYRA: Also true.

CHRISSY: Which is why I want you to write to him again for me.

CYRA: Wrong-a-mundo.

CHRISSY: Please —

CYRA: No, negative, nada, nein. Write to him yourself!

CHRISSY: I did! For two years! He hated me!

CYRA: But now he's seen your picture. Once a guy has seen *your* picture, all *you* have to do to get him like you is stand there and *breathe*.

CHRISSY: Not this guy.

CYRA: Does he have eyes with which to take in the perfection that is you?

CHRISSY: This guy is different, Cyra. *(Chrissy shows Rocky's picture to Cyra.)*

CYRA: *(Ho-hum.)* Yeah, he's cute. So?

CHRISSY: Cute? This isn't just cute! This is . . . this is gorgeous! This is I-have-to-have-him-or-I-will-die gorgeous! Just write one more letter from me, this'll be the last time, I swear it —

CYRA: Read my lips: no. Write it yourself.

CHRISSY: I can't! I'm not like you. I don't know how to say things, especially to a cute guy! It's like the words just won't come out of my mouth! And it's just as bad on paper! There's my pen, and there's all this white space, and what comes into my mind is just a big . . . nothing.

(Chrissy hands Cyra pen and paper. Cyra hands it back.)

CYRA: At least try. Come on, I'll help you.

CHRISSY: *(With a sigh.)* Oh, all right. I'll try. So, how should I start?

CYRA: Dear Rocky . . .

CHRISSY: *(Writing.)* Dear Rocky . . .

CYRA: Okay, tell him how you feel.

CHRISSY: How I feel.

CYRA: Your deepest, innermost feelings . . .

CHRISSY: My deepest, innermost feelings. Right. Right. Dear Rocky . . . These are my deepest, innermost feelings. I feel . . . I feel . . . I feel like barfing because I don't know what to say in this stupid letter —

CYRA: Try again. Deeper. More personal.

CHRISSY: More personal. Okay. Dear Rocky . . . I know this is really personal but . . . I've got killer cramps because I'm about to get my —

CYRA: *(Grabbing the pen and paper.)* Never mind. I'll write it.

THE DANCERS
by Horton Foote

American (Southern): One Male and One Female

THE PLAY: This touching one-act play centers on the shy Horace Robedeaux and his eventual coming-of-age into a confident and honorable man.

THE SCENE: Horace Robedeaux (18) has found a new friend and confidante in Mary Catherine (17). With Mary Catherine's gentle guidance, he begins to overcome the two things he fears the most: dancing and talking to girls.

TIME AND PLACE: Harrison, Texas (a fictional East Texas town). 1952. Early summer. Mary Catherine's living room.

HORACE: [Good night, sir. *(He goes out upstage left.)*] What does your father do?

MARY CATHERINE: He works in a garage. He's a mechanic. What does your father do?

HORACE: He's a judge.

MARY CATHERINE: My father worries so because he can't afford to send me to college. My mother told him that was all foolishness. That I'd rather go to business school anyway.

HORACE: Had you rather go to business school?

MARY CATHERINE: I don't know. *(A pause.)* Not really. But I'd never tell him that. When I was in the seventh grade I thought I would die if I couldn't get there, but then when I was in the ninth, Mother talked to me one day and told me Daddy wasn't sleeping at nights for fear I'd be disappointed if he couldn't send me, so I told him the next night I decided I'd rather go to business school. He seemed relieved. *(A pause.)*

HORACE: Mary Catherine. I . . . uh . . . heard you say a while ago that you didn't dance because you lacked confidence and uh . . . then I heard you say you talked it over with Emily and she told you what was wrong and you got the confidence and you went ahead . . .

MARY CATHERINE: That's right . . .

HORACE: Well . . . It may sound silly and all to you . . . seeing I'm about to start my first year at college . . . but I'd like to ask you a question . . .

MARY CATHERINE: What is it, Horace?

HORACE: How do you get confidence?

MARY CATHERINE: Well, you just get it. Someone points it out to you that you lack it and then you get it. . . .

HORACE: Oh, is that how it's done?

MARY CATHERINE: That's how I did it.

HORACE: You see I lack confidence. And I . . . sure would like to get it . . .

MARY CATHERINE: In what way do you lack confidence, Horace? . . .

HORACE: Oh, in all kinds of ways *(A pause.)* I'm not much of a mixer . . .

MARY CATHERINE: I think you're just mixing fine tonight.

HORACE: I know. That's what's giving me a little encouragement. You're the first girl I've ever really been able to talk to. I mean this way . . .

MARY CATHERINE: Am I, Horace? . . .

HORACE: Yes.

MARY CATHERINE: Well, I feel in some ways that's quite a compliment.

HORACE: Well, you should feel that way. *(A pause.)* Mary Catherine . . .

MARY CATHERINE: Yes, Horace?

HORACE: I had about decided to go back home tomorrow or the next day, but I understand there's another dance at the end of the week . . .

MARY CATHERINE: Uh huh. Day after tomorrow.

HORACE: Well . . . I . . . don't know if you have a date or not . . . but if you don't have . . . I feel if I could take you . . . I would gain the confidence to go . . . I mean . . .

MARY CATHERINE: Well, Horace . . . You see . . .

HORACE: I know I'd gain confidence. My sister is a swell dancer and she'll let me practice with her every living minute until it's time for the dance. Of course I don't know if I could learn to jitterbug by then or rumba or do anything fancy, you understand, but I know I could learn the fox-trot and I can waltz a little now . . .

MARY CATHERINE: I'm sure you could.

HORACE: Well, will you go with me?

MARY CATHERINE: Yes, Horace. I'd love to . . .

HORACE: Oh, thank you, Mary Catherine. I'll just practice night and day. I can't tell you how grateful Inez is going to be to you . . . Mary Catherine, if we played the radio softly could we dance now?

MARY CATHERINE: Why certainly, Horace.

HORACE: You understand I'll make mistakes . . .

MARY CATHERINE: I understand . . . *(She turns the radio on very softly.)*

HORACE: All right.

MARY CATHERINE: Yes . . . *(He approaches her very cautiously and takes her in his arms. He begins awkwardly to dance. Mary Catherine is very pleased and happy.)* Why, you're doing fine, Horace. Just fine.

HORACE: Thank you, Mary Catherine. Thank you.

(They continue dancing. Horace is very pleased with himself although he is still dancing quite awkwardly. The lights fade.)

THE DAYS AND NIGHTS
OF BEEBEE FENSTERMAKER
by William Snyder

American (Southern): Two Females

THE PLAY: Set in an American city with definite Southern leanings, the play follows the life of the ambitious, but ultimately unfulfilled Beebee Fenstermaker. Beebee has just graduated from college, and instead of living in her old hometown, waiting for life to happen to her, she decides to move up to the city and become an author. After her savings run out, she is forced to take a nine-to-five job and watch her passionate ambitions slowly slip away . . . victim of a lack of drive, talent, and miscellaneous heartbreaks along the way.

THE SCENE: Beebee (20 to 24) has been living in her apartment in the city for two years and is amazed that the time has passed her by so quickly. Her friend Nettie Jo (20 to 24) stops by on her way out and the two women get into a heated discussion about goals and plans and lifestyles.

TIME AND PLACE: Beebee's apartment. An American city (in the South?). Early evening. Present.

The lights in Beebee's apartment come up full. Nettie Jo enters dressed for a date.

NETTIE JO: Beebee?

BEEBEE: Hey, Nettie Jo. *(Nettie Jo stands in front of armchair and takes a modeling pose. Beebee gets a sketchbook and pencil out of coffee table drawer, sits on sofa and begins to sketch Nettie Jo.)*

NETTIE JO: You antsy about something?

BEEBEE: *(Shakes her head.)* Uh-uh.

NETTIE JO: Ever since you dropped your novel and took up art, you seem much more moody to me.

BEEBEE: I haven't dropped my novel. I put it aside to let the ideas solidify.

NETTIE JO: Since you put it aside then. You seem much more moody to me. *(Crosses to kitchen, gets coke out of refrigerator, and opens it.)*

BEEBEE: I don't think I am.

NETTIE JO: I do. I think you are.

BEEBEE: Hold still, Nettie Jo.

NETTIE JO: *(Returns to her position in front of armchair.)* Don't you want me to be evanescent?

BEEBEE: Not tonight.

NETTIE JO: That's the way I feel tonight.

BEEBEE: You look very pretty.

NETTIE JO: Thank you *(She smiles.)*

BEEBEE: Don't smile.

NETTIE JO: How's your new art teacher?

BEEBEE: I stopped goin' to him.

NETTIE JO: Stopped goin' to this one too? Why?

BEEBEE: He was talkin' more than he was teachin'.

NETTIE JO: Who will you go to now?

BEEBEE: Nobody for a while. I thought I'd work on my own. Hold still, Nettie Jo. I wish you'd have your hair cut. All I can see is hair.

NETTIE JO: Most people like it long. *(Sits in armchair.)* Mother could sit on hers. I've got a picture of her doin' it. Lookin' up into a sterlin' silver hand mirror. *(Poses like her mother.)*

BEEBEE: Come on now, Nettie Jo.

NETTIE JO: How many teachers have you been to?

BEEBEE: What difference does it make?

NETTIE JO: Two or three anyway.

BEEBEE: What difference does it make? None of them fit the bill. I don't either, I guess. When I first go to them they all think I'm wonderful. They say how expressive and sensitive and all that. *(Nettie Jo pulls at her skirt to even the hem.)* Nettie Jo will you hold still? *(Nettie Jo resumes posing.)* And the first few days I am good. Then I get so bugged I freeze up and I get just horrible. And I stay horrible. And I tell myself I'm not doin' it for them. And all right so I'm horrible now, if I was good once I'll be good again. But I'm not. Well, I'll have to work harder, that's all. Keep workin' is the important thing. *(Closes sketchbook and puts it in coffee table drawer.)*

NETTIE JO: *(Sits in armchair.)* I wish you'd date more.

BEEBEE: I've told you a thousand times those T. D. Hackameyer boys don't interest me.

NETTIE JO: You don't give yourself a chance to meet anybody else. Then when you do you never will date 'em more than once. I wish I had a nickel for every boy I've had Tommy bring up here that you've turned thumbs down on.

BEEBEE: Nettie Jo, stop talkin' like my mother.

NETTIE JO: I think you're workin' too hard.

BEEBEE: *(Rises.)* And I think you're just breezin' along with the breeze, aren't you, Nettie Jo? Lettin' the rest of the world go by.

NETTIE JO: I might as well. I certainly can't change it.

BEEBEE: *(Circling Nettie Jo.)* You go right down the years sittin' on your one spot. You sit on your one spot at the office. You sit on your one spot in your folks' split-level ranch house. You have no outside interests other than men. No hobbies, handicrafts, or sports. No religious convictions or philosophical leanin's. Just sittin'. One spot Nettie Jo Repult. The girl who never gets off her behind. *(Moves around to upstage right area.)*

NETTIE JO: Correct, Beebee. And I'm having a grand time doin' it.

BEEBEE: You live a day at a time with never a passin' thought for tomorrow or the day after.

NETTIE JO: Correct, Beebee.

BEEBEE: And what beats me is you're satisfied.

NETTIE JO: I don't have any ambition, Beebee.

BEEBEE: That's the kind sails right to the top like a gas balloon.

NETTIE JO: What do you want me to do?

BEEBEE: I don't know. But there's somethin' wrong about bein' so satisfied with everything the way it is and goin' along with the crowd. You have to gain special recognition in some way. In *some* way, Nettie Jo. If you don't you end up nothin' — a nonentity. Another face in the crowd. And that's like bein' dead. Do you want to wind up dead without one person to remember your name?

NETTIE JO: *(Rises, crosses to bureau and gets nail file.)* If I'm dead, why should I care if people remember my name? *(Crosses back to armchair, sits and files nails.)* And I've got enough to keep in mind without worryin' whether I'm leavin' behind some mark that I won't even be able to look at. Anyway, what's wrong with bein' another face in the crowd?

BEEBEE: It's death in life, that's what. It's walkin' through the world without touchin' a thing. It's blendin' in instead of stickin' out. And God knows folks try to push you into the wallpaper from the minute you're born. Startin' with your family. She gets this from so and so. That from somebody else. Eyes, ears, character, bad habits, good habits. Just when you think you finally got somethin' on your own, as sure as Christmas somebody comes along and says, "Isn't that exactly like Uncle Whatchamacallit."

There you are locked tighter than a Chinese puzzle without knowin' where one person ends and the other ones begin. *(Sits on coffee table.)* Then your mother starts sayin' why aren't you more like people your own age? Why don't you join a sorority, a club, go to dances?

NETTIE JO: Did you ever do any of those things, Beebee?

BEEBEE: No.

NETTIE JO: Why?

BEEBEE: I didn't want to. *(Pauses, then reflectively.)* The funny thing is, if I had gone along with the rest, I would have been last in line.

NETTIE JO: Why?

BEEBEE: They weren't interested in me and I wasn't interested in them. It was like they had something extra. A gift I didn't have. And it made me feel cut off.

NETTIE JO: What gift was that?

BEEBEE: *(Absorbed in her words.)* The gift of ease. Of comradeship. Of . . . be-longin' to somethin'.

NETTIE JO: Beebee, I don't know if you realize it or not but you just contra-dicted yourself.

BEEBEE: How? I didn't.

NETTIE JO: You just finished sayin' the last thing you wanted to be was part of a group.

BEEBEE: And I meant it. But a person can still be momentarily seduced by the *idea* of somethin' they think is *wrong*.

NETTIE JO: Beebee, do you want to be like me?

BEEBEE: Like you! *(Rises, crosses downstage left then circles around Nettie Jo.)* Like you, Nettie Jo. Nettie Jo, like you! Why Nettie Jo, you're the last person to step on grass I'd want to be like. Why I'd take a flyin' leap off anything high enough if I thought I was anything approachin' bein' like you.

NETTIE JO: If that's so, it makes me wonder sometimes why I'm your only friend.

BEEBEE: *(Holds upstage right above coffee table.)* You're not.

NETTIE JO: Who else do you see?

BEEBEE: I live in the same apartment building with you. I couldn't get away from you if I tried.

NETTIE JO: You haven't tried very hard. In fact it's been just the opposite. You're always askin' me up here every hour of the day or night on any pretext other than just to visit. I don't know why you can't admit some-times you'd just like to visit.

BEEBEE: *(Crosses to downstage right between coffee table and bed.)* Well I'm admittin' now that I'm gonna avoid you from now on like the bubonic plague!

NETTIE JO: Okay, Beebee, but I'll tell you this. For my money and for all your talkin' — you're not much further along than me.

BEEBEE: I'm not huh? I'm not huh?

NETTIE JO: No.

BEEBEE: All that proves is that you're blind in one eye and can't see good out of the other.

NETTIE JO: And you can see out of both of yours I suppose.

BEEBEE: At least I use mine for somethin' besides Maybelline!

NETTIE JO: Maybe so, but two years ago you said . . .

BEEBEE: *(Stunned.)* Two years ago?

NETTIE JO: Yes, Beebee, two years ago. I met you two years ago.

BEEBEE: What month is this?

NETTIE JO: June.

BEEBEE: I thought it was the tag end of May.

NETTIE JO: No, it's the second of June. You were doin' all that talk about love and a career bein' God's answer to hundred-proof bourbon. And I thought it was a fine idea. Still do for that matter. But what have you done?

BEEBEE: What do you mean what have I done?

NETTIE JO: What have you got to show for your two years besides a stab at a novel and a few weeks of art school. What have you settled on?

BEEBEE: I've settled on paintin'.

NETTIE JO: With writin' on the side and music in the background. Well, I'm sorry, Beebee, but I don't see where all your "doin'" gives you any right to criticize my "sittin'" — cause from where I'm sittin', your doin' don't look like much. *(Beebee sits on coffee table. Pause.)* Oh, Beebee, I didn't mean to say all that.

BEEBEE: Never mind, Nettie Jo.

NETTIE JO: When you jumped on me with all fours you just got my back up.

BEEBEE: I don't blame you.

NETTIE JO: *(Rises and crosses to Beebee.)* Beebee, I'm worried about you.

BEEBEE: Well don't be.

NETTIE JO: *(Kneels beside Beebee.)* The thing of it is I'll be leavin' pretty soon.

BEEBEE: Leavin'?

NETTIE JO: See. Tommy's asked me to marry him. And I'm goin' to.

BEEBEE: Married. *(Moved.)* Oh. Oh, Nettie Jo. How wonderful. *(She hugs Nettie Jo.)* When did it happen? How wonderful. He's a very nice boy.

NETTIE JO: I think so.

BEEBEE: Where will you live?

NETTIE JO: *(Crosses to armchair.)* He's had a real good job offered to him in L.A. so we'll be movin' out there.

BEEBEE: Soon, you say.

NETTIE JO: In about a month. It'll take me that long to quit my job and give up this place and get ready.

BEEBEE: Well. Oh, Nettie Jo. It's wonderful.

NETTIE JO: *(Crosses to Beebee.)* I wish you were comin' to California with us.

BEEBEE: *(Crosses to bureau.)* Nettie Jo stop.

NETTIE JO: *(Follows Beebee.)* I do. We could all take an apartment together.

BEEBEE: Now wouldn't that be fun.

NETTIE JO: It would. I know Tommy wouldn't mind.

BEEBEE: You ought to try asking him.

NETTIE JO: I already have. And he thought it was a wonderful idea.

BEEBEE: Nettie Jo.

NETTIE JO: The thing of it is I think a change of scene might give you a fresh viewpoint.

BEEBEE: Well, thanks, Nettie Jo but . . .

NETTIE JO: My thought is a fresh scene and fresh faces might help you get settled on somethin'. And I'd certainly feel better about you. Will you think about it?

BEEBEE: *(Distracted.)* What?

NETTIE JO: I say will you think about it.

BEEBEE: Yes, I'll think about it.

NETTIE JO: Well. I'll see you later. I'll come up when I get home if it's not too late.

BEEBEE: Good-bye, Nettie Jo. *(Nettie Jo exits. Beebee crosses upstage center. With emotion.)* Two years! That's three hundred and sixty-odd days times two! And how many hours and how many minutes and how many seconds? God, what have I been doing all this time? *(The sound of ticking begins under and increases in volume as the speech progresses.)* You must have put me in a trance. I'm so dogged by time all I been doing is lettin' it go by. I been here two years! People ask me what are my interests, and I say I'm a writer/pianist or a pianist/writer or a pianist/painter or a writin' piano playin' painter. When all I am is a nine-to-five worker at T. D. Hackameyer's with an unfinished novel, a grubby sketchbook, and an

apartment that's drivin' me stark starin' crazy. I need somebody! Somebody for me! If I had somebody I'd know what to do and how to do it. Well, what do you want, Miss Beebee? *(Fiercely.)* I want man in the image of God! Isn't that what you're supposed to be producin'? Then do it goddamit! If I'm my own worst enemy make me not my own worst enemy. I've got strings attached and they're tying me in knots! *(The ticking has become almost louder than her voice. It stops abruptly.)*
(Blackout and curtain.)

EARLY DARK
by Reynolds Price

American (Southern): One Male and One Female

THE PLAY: Set in North Carolina in 1957, *Early Dark* traces the journey of love taken by Rosacoke Mustian and the man who tortures her mind, Wesley Beavers. As she struggles with deciding the path of her life and the illogical nature of affection, Rosacoke endures the callous nature of her family, the seeming insensitivity of her object of affection, and the cruel accidents of nature.

THE SCENE: It has been years since Rosacoke (20) has seen Wesley (22), and he is already planning to leave again. After a Sunday afternoon picnic and swim, the lovers are left alone to sort out their true feelings for the future of their relationship.

TIME AND PLACE: July 1957. Late afternoon. North Carolina. A swim hole and picnic area and the surrounding forest.

WESLEY: *(Still distant.)* Rosa, you got anything I can drink?

ROSACOKE: What you mean?

WESLEY: I mean I'm thirsty.

ROSACOKE: You're standing in several thousand tons of spring water. *(Goes on watching as Wesley approaches, soaked and serious.)* The drink stand is closed. We're on our own.
(Wesley nods, extends a hand to her hair, stops short of a touch, moves off to the bathhouse. Rosa thinks they are leaving, goes to find her shoes and hat. She puts on her shoes as Wesley appears in the bathhouse door, having added a shirt to his trunks.)

ROSACOKE: Who stole your pants?

WESLEY: Rosa, come here.
(Wesley waves her to him. She goes, takes his proffered hand; and he leads them off on a walk around the lake. After six slow steps and silence from Wesley, Rosa stops.)

ROSACOKE: Aren't we going home? Mr. Mason has shut it; maybe we should go.

WESLEY: Maybe I can find some drinking water.

ROSACOKE: *(Accepting his lead again but with protest.)* Wesley, there is water at every gas station between here and home. Why have we got to go tearing through some strange somebody's bushes?

WESLEY: *(Stops.)* Please hush, Rosa. *(Strokes her hair.)*

ROSACOKE: *(Steps away, touches her hair quickly.)* Sun has bleached me till I look like a tramp.

WESLEY: What would you know about a tramp, bleached or black?

ROSACOKE: I know you don't have to go to Norfolk to find one.

WESLEY: What do you mean?

ROSACOKE: You know who I mean.

WESLEY: If it's Willie you mean, she'll be in Norfolk tomorrow morning with all the other tramps you know.

ROSACOKE: What's she going for?

WESLEY: To ease her pain. *(Smiles.)* No, she's got a job.

ROSACOKE: Doing what?

WESLEY: Curling hair.

ROSACOKE: What does she know about curling hair with that mess she's got?

WESLEY: I don't know but she's moving up, bag and baggage.

ROSACOKE: What was she asking you about then?

WESLEY: Would I ride her up.

ROSACOKE: On that motorcycle? — a hundred thirty miles?

WESLEY: Yes.

ROSACOKE: Then she's crazier than even I thought she was. *(Moves two steps away.)* Are you taking her?

WESLEY: Don't know yet.

ROSACOKE: When will you know?

WESLEY: Time I'm home tonight.

(Wesley goes to her, takes her hand again; they walk on farther to trees above the lake. Rosa finally pulls at his lead.)

ROSACOKE: We'll both catch terrible poison-oak — which Milo will laugh at till Christmas at least — and you won't find any water up here.

WESLEY: Maybe water's not what I'm looking for.

ROSACOKE: I don't notice gold dust lying around — what are you hunting?

(Wesley leads her to a large tree and sits beneath it. Rosa holds his hand but doesn't sit.)

ROSACOKE: Night'll come and catch us here, and we'll get scratched to pieces stumbling out.

(Wesley looks up, not smiling; pulls her hand. She sits beside him and smooths her hair. He takes her smoothing hand, lifts her hair and kisses her

neck. She sits upright, eyes open, face clenching. Wesley works on till she pulls away.)

ROSACOKE: How much else did you learn in the Navy? — harmonica playing, motorcycle riding, gnawing on girls like sides of meat. Uncle Sam got his money's worth in you. *(Wesley sits far back, his face all dark.)* Wesley, where are you?

WESLEY: I was right there with you. *(Waits.)* I'm here, I guess.

ROSACOKE: You guess. You *guess?* Do you guess I'm made out of brass like Willie to trail behind you and beg for notice? You guess I can sit on another seven years, wondering who Wesley is and where Wesley is and is Wesley ever coming home, calming down, resting long enough to have him a life? You guess I can live on in mystery like this till you finally decide to come out of cover and speak your mind? — say "Rosa, I'm ready to carry my share" or "Rosa, get your fool self home to your Mama." All I'm asking you to do is say. Do you guess you love me or that I love you?

WESLEY: *(Waits, still dark; then his voice half-strange.)* I've answered that the only way I know how. I'm here by you. *(Moves forward far enough to take light again.)*

ROSACOKE: *(Studies him closely.)* I love you, Wesley. When I see you, I do. I know this isn't what a girl ought to say; but when you have sat silent seven whole years, waiting for somebody you love to speak and you don't know one reason why you love them or even what you want them to say — then there comes a time when you have to speak. I've spoken and I'm here.

WESLEY: I knew that, Rosa. Wesley is here.

(He begins his answer the way he can — gently kissing her eyes, lips, neck; then moving downward. At first she responds, then balks and stops him with her hand.)

ROSACOKE: Is that everything you want out of me?

WESLEY: It's right much, Rosa. *(Waits.)* We're not exactly strangers. Listen, if you're thinking of Mildred's trouble, you'll be all right. It's why I left the funeral — *(Touches his shirt pocket.)*

ROSACOKE: *(Stands suddenly.)* Take me home please. It's nearly night.

WESLEY: Of course it's night. What the hell you want — floodlights?

ROSACOKE: I said take me home.

WESLEY: You say a lot, Rosa — more than you understand. Try living those words. *(She does not turn, so Wesley stands.)* You know I'm going to Norfolk tomorrow. You know that, don't you?

ROSACOKE: I know it. *(Moves to leave.)*

WESLEY: And that maybe I'm riding Willie up there?

ROSACOKE: You can ride Willie up the seaboard coast, if she's what you want. Just take care she doesn't have Mildred's trouble either.

(Rosa leaves and waits near the bathhouse — full night now. Wesley follows separately, slowly; enters the bathhouse, comes out with his clothes. Facing Rosa, three steps away, he slides off his trunks; stands bare before her — to punish and tempt her. Then slowly, still watching her, he dresses. She bears the sight with no visible response.)

WESLEY: You ever know that you really want me — not a dream about me but a person you can see and touch: *not you* — you let me know.

(Rosa nods, moves quickly off. Wesley follows slowly.)

EARLY DARK
by Reynolds Price

American (Southern): One Male and One Female

THE PLAY: Set in North Carolina in 1957, *Early Dark* traces the journey of love taken by Rosacoke Mustian and the man who tortures her mind, Wesley Beavers. As she struggles with deciding the path of her life and the illogical nature of affection, Rosacoke endures the callous nature of her family, the seeming insensitivity of her object of affection, and the cruel accidents of nature.

THE SCENE: Rosacoke (20) is surprised to have to face Wesley (22) for the first time in many months. Having kept to herself, agonizing over the secret she has held since the last time they met, she is forced to finally reveal herself and her true need for Wesley. Wesley is determined to follow through with her *this* time.

TIME AND PLACE: Christmas Eve. 1957. North Carolina. Early evening. The front room of Mr. Isaacs — after Rosacoke has delivered Christmas candies to the elderly, housebound Mr. Isaacs.

WESLEY: *(Tentatively.)* Merry Christmas, Rosa.

ROSACOKE: *(Surfaces slowly from reverie.)* Why have you trailed me?

WESLEY: Your mother sent me home to get you. Sissie and you were here. Willie's eloped with Heywood Betts, and you've got to be in the pageant tonight, so they need you to practice.

ROSACOKE: No.

(She strains at control but intends to leave; she takes two steps around Mr. Isaac's chair. He claws at her coat. Rosa shakes her head slowly as if a paralysis were flooding her. Then, she gives a low groan and runs from the room — out the front door, Wesley a few strides behind her. At the edge of the yard, he touches her shoulder. She stops there, beyond him.)

WESLEY: Please tell me what hurts you.

ROSACOKE: Nothing you can cure.

WESLEY: You don't know that. *I* don't know that till you tell me the trouble.

ROSACOKE: It's *my* trouble and if you don't know by now —

WESLEY: I don't know anything about you, Rosa; and I've known you seven years. Six weeks ago you welcomed me, then turned yourself like a weapon against me — won't answer my letters, won't tell me anything. You don't have the right. *(With both hands he takes her arms at the elbows, holds her firmly but gently.)* We've got to go practice. Everybody's waiting. Come on with me. *(Rosa shakes her head no.)* Rosa, Willie has gone. You've got to take her part or your mother's show will fail.

ROSACOKE: Marise Gupton can do it.

WESLEY: You haven't seen Marise lately then. She's the size of that house. *(Points behind him, glances back. Sammy stands in the door. Wesley waves him in.)*

WESLEY: It's all right, Sammy.

(Sammy nods and goes.)

ROSACOKE: It's not all right.

WESLEY: *(Still behind her, he reaches for her left hand. She lets him hold it.)* Why?

ROSACOKE: *(Frees her hand; turns to face him, calm but tired.)* Marise Gupton is not the only person working on a child.

WESLEY: What do you mean?

ROSACOKE: I mean Rosacoke.

WESLEY: *(Thinks a long moment.)* And Wesley then. *(Rosa shakes her head no, not fiercely but firmly. With his hand in the air, he asks her to wait.)* Understand this one thing and answer — you don't know nobody but me, do you?

ROSACOKE: I don't know you.

WESLEY: Don't lie to me — you know what's here. *(Waits.)* You don't know anybody else, do you, Rose?

ROSACOKE: You know I don't.

WESLEY: *(Draws one long breath, slowly exhales it; makes no try to touch her again but extends his offer in a mild half-whisper.)* Come on then. We got to go practice. *(He turns to go and has gone four steps before he knows he is walking alone. He stops and half-turns. Rosa is facing her home but has not moved. Wesley comes back to her; by now his voice is almost happy.)* Rosa, why didn't you tell me sooner?

ROSACOKE: What good would that have done?

WESLEY: Good? — maybe not. But it would've been fair.

ROSACOKE: I can't see I owe you two more words.

WESLEY: Try one. Try *Wesley.* Wesley's my name.

ROSACOKE: *(Smiles.)* I'll try to remember that. *(Takes a homeward step, turns.)*

Weapons, Wesley — I have lain down and got up and worked through years with you driven into my chest like a nail.

(Wesley takes that, full face; then slowly comes toward her, begins quietly as if to himself.)

WESLEY: Rosa, you aren't the only human made out of skin. What do you think us others are? What do you think I've been these long years? — asbestos? wood? I'm not, not now if I ever was. I may not have talked as well as you. Or planned as far. I may have disappointed you hundreds of times, but I'm still the person you claimed to love and plan a life on. I've shied from plans. *(Waits.)* I'm not shying now. We'll leave here after the pageant tonight and be in South Carolina by day — we won't need a license; that's where everybody goes. We can spend a night somewhere, be back by Christmas eve —

ROSACOKE: I'm not everybody. I'm just the cause of this one baby. It's mine — something really mine from the start; I'll have it on my own.

WESLEY: And shame your mother and feed it how and tell it what? Not a hundred percent yours, it's not. Remember that along with my name. *(Rosa watches him closely but doesn't answer.)* Do something about me. Tell me "go" or "stay." *(Silence still.)* We can live. I've paid up all my debts; every penny I make from here on is mine.

ROSACOKE: *(Genuinely thinking aloud.)* Let me get this straight. You offer to drive me to South Carolina and marry me at dawn in some poor justice of the peace's living room, then give me a little one-day vacation and bring me home for Christmas with my family that will be cut again by this second blow, then take me on to Norfolk to spend my life shut in two rented rooms while you sell motorcycles — me waiting out my baby, sick and alone, eating what we could afford and pressing your shirts and staring out a window in my spare time at concrete roads and people that look like they hate each other — That's what you're standing here, offering me, after all these years?

WESLEY: Yes. It was all I ever had to offer. I never said I was anything but Wesley. All the rest you made up yourself and hung on me. Sure, that's one way of seeing my plan; but if everybody looked at their chances like that, people would have gone out of style long ago.

ROSACOKE: Maybe they should've.

WESLEY: You don't mean that.

ROSACOKE: I think I do. I haven't been sleeping.

WESLEY: You're talking like the old Wesley now.

ROSACOKE: You said there was just one Wesley all along.

WESLEY: *(Shakes his head slightly.)* There's Wesleys you never dreamed of, Rosa.

ROSACOKE: *(Opens her mouth to answer, finds only a kernel of what seems knowledge.)* That may be so. But — look — I'm free. I'm standing here seeing you and, Wesley, I'm free.

WESLEY: You're wrong. And I'm sorry. We've got till tonight. Believe I'm serious — whatever it means weeks or years from now — and tell me tonight. *(Rosa starts to answer.)* Please. Tonight.

(As Rosa faces him — silent, not moving — a piano begins to play "Joy to the World." After six bars Rosa moves toward the sound; Wesley follows. When the light has dimmed, Baby Sister — hidden — sings the whole first stanza.)

FULL MOON
by Reynolds Price

American (Southern): One Male and One Female

THE PLAY: In the dark of the night, in a town in Eastern North Carolina, the moon, the gin, and the sensations of love send Reynolds Price's main characters (Kerney Bascomb and Kipple Patrick) into a whirl of emotion and passion. In the light of day, reality creeps back in and the dreams and plans made in the moonlight receive full, careful consideration.

THE SCENE: After an evening of drinking and dancing, Kerney (19) and Kip (21) continue to dance around each other in a lover's duet as they ponder the future.

TIME AND PLACE: Eastern North Carolina. 1938. Kerney's front yard/porch. Midnight. A late summer's evening.

KIP: I've looked far ahead as my eyes reach. And Kerney, I want us to leave here soon and marry each other.

KERNEY: We could always leave and marry other people.

KIP: *(With sudden calm force.)* Don't talk that trash.

KERNEY: *(Calm too.)* I'll say any goddamned thing I feel.

KIP: Your father'll hear us.

KERNEY: My pa could teach us worlds about swearing.

KIP: All your pa wants to teach Kip is *running* lessons — how to run as far as Bangor, Maine and never see you.

KERNEY: And your pa's not that stuck on me.

KIP: That's a lie. He told me, not two days ago, "Kip, she's an elegant piece of construction with a mind like a steel trap. Don't let her vanish."

KERNEY: *(Laughs and nods.)* Your pa would call a two-headed cross-eyed brunette gorgeous if she kept you home.

KIP: We wouldn't live with him.

KERNEY: But in sight and earshot.

KIP: McDuff is no village. We'd move across town —

KERNEY: Across the tracks maybe? *(Half-sings.)* Out near Sugartown, where the sweet darkies dwell —

KIP: *(Ignoring her hint and fervent to hide the problem she has raised.)* Kerney, my father's been good to me. Now he faces me leaving. I don't see you abandoning yours.

(Kerney thinks through that. It is the first time she has faced the full prospect of leaving home. Her face slowly mirrors the mind's desolation. At no other moment will she seem more alone. When she speaks, she's resolved.)

KERNEY: I-*will*-leave — though, when the time really comes.

(At the end she is smiling. Kip sees it, shivers slightly.)

KIP: Got any hint who you're leaving with?

KERNEY: I've entertained more than one bid and you know it. Yours still in force?

KIP: *(Waits incredulous.)* God on high, woman! Kipple Patrick loves you. He's said it all ways, in more than one language, since you were a child.

KERNEY: Ego amo te. Je t'aime. Yo te amo. And what about African? Mumby-Jumby-Boo! I'll need to learn it in African, won't I? — to keep your attention.

KIP: You're not drunk. Why the hell turn vicious?

(Kerney takes fire from his word vicious. *She waits blankly for a moment, then contorts her face and gives a sudden, muted but impressive cat's warning growl and a single clawing gesture in the air.)*

KERNEY: *(Suddenly calm.)* Something mean got in me, some truth-telling demon.

KIP: Get it out fast.

(Kerney prowls in the effort to clear her mind. She has a fierce need to exorcise what she has heard in town gossip but has not discussed with Kip.)

KERNEY: I need to hear you say it again. Make your bid again please.

KIP: You're not at an auction. It's a heartfelt proposal.

KERNEY: Say it.

KIP: *(Waits.)* Let's clear out of here. We'll catch a train to South Carolina, get married down there where you don't need a blood test and spare our fathers the cost and worry. What we save, we can put toward buying a house.

KERNEY: Sounds easy as buying a red toothbrush.

KIP: It's not that new an invention, girl — holy matrimony. A man and a woman choose each other and say so in public. Ninety people in any odd hundred have done it.

KERNEY: A hundred people in any odd hundred are going to die. I don't think I plan to be that normal.

KIP: *You* won't be normal — don't lose sleep on it.

KERNEY: Now tell me why I should do what you say?

KIP: Say *we* for once. Why should *we* elope?

KERNEY: I'm all *for* elopement. Big weddings are nothing but a sinful waste. No, tell me why to get married at all. And why is it holy?

(Through the following Kerney reveals a genuine innocence — she does not know and wants to. Kip shows the delighted patience of a good teacher.)

KIP: I guess most girls learn this from their mothers, so you got left out. But I just thought — Lord, with all we've done, from rafters to floor — you were some great expert on love and life.

KERNEY: I did what you and Jeffer Burns taught me. It didn't seem holy.

KIP: Don't mention Jeffer Burns. *(Waits.)* You enjoyed yourself, true?

KERNEY: I liked being present and helping you out. It seemed like something you needed, right then, to go on living. Like you were out to get my blood.

KIP: I never meant harm.

KERNEY: Never — you didn't. It *seemed* like, seemed that urgent.

KIP: And it's not for you? I'm a young man, girl. Men are built that way. But hurt you? God, I want you to last — here in my life.

KERNEY: Why not another girl — same hills and valleys — that can cook, clean house, do long division? I can't walk straight, much less keep house.

KIP: You, Kerney. You or life alone.

KERNEY: I'm looking at life alone myself. *(Waits, laughs.)* If I die tonight you'd marry by fall.

KIP: Me and my wife'll sweep the dead leaves off you.

KERNEY: *(Laughs.)* See?

KIP: — If you're *dead*. But if you're drawing breath on Earth — with Jeffer Burns or Gary-damned-Cooper — I'll be the most miserable soul upright.

KERNEY: Is it holy though? Why won't you tell me?

KIP: *(Waits, then smiles.)* I can't say I'd ask God to watch every minute. But I think he blesses love, lasting love.

KERNEY: Church love, altar love. Church marriage makes you say "Forsaking all others." You ready for that?

KIP: I've copied the Methodist marriage vows. Once we're joined by the justice of the peace, we'll read each other the vows in private.

KERNEY: You didn't! *(Laughs.)* If I know you, there'll be precious little reading. But "Forsaking all others" — talk about that.

KIP: Who's been filling your head with filth? I'll come to you clean.

KERNEY: *(With increasing force.)* I've heard that concubines flourish hereabouts. I'll need an oath that I'm all you've got before I let my body start babies. *(Tries to lighten her tone.)* Now if we perform this private wedding in our honeymoon nest, will you sing "Oh, Promise Me" and other crowd favorites? *(Then quickly.)* Kipple, Kipple — I don't mean to mock. God knows, you can't marry me in church. Orange blossoms and satin just will not hang on skin as wicked as this skin has been.

(Kip thinks then gently takes Kerney's wrist, kisses it, trails his lips delicately up the skin.)

KIP: Sweet, sweet, sweet.

(Kerney bears him a moment, then pulls away — no harshness or fear. She walks to the dark edge of the pool of moonlight. Kip moves to follow. She stops him with a gesture, then studies him.)

KERNEY: Kip Patrick, I may need you.

KIP: Is that the same as "Kip, I may love you"?

KERNEY: It could well be — any minute, any day.

KIP: You're welcome to phone me collect, from any phone on the planet Earth, if and when you can truly say yes.

KERNEY: I can save you some cash — *(Faces him fully.)*

(Kip is oddly cautious. He waits a moment, then steps to within an arm's length of her. She pulls him down to sit beside her.)

FULL MOON
by Reynolds Price

American (Southern): One Male and One Female

THE PLAY: In the dark of the night, in a town in Eastern North Carolina, the moon, the gin, and the sensations of love send Reynolds Price's main characters (Kerney Bascomb and Kipple Patrick) into a whirl of emotion and passion. In the light of day, reality creeps back in and the dreams and plans made in the moonlight receive full, careful consideration.

THE SCENE: As part of his passion-induced promise to Kerney, Kip (21) must sever all ties with his former mistress, Ora Lee (22). The passion they once shared, against all social protocol of the time (Kip is white, Ora Lee is black), returns to Kip the moment he sets eyes on Ora Lee — making his promise to Kerney a difficult one to keep.

TIME AND PLACE: Eastern North Carolina. 1938. Ora Lee's front yard/porch. Shortly after midnight. A late summer's evening.

Ora Lee stands in a long white nightgown, thrusting her arms into an ancient oversized sport jacket. She stops short of Kip by several steps.

KIP: Thank the good Lord.

ORA LEE: Hold your thanks till you see who I am.

KIP: I'd know you anywhere.

ORA LEE: I don't know how. Seems like they used to call you Kipple Patrick.

KIP: *(His liquor shows in a shaky bow.)* At your service.

ORA LEE: I don't need nothing you selling or giving.

KIP: I hope to be buying.

ORA LEE: God, strike him dumb! I never took a penny —

KIP: Just a good many greenbacks, three or four rings, a locket with a curl of your best friend's hair, a pretty wristwatch — right many nice gifts down through the sweet years.

ORA LEE: That gin don't smell too sweet — Kerney Bascomb's gin.
(The sound of Kerney's name shocks and confuses Kip. He responds with a harshness that, though unnatural, begins to show him the awfulness of his purpose here.)

KIP: *(Waits, grins.)* You put on some of your bleaching cream and go spying on the dance? Didn't see you there.

ORA LEE: You ain't been seeing nothing dark as me these days.

KIP: My eyes can always find you.

(Ora sees him at last with revulsion. She cannot speak yet but she mimes spitting at him.)

KIP: *(Laughs.)* You knew our game.

ORA LEE: *Game?* What kind of game — you telling me all I hope to hear, through all these years? Then just because Jeffer Burns saw the light on that Bascomb bitch, you take your face right out of here. Well, keep it gone. I'm thriving, sucker.

KIP: *(Stung, but hiding it.)* I heard you were. Dave Robbins been seen riding out this way.

ORA LEE: I been needing to tell you in person. Dave Robbins know the pathway to Paradise now.

KIP: Davey's all right, a safe old boy.

ORA LEE: He take his time but he touch all bases.

KIP: *(Laughs.)* Whoa! Still, Dave's not all that strong in the head. *(Taps his forehead.)* Wrecks his car every week, bad judgment. *(Mock whisper.)* Small brain —

ORA LEE: You the big brain, sure. Everybody knows Kip's right most days. Hell, you could dress me, ride me to Raleigh to the Governor's Mansion, say I was yours — me and my brown butt — and the Governor's wife would shake my hand and set me down like an actual lady that she couldn't smell.

KIP: It'd be fun to try.

ORA LEE: Some other year. Ora's tired this year. Needs to head back to sleep.

KIP: That pains me to hear.

ORA LEE: It'll pain you a heap-damned-worse if I stay. I'm too naked though to be in the night and too tired of you.

(Ora turns toward the house.)

KIP: Want to take a short ride?

(Ora continues walking till she reaches the porch steps.)

ORA LEE: *(Mocking her own accent.)* I tell you what's the truth, white man — Ora Lee's night-riding days are past.

KIP: What about Dave Robbins, his big green roadster?

ORA LEE: That's a whole nother business — Dave drives me in *daylight.*

(She climbs the steps and stands on the stoop.)

KIP: You going to say good-bye at least?

ORA LEE: For a crisp new five-dollar bill, cash money.

KIP: Your words come high, lot higher than your —

ORA LEE: Kipple, Kip — leave yourself *something* here.

KIP: Like what?

ORA LEE: Not meanness, not trash.

(Kip by now sees half the awfulness implicit in his being here at all, yet he cannot want to leave.)

KIP: Could we start this over someway — do it right?

ORA LEE: I didn't mean that. You too old, Kipple, to play this game. Too old and white — too white in the heart. God keeping score of your life now. Angels watching your hands.

(Kip looks at both hands.)

ORA LEE: You go on home. *(Points.)* That road yonder, right past Kerney Bascomb's. Don't blow no horn now and wake her up. She need all the beauty sleep she can get; might help her dry little titties grow.

KIP: *(With controlled force.)* Keep that name out of your *mouth* forever.

ORA LEE: *(Smiles.)* My mouth ain't dirty — didn't used to be.

(Kip shuts his eyes and waits to calm. But his bafflement rises. He wipes his lips slowly with the back of a hand.)

KIP: *(Nods his head firmly.)* Filthy — tonight.

ORA LEE: *(Waits.)* Be nice now, son. Don't make bad blood. You be needing me — you and your poor daddy — when the nigger folk rise.

KIP: *(Smiles.)* They all eating yeast?

ORA LEE: Oh no. Eating knives. Eating cold wind and rain.

KIP: Remember me then. I'll lean on you.

ORA LEE: Don't lean too hard; I might not know you. Might hand you over to the first hungry child.

KIP: Throw your mind back — four summers ago, way deep in the trees. First time you showed me all your sweetness.

ORA LEE: Seem like I'm forgetting right much these days.

KIP: But work on it, Ora. Next time we'll find out what we got left.

ORA LEE: Next time I'll be too bright for you to see. I'm getting more splendid by the night now, boy. Be good to your eyes; don't glance at Ora — her and her son and all her kin. She'll blind you fast.

(She launches a final dazzling smile, then slowly goes in. Kip stands a moment, fixing the memory. Then he shakes his head in confusion and leaves.)

FULL MOON
by Reynolds Price

American (Southern): One Male and One Female

THE PLAY: In the dark of the night, in a town in Eastern North Carolina, the moon, the gin, and the sensations of love send Reynolds Price's main characters (Kerney Bascomb and Kipple Patrick) into a whirl of emotion and passion. In the light of day, reality creeps back in and the dreams and plans made in the moonlight receive full, careful consideration.

THE SCENE: Kip (21), still feeling the effects of his earlier drinking, and reeling from the dismissal by Ora Lee, returns to Kerney's (19) window fortified by the knowledge that he kept his promise. Kerney begins to consider the sincerity of Kip's attentions but remains fiercely protective and mysterious about her final decision.

TIME AND PLACE: Eastern North Carolina. 1938. Kerney's front yard/porch. A late summer's evening.

After a long wait Kerney appears, full-length in the window. She wears a long nightgown but seems wide awake. It takes her awhile to notice Kip.

KERNEY: Go *on* —
KIP: Where?
KERNEY: *Fly,* to the stars — I know you can.
KIP: Girl, are you still drunk?
KERNEY: I never was but I know who is.
KIP: Come save me then.
KERNEY: I'm no missionary. Save your own soul.
KIP: My body's the problem.
KERNEY: I thought you'd have that cooled down by now.
KIP: No ma'am, still steaming. I've been out seeing to the orders you gave me.
KERNEY: Pa and Walter Parker are asleep. You ought to be.
KIP: *(Holds up his arms for her to join him.)* One short look — at just your face — and then I'll fly.
(Kerney thinks, then slowly climbs through her window, crouches on the ledge and — almost dizzy — sits there.)

KERNEY: You'll kill me yet.

(Kip stays in place.)

KIP: That's not my intention.

KERNEY: What is?

(Kip studies her slowly, hoping to calm the sadness from Ora.)

KIP: Watching you, all dazed and helpless.

KERNEY: Get one thing into your dazed head — Kerney's as helpless as a Mexican rattlesnake.

(She springs from the window ledge to the ground and approaches Kip.)

KERNEY: What did you tell her? *(When Kip looks puzzled.)* You said you obeyed some orders of mine.

KIP: The way's clear now.

KERNEY: What did you tell her?

KIP: I'm not here begging for *your* secrets, notice.

KERNEY: *(Waits.)* Your concubine was never a secret.

KIP: That's a scandalous lie.

KERNEY: I've known it forever. So have Pa and Walter Parker. And all my friends. So's every colored person between here and Raleigh.

KIP: We won't get anywhere, telling lies. I came here to tell you I did what you asked. Think it over in your spare time, hear?

KERNEY: *(Studies him slowly, nods.)* Now go on to bed.

(She moves toward her window. For a moment Kip balks, stunned by her apparent refusal in the face of his news. But then as she reaches to climb back in, he takes her arm. She pulls free and stays by the window. Again Kip is won by her presence and tries to raise the tone.)

KIP: Those Mexican rattlers you spoke about? They look right fine, undressed for bed.

KERNEY: You don't want to corner one.

KIP: You never hurt a gnat. *(Studies her again.)* You need me, girl.

KERNEY: You'd make a nice hat rack to stand in the hall.

KIP: You'd make a fine statue for the Temple of Venus.

KERNEY: *(Takes a step toward him.)* I'll make you a practical proposition, son. Get somebody sober to drive you to Raleigh. Find you an artist and I'll pose for him, long as it takes to make you a perfect life-sized *me* — real hair, china teeth: your own Kerney Bascomb. Then tease her, squeeze her, do anything you need to that I don't have to watch. *(Turns to her window.)*

(Kip's head has begun to clear. His voice is firm.)

KIP: This is so damned childish. I beg your pardon.

KERNEY: I can sleep tomorrow. I'm not as accustomed to gin as you and I'm —

KIP: We're both heading south.

KERNEY: With the wild geese or what?

KIP: With the man you'll spend your grown life beside.

(Kerney moves closer to see his eyes. Then she steps well back.)

KERNEY: I'm no orphan dog. I don't follow strangers.

KIP: You've known me most of the days of your life. I'm your heart's choice.

KERNEY: *(Laughs one note.)* Brace yourself, boy. *(Waits.)* My heart hasn't chose.

(Kip approaches and reaches for her hand. Kerney draws back.)

KERNEY: I'm thinking. But I have not chosen. I have real duties — I'm all Pa's got.

KIP: He's got his *life* — his law practice, this house for a home. He's got Walter Parker.

KERNEY: If I leave now he'll howl like the wind through a burnt-out barn.

KIP: Brace yourself now: that's-the-way-life-is. You *want* to leave here. You said you were trapped.

KERNEY: It's the trap I *know* — no mean dark corners.

KIP: If it's my dark corner you're worried about, I told you that's gone.

(This late, and near her father's window, Kerney will not deal with the subject of Ora. She shakes her head no.)

KIP: *(A new calm tack.)* I know for a fact that your father wants you to have a grown life. *(Waits.)* I asked him.

KERNEY: Don't start a clean day with a lie, Kip Patrick.

KIP: *(Raising his hand to swear.)* Two whole days ago, in his office. I'd gone in to ask him about a land problem, my family's land. And when we were finished, your father sat back and asked a few questions about my life — any hopes I had. I didn't feel like he was fishing hard, but finally the trust in his face made me tell him. I said "Mr. Bascomb, I'm in love with Kerney."

KERNEY: No wonder he was so blue tonight.

KIP: Blue? No, lord, he was pink with joy. He said "She mentions your name more than seldom." Then we sang your praises in all major keys.

KERNEY: How sad for you both.

KIP: No! By the end we were whooping like monkeys. *(When he sees a sign of anger in Kerney.)* Whooping in *love,* child — pure brotherly love. He told me about you before I knew you — how you set fire to your granddaddy's hair, how you lamed the gray horse, how you took the good rolling pin and squashed your goldfish.

KERNEY: To see how they worked. But you never got serious with him again?

KIP: Sorry. I told him he couldn't change my heart, no matter what terrors he dredged up from the past.

(Kerney moves quickly to the edge of dark — her back to Kip, facing the audience. This is hard to hear.)

Then he finally gave me a reason to hope.

(Kerney crouches to the ground and covers her ears.)

He said "I'll give her to the man she chooses, no sooner than that." I said "Will you bless him?" He walked all the long way back to his desk. Then he faced me and nodded. "It'll be God's will."

KERNEY: *(Faces Kip, stands.)* That proves you're lying. Pa's an old agnostic.

KIP: *(Smiles.)* Ah! I too smelled a lawyer's trick. I said "Sir, you're no church-going man." He said "True, Kipple, but that's owing to the scenery: those ladies' hats, those fat preachers stuffed down in swallow-tailed coats."

KERNEY: *(Nods.)* His voice.

(Disheartened, she moves a little farther from Kip.)

KIP: Marry me.

KERNEY: Why?

KIP: *(With smiling impatience.)* I've done the last big deed you demanded. You're changing ground fast as a Mexican rattler.

KERNEY: *(Waits.)* I need to know what drives a person as smart as you to give up freedom and all his sins and crave wild me.

KIP: *(Waits.)* You know about the beauty part, but there's so much more. *(Tries to see her in the dark.)* — How scary you are, what a daring soul. Everybody else we know is groggy. I've been a stunt pilot all my life and so have you. I need a brave wife.

KERNEY: I'm weak as water.

KIP: You're a damned *power* plant. You glow in the dark. You'd gnaw your arm off, neat at the shoulder, if you got caught. You've got a mind in all that hair, that glorious hair —

KERNEY: Just stay out of the beauty department.

KIP: I can see children all in your eyes, all lovely as you —

KERNEY: No healthy young man ever wants children. Tell that to some sucker-homebody, not wise old Kerney.

KIP: *(Waits, then with new firmness.)* All right, goddammit — I feel like I'm strong and need to bear weight. You're what I want to lift and carry. I want to bear you forward through life, whatever years are left.

(As Kip's explanation grew, it gradually fascinated Kerney with its passion; and eventually it touched her. She moves back nearer, into the moonlight.)

KERNEY: All this moonlight and all that honor — Kip, I think you mean it. And a lot of the time, I want to step toward you. But there's still big trouble, deep back in my head. *(Waits.)* I'm such a part of my father's life, so maybe I've had all the marriage I need. More likely though, I don't have the talent. I just can't say, tonight or next week, where I'm likely to be six minutes from now, much less sixty years.

KIP: Do you love me?

KERNEY: Now you sound like Jeffer.

(Kip turns and begins to leave.)

KERNEY: I may well need you someday soon. *(When he stops to listen.)* But maybe right now, here tonight, it's your age that's the problem. Your glands and all —

KIP: *(Calm but strong.)* My glands cranked up more than eight years ago. By now I've learned how to screen glands out of my hopes and dreams.

KERNEY: *(Nods in innocence.)* I'll try to answer you as soon as I can. Right now my tired runaway mind wants to stand in a field, with shade and a pear tree and no-other-thing.

KIP: You scare me.

KERNEY: I told you I would. I scare myself so bad I can't breathe.

KIP: *(Believing her, relenting a little.)* I've told you my feelings. I won't try again. Remember my question — will you stay by me, through whatever comes, till you or I end? Like it or not, we were both born with faces people fly up against like moths to a light —

KERNEY: Or me to the moon.

(Through the following Kip slowly walks over and stands close to Kerney.)

KIP: So nobody's going to leave us alone. If we don't choose each other soon, we'll be worn down with people coming at us. That's not pride; it's a flat damned fact.

(Kip takes Kerney's hands. Suddenly she raises the joined hands and kisses each, entirely sincere. Kip is moved but after a moment he withdraws both hands and steps back.)

KERNEY: Soon, soon. You've got my word.

(Kip turns and walks away slowly. As he sinks into darkness, Kerney can't help teasing.)

KERNEY: Take several more words — all my favorites. Take — *(Waits, then with hushed but exaggerated relish.)* Alabaster. Camomile. Resurrection. Take *cellar door.*

KIP: *(At a distance.)* Get serious; that's two.
   (Kerney reaches for her window ledge.)
KERNEY: Take *forsaking all others.*
KIP: Take *hush your mouth.*
   (At the sound of Kip's car, Kerney waves once. Then she makes the small leap and enters her window.)

HOME FIRES
by Jack Heifner

American (Southern): Two Females

THE PLAY: In a small Texas town during World War II, the Morris family tries to stay afloat after being abandoned by their father and husband. They make ends meet by turning their beautiful home into a boarding house for the young women who come to their town to work in the factories while the men are away at war.

THE SCENE: June (20 to 22) is a young woman with a past and no idea about the future; Susanna (15) craves a "past" and anxiously awaits a future — a future she hopes will prove more exciting than the present in which she lives. June sets her straight.

TIME AND PLACE: 1940s. A modest home in a small Texas town. The living room/dining room. Early eve.

JUNE: *(Eats more biscuits during the following.)* Why are you sitting in the corner?

SUSANNA: Trying to do my homework.

JUNE: Oh, I hate to use my brain. But I guess I could think if I put my mind to it. *(She laughs and continues eating.)* You know how everybody always loves their mother's cooking?

SUSANNA: No. *(She doesn't really want to listen but it's better than doing homework.)*

JUNE: Well, I hated mine. She loved to try fancy dishes . . . little birds with berry sauce and dainty tarts with curlicues on top. Real tea-party food she learned someplace. She liked to pretend we were wealthy and eating high on the hog. But I hated it. I'm a meat and potatoes girl. You should have seen the look on my dad's face when he'd come in after a hard day working in the fields. He'd come in and have to sit down and try to eat some baby bird drowned in cherries. *(She lets out a big laugh.)* You know, I think that's finally how I ended up in the orphanage. I think it was those little birds that caused him to kill her. He did it just so he could move to the state penitentiary and get a decent meal. *(She laughs again. Susanna is suddenly interested.)*

SUSANNA: Are you serious?

JUNE: I'm just joking.

SUSANNA: *(Relieved.)* Good. For a moment I thought he'd really killed her.

JUNE: Oh, he killed her all right. I was just joking about his motive. It wasn't the birds. It was adultery.

SUSANNA: Golly, June, I knew you grew up in an orphanage, but not the other.

JUNE: Honey, it was the best thing that ever happened to me. I had a ball at that State Home for Girls.

SUSANNA: June, tell me . . .did it take a lot of courage to leave your orphanage, which I guess would be just like your home, and go off not knowing what to do?

JUNE: Well, me and Alice . . . we met up. We were working in a bean factory at the time.

SUSANNA: A bean factory?

JUNE: I weighed the cans to make sure there was just the right amount in them. Alice had a much better job. She was a "snipper." She'd cut the ends off green beans. I was in pintos. Anyway, we got to know each other. Moved into a nice little garage apartment. Had a sweet little life going. But Alice's family was very prominent in the town. Her daddy was the mortician. Buried my mama, actually. They had all kinds of money and wanted Alice to marry some guy. A foot doctor, I think. She wouldn't have anything to do with it. She just wanted her own life, and they were against it.

SUSANNA: Why?

JUNE: They hated her hanging around me. I wasn't their type. The orphanage and all. Not that I think being a mortician is such a swell thing to be. It's sort of a *nasty* profession. But they kept on complaining I was a bad influence on Alice. Finally, she just couldn't bear her family telling her what to do anymore; and we heard there were some factories down here needing help. So that's how you ended up with the two of us.

SUSANNA: And are you happy, June?

JUNE: Happy? I really don't have a happy past, so I'd have to say I'm as happy as I've ever been in my life. Aren't you happy?

SUSANNA: I don't know. I look in the mirror and I feel incomplete.

JUNE: Why? You got two eyes, two ears, a nose, a mouth — the works!

SUSANNA: Yes! I was just looking at my features. Don't they look familiar? Haven't you seen these lips at the movies?

JUNE: I can't afford to go to the movies. So what's your point?

SUSANNA: I just feel like life should be more exciting. Every day just sort of goes into the next and nothing happens.

JUNE: That's the way it is. Same thing, one day after the other — then *pow!*

SUSANNA: Yes! Suddenly you're alive!

JUNE: No. Suddenly you're dead. That's what changes things.

SUSANNA: Now, I'm really depressed.

LU ANN HAMPTON LAVERTY OBERLANDER
by Preston Jones

American (Southern): One Male and One Female

THE PLAY: Starting with the teenaged Lu Ann, the play traces the loves and losses of an exuberant, friendly, simple Southern girl as she makes her way in the world, surrounded by the many types of eccentric characters the rich world of Texas has to offer.

THE SCENE: At the start of the play, Lu Ann and Billy Bob (both 17) make plans for the senior picnic and beyond.

TIME AND PLACE: 1953. Late spring. The front porch of Lu Ann's modest home in Bradleyville, Texas — a small, dead West Texas town in the middle of a big, dead West Texas prairie between Abilene and San Angelo. The new highway has bypassed it and now the world is trying to.

The time is 1953. The act is set in the living room of Claudine and Lu Ann Hampton's home in Bradleyville. A small frame house in a small frame town. The room is modestly furnished in Sears-catalogue-type furniture — sofa, table, chairs, radio, etc. A door upstage left leads to the kitchen. Upstage center door leads to bedrooms. Stage right is a small front porch section with a functional screen door.

As the scene opens, Claudine slams through the kitchen door with bowl of tangerines, sets it on end table. She is a heavy-set women in her early forties, her hair is grayish blond. She is dressed in house dress and apron — takes apron off and puts it on sofa back. Notes time and looks out porch door, then goes upstairs, picking up sneakers from landing. Lu Ann runs on and into living room. She is dressed in the blue-and-gold uniform of a Bradleyville cheerleader. She is well built and very blond. She is also very pretty. Small-town pretty, healthy pretty, clean pretty, Pepsodent and Ivory Soap pretty.

BILLY BOB: *(Offstage.)* Lu Ann! Lu Ann! Wait up, will ya! *(Following Lu Ann on. Billy Bob Wortman is tall and lanky. He wears a white shirt, Levi's, boots, and a letter sweater. His crew-cut hair has been died green.)*
LU ANN: Ma! I'm home!

CLAUDINE: *(Offstage.)* About time!

LU ANN: Well, ah thought ah would die! Ah just thought ah would curl up and die right there on the gym floor. When the coach introduced the basketball team and you-all come out there with your hair all dyed green. Well, sir, mah eyes liked to jumped plumb outta mah head! Why, Mary Beth Johnson jest hollered. That's right, jest hollered right out loud.

BILLY BOB: It was Pete Honeycutt's idea.

LU ANN: Why, ever'one jest laughed and shouted and carried on so. Eveline Blair came runnin' over to me shoutin', "Look at the basketball boys, look at the basketball boys!"

BILLY BOB: It was Pete Honeycutt's idea.

LU ANN: *(Gestures to porch — they go out.)* After the assembly we cheerleaders all got together and decided we'd do something funny too.

BILLY BOB: Aw, like what?

LU ANN: Now wouldn't you like to know? Mr. Green-headed Billy Bob Wortman.

BILLY BOB: Aw, come on, Lu Ann, what are you-all fixin' to do?

LU ANN: Oh, ah don't know, somethin', somethin' real neat.

BILLY BOB: You cain't dye you-all's hair. Pete Honeycutt already thought that one up.

LU ANN: Eveline Blair thought up different shoes.

BILLY BOB: Different shoes?

LU ANN: You know, come to school wearin' one high-heel shoe and one saddle shoe. Somethin' *neato* like that.

BILLY BOB: Yeah.

LU ANN: Ah don't know, though, it might be kinda tricky doin' the Locomotive in a high-heel shoe.

BILLY BOB: Might be at that.

LU ANN: But it might be fun.

BILLY BOB: Shore.

LU ANN: *(Sitting on swing.)* Maybe we can wear them out to the senior picnic.

BILLY BOB: *(Joins her.)* Shore!

LU ANN: We're still goin' in your daddy's Hudson, ain't we?

BILLY BOB: Well, uh, naw, we gotta use the pickup.

LU ANN: The pickup!

BILLY BOB: Yeah, my dad wants the car to go over to Big Spring.

LU ANN: But it's the senior picnic! Mah God, ah don't want to go to mah one and only senior picnic in a danged-old pickup.

BILLY BOB: Well, goshalmighty, Lu Ann, ah cain't help it.

LU ANN: What the heck good is it for your dad to have a bran'-new, step-down Hudson Hornet if *we* never get to use the danged old thing.

BILLY BOB: Seems like ever'thin' ah do is wrong.

LU ANN: Boy, that's the truth.

BILLY BOB: Gawlee, Ruthie Lee Lawell and Pete Honeycutt are goin' in his pickup.

LU ANN: So what.

BILLY BOB: Well, nuthin', ah jest mean that it don't seem to bother Ruthie Lee none.

LU ANN: Heck no, it don't bother Ruthie Lee none. Mah Gawd, she almost lives in Pete Honeycutt's pickup seat. I'll bet her bra spends more time on the danged gear shift than it spends on her.

BILLY BOB: *(Shocked.)* Lu Ann Hampton! You know that ain't true.

LU ANN: It is so, too. I seen 'em when they was parked out to the drive-in and she was danged near naked.

BILLY BOB: I never saw nuthin'.

LU ANN: 'Course you never saw nuthin'. You was too busy watchin' the movie. Mah Gawd, you was more worried about old Gary Cooper than Grace Kelly was.

BILLY BOB: Ah liked that movie.

LU ANN: Boy, you shore did.

BILLY BOB: Well, ah did.

LU ANN: No wonder Ruthie Lee has so many chest colds in the wintertime.

BILLY BOB: If Pete and Ruthie Lee was actin' like the way you said, that jest means they don't have any respect for each other.

LU ANN: Or for Gary Cooper.

BILLY BOB: Reverend Stone says that goin' on like that is a sinful sign of no respect.

LU ANN: Oh, brother.

BILLY BOB: People that behave thataway out to drive-ins and such-like is be-havin' plumb un-Christian.

LU ANN: Well, at least they were sharin' somethin' more than a danged ol' box of popcorn.

BILLY BOB: A true Christian is pure in mind and body.

LU ANN: I wish you'd stop preachin', Billy Bob. Mah Gawd, ever' time we have somethin' important to discuss, you come up with a danged sermon.

BILLY BOB: What in the world are we discussin' that's important?

LU ANN: Your daddy's step-down Hudson Hornet, that's what!

BILLY BOB: My daddy's . . . For cryin' out loud, Lu Ann, sometimes you drive me absolutely nuts!

LU ANN: Well, you don't have to yell, Billy Bob.

BILLY BOB: Ah told you, an' told you, an' told you that we cain't have the Hudson.

LU ANN: Well, why not?

BILLY BOB: 'Cause my daddy's got to go over to Big Spring!

LU ANN: Well, it seems plumb funny to me that your daddy picked the very day of the senior picnic to go over to Big Spring. Ah mean, doesn't he know that the senior picnic is just about the most important event in our whole schoolin' career?

BILLY BOB: Ah don't know if he does or not, he jest . . .

LU ANN: Don't hardly seem fair to look forward to somethin' all these years only to have your daddy come along and mess it up.

BILLY BOB: Daddy ain't messed up nothin', he jest . . .

LU ANN: He's only doin' it for spite, Billy Bob.

BILLY BOB: No, he ain't, he jest . . .

LU ANN: And spite in my book is jest plain sinful and un-Christian. *(She turns to go.)* Good night, Billy Bob.

BILLY BOB: *(Grabbing her arm.)* Now wait a minute, Lu Ann. *(They are very close now.)* Oh, boy, uh, uh. Ah will talk to Dad tonight and ask for the car again, okay?

LU ANN: Swell, Billy Bob. *(She kisses him.)* Good night, now.

BILLY BOB: Good night. By gollies, Lu Ann, ah'm gonna make danged sure we git that car.

LU ANN: Fine.

BILLY BOB: Danged sure! *(He exits.)*

(Lu Ann watches him for a moment and then enters the house.)

LU ANN HAMPTON LAVERTY OBERLANDER
by Preston Jones

American (Southern): Two Males

THE PLAY: Starting with the teenaged Lu Ann, the play traces the loves and losses of an exuberant, friendly, simple Southern girl as she makes her way in the world, surrounded by the many types of eccentric characters the rich world of Texas has to offer.

THE SCENE: Lu Ann's brother Skip (20 to 22) has returned home from the war in Korea where he served as a supply truck driver, never anywhere near the front. He brings his friend Dale (20 to 22) home to meet his charming and attractive sister in the hopes of charming Dale to go along with him in his latest "get rich quick" scheme.

TIME AND PLACE: 1953. Late spring. The living room of Lu Ann's modest home in Bradleyville, Texas — a small, dead West Texas town in the middle of a big, dead West Texas prairie between Abilene and San Angelo. The new highway has bypassed it and now the world is trying to.

DALE: *(Going up to Skip.)* Gawlee, Skip, what are you tryin' to do, ah never saved your life or nuthin'.

SKIP: Shore, shore, I know. So what, we'll jest have some fun with little sister, okay?

DALE: Well, shore, ah guess.

SKIP: Whattayou think of Lu Ann — nice, huh?

DALE: *(Sincerely.)* She's real pretty.

SKIP: Yes, she is. She's mah one-and-only sister and you are mah one-and-only buddy. Only buddy ah got in the whole lousy world.

DALE: Aw hell, Skip.

SKIP: The only one. You saw how them slobs down at Red's acted. Lived in this lousy town all mah life, served mah stinkin' country in Ko-rea, and they wouldn't even buy me a lousy beer.

DALE: Aw come on, Skip, you know that ain't true.

SKIP: The hell it ain't.

DALE: You got lots of friends in this-here town. What about that-there lodge you joined the other day?

SKIP: The Knights of the White Magnolia? Hell, Dale, none of them fellers are friends of mine. Ah joined that-there lodge to get ahead in this town. Damn right, that lodge is jest a steppin' stone, buddy. I've got ideas that's gonna put this little old town right on its ear.

DALE: By gollies, Skip, if anybody can do it, you can.

SKIP: You're damn right I can. I got plans, buddy, big plans. Remember Corporal Rosenberg?

DALE: Yeah. Old Four-Eyes, the motor-pool clerk.

SKIP: That's the guy. Well, he had two college degrees. That's right, *two* — an A.M. and a F.M., some damn thing like that. Well, one afternoon when we was havin' some beers over to the N.C.O. club, he told me that even with all his education he wished he had my common sense.

DALE: No kiddin'.

SKIP: That's right. You see, Dale, all them college chumps like Rosenberg is good for is like one thing at a time — you know. But common-sense guys like me can move around, ya see. We can be goin' with three or four deals at once. Hell's fire, ah got me a couple of real-estate ideas figgered out over to Sweetwater that are flat gonna make a bundle.

DALE: Gawlee.

SKIP: Damn right. And that ain't all. After ah talk to old man Cullers over to the bank, and git me a little capital together, ah'm really gonna put 'er in high gear. You see, Dale, I got all these-here opportunities right out in front of me. And ah got the common sense as how to move out and latch hold of 'em.

DALE: Yeah!

SKIP: But you gotta be careful, you know what ah mean?

DALE: Well, ah . . .

SKIP: You just cain't go rushin' straight into things like a damn fool. No, sir. You gotta move kindly easy-like. Keep your eyes open and slip around. In business you got to know ever' side of things affore you decide to pick up the cards.

DALE: Yeah, ah speck so.

SKIP: Did you know that ah wasn't back in this town of Bradleyville more than five minutes affore old Derwood Herring was over here wantin' me to go in with him in the Western Auto?

DALE: Them Western Auto stores is damn good outfits.

SKIP: Hell, yes, they are!

DALE: We got one over to San Angelo.

SKIP: You know what ah told him? I said, "Now look here, Derwood, I appreciate the hell outta you comin' over here." You see, Dale, in business matters you always gotta be polite. "But ah just ain't the kind of feller just to jump on into things this way. No sir. Ah gotta put my mind to work on it. Look at ever' side of this-here deal. Now, you jest come around again, say, in a month or two, and maybe ah can figger out somethin' for you."

DALE: What did he say to that?

SKIP: What could he say? Hell, Dale, Derwood ain't dumb. He knows the truth of things. He just sorter mumbled somethin' like "Well, all right, Skip, if that's how you feel." Then he got the hell out.

DALE: Did he ever come back?

SKIP: Naw. The back-stabbin' SOB went straight over to Earl Parker's place and got him to go partners.

DALE: That was a damn dirty thing to do.

SKIP: Ah was glad, Dale, glad he done it. Who the hell would want to spend the rest of their life runnin' a Western Auto store for Christ's sake?

DALE: Them places ain't much account anyway.

SKIP: Hell, no, they ain't.

DALE: We got one over to San Angelo that ah never liked much.

SKIP: When these real-estate outfits work out, why in ten years or so ah'll not only own that damn Western Auto store but the whole damn block it's sittin' in.

DALE: You'll do 'er, too, buddy!

SKIP: You see, Dale, time don't mean a damn thing in the business world. It's what you do with it that counts. How would you like to come over here someday and have old Skip drive you on down to the country club in his new Cadillac, sit around the bar over there with Floyd Kinkaid and all them rich bastards, and talk about wells and such like?

DALE: Boy, that would be somethin'.

SKIP: Can't ever tell, buddy. Why, hell's fire, ah might even buy into that livestock-haulin' outfit you're fixin' to go to work for.

TREMULOUS
by Le Wilhelm

American (Southern): Two Females

THE PLAY: In this timely and poignant one-act, two lonely and desperate teenaged friends make a pact and meet to carry it out. As they discuss the details of the plan, and the fallout they could expect (or wish for), the desire and drama of actually going through with it seems to dwindle, and renewed hope and acceptance takes its place.

THE SCENE: The climax of the play finds Beth and Mary (both 15) justifying their morbid decision with conflicted resolve to follow through.

TIME AND PLACE: The present. Early afternoon. An apple orchard.

BETH: Are you all right?

MARY: Uh huh.

BETH: Momma isn't going to sleep tonight.

MARY: I don't want them to worry about us.

BETH: I don't mean because of that. I took all her sleeping pills. She can't sleep a wink without them.

MARY: Oh.

BETH: She'll tear the house apart looking for them.

MARY: Do you know how many we should take?

BETH: Six. No more than seven. Each of us needs to take six. I asked her about it once.

MARY: Didn't she think that was odd?

BETH: No. I acted like I was worried about her taking an overdose.

MARY: You think we should take a couple more just to be sure?

BETH: No. If you took too many, you might throw up. Six should be more than enough. Don't worry.

MARY: Okay, I trust you.

BETH: She caught me crying yesterday. Just looked at me and said, "Oh, Beth, it's the curse again, isn't it?" No matter what happens to me, she always blames the curse. I almost told her that it didn't have anything to do with my being a woman. That it's 'cause I'm all hollow inside. Everywhere there's all this energy and life going on and flooding over me, but I'm just this dead thing, Momma, and dead things aren't bothered by the curse of being a woman. They're just lonely. Always lonely.

MARY: You're not lonely when you're with me, are you?

BETH: Uh huh, but it's not too bad.

MARY: I wrote something about it in my book. Not on the last page, 'cause we agreed we weren't going to leave any notes. So I put it in the middle on a blank page I found. I wrote, "If anything ever happens to me, no one should blame themselves. It wasn't anyone's fault. I just didn't belong here." *(Looks up to change the mood.)* One thing good about killing ourselves is we won't have to worry about Ms. Connard's math test on Monday.

BETH: No. It should make the rest of the class happy that we're not part of the class anymore.

MARY: I don't think people'll be happy, Beth. They might not care.

BETH: Of course they'll be happy.

MARY: No, they won't.

BETH: Think about it, Mary. Who are the best students in the class.

MARY: Us.

BETH: And?

MARY: And what?

BETH: And Ms. Connard grades on the curve. Without us, the curve will be greatly altered. A lot of people are going to be getting better grades.

MARY: Maybe even Jason will pass.

BETH: Jason?

MARY: You're right. He probably won't, even with us gone. *(She has finished Beth's nails.)* There you go. All done.

BETH: They look great.

MARY: Now what's in the basket?

BETH: Just wait. Not yet.

MARY: Yesterday, I changed my list.

BETH: The ten reasons you want to die?

MARY: Yes. I was trying to find something . . . something to make . . . to give me a reason for not doing this. Sometimes I get confused about it . . . so I had read somewhere that this astronomer guy . . . Carl Sagan was inspirational.

BETH: I watched his show on PBS a couple of times. He died recently, didn't he?

MARY: I think I heard that. Anyway, I read some things he wrote about the universe. And in this one thing, he was explaining how the earth was a rather unimpressive planet that was circling a very ordinary star. That ordinary star is our sun. And that there were millions of suns and millions and millions of planets and that was just in our universe and that we were probably just one universe that made up a group of universes and maybe our whole universe would be only a dot if we stood back and looked at it all, and that maybe there was no end to anything, that it just went on and on beyond any comprehension. And I suppose it was supposed to somehow make me understand something, but it just made me feel even more insignificant. Like here I am an insignificant life among others like me, living on an insignificant planet which was orbiting an insignificant sun. I thought about all this, what he was saying, and I placed it on my "ten reasons I want to die" list. Right after having to take showers with everyone after gym.

BETH: I brought us champagne to drink.

MARY: Champagne?

BETH: Good champagne. French.

MARY: Where'd you?

BETH: They've got lots of bottles around the house. And I brought some pretty glasses. Real champagne glasses.

MARY: I've never had any. Is it good?

BETH: Not really. But it bubbles in your mouth. Tastes strange, but the bubbling's fun. I thought we'd take the pills and then have a glass of champagne and then we'd just sit and wait to die.

MARY: I hope we don't have to wait too long.

(After a moment.)

BETH: It's time, isn't it?

MARY: Yes.

BETH: Are you afraid?

MARY: Very.

BETH: Me, too.

MARY: I know people die all the time.

BETH: Me, too.

MARY: That's what I keep telling myself, but it doesn't help much.

BETH: I think most people are afraid to die.

MARY: I wonder what it'll be like.

BETH: No one knows. That's why we're all afraid.

MARY: Let's say it's going to be wonderful. All right?

BETH: All right.

MARY: If it's really bad, all that'll mean is we'll be disappointed. Won't be the first time.

BETH: No. But it might be the last.

MARY: *(Laughs a little.)* I guess that's right.

BETH: Now's the time when an angel is supposed to show up.

MARY: An angel?

BETH: Yeah, an angel. Haven't you ever seen those shows when something's about to happen, someone's about to die, and an angel showed up and straightens everything out and then it's all better.

MARY: I hope you're not counting on that.

BETH: I'm not.

MARY: It's time, Beth. *(Beth takes the pill bottle out. She is too nervous to get it open.)* Here, let me do it.

A YOUNG LADY OF PROPERTY
by Horton Foote

American (Southern): Two Females

THE PLAY: Young Wilma Thompson dreams of flying away to Hollywood, but the home her mother left her holds her closer to reality. As the people in her life come and go and swirl her dreams all around, she continues to search for the calming sanctity of the swing on "her" front porch.

THE SCENE: After pestering the post office yet again for news of her expected letter from a film director, Wilma and her best friend Arabella (both 14) head off home.

TIME AND PLACE: Harrison, Texas (a fictional East Texas town). 1930s. Downtown. Early evening (twilight).

Wilma and Arabella go outside the area and walk directly down the center of the stage and pause at the apron looking up and down. They are now on the sidewalk area.

WILMA: I'd like to scratch that old cat's eyes out. The idea of her saying old lady Leighton is going to be my mother. She's so nosy. I wonder how she'd like it if I asked her if Mr. Russell Walter was going to ask her to marry him after she's been chasing him for fifteen years.

ARABELLA: Well, just ignore her.

WILMA: I intend to.

ARABELLA: What are you going to do now, Wilma?

WILMA: Fool around until the six o'clock mail.

ARABELLA: Don't you think you ought to go home like your aunt said?

WILMA: No.

ARABELLA: Have you told your Aunt Gert about the letter you're expecting yet?

WILMA: No.

ARABELLA: When are you going to tell her?

WILMA: Not until it comes. I think I'll go over and see my house. Look at how those tenants left it. I may have to sell it yet to get me to Hollywood.

ARABELLA: Wilma, is that house really yours?

WILMA: Sure it's mine. My mother left it to me.

ARABELLA: Well, do you get the rent for it and tell them who to rent to like Papa does his rent houses?

WILMA: No. But it's understood it's mine. My mother told Aunt Gert it was mine just before she died. Daddy had put it in her name because he was gambling terrible then, and Aunt Gert says Mama was afraid they'd lose it. I let Daddy rent it and keep the money now. Aunt Gert says I should as he is having a very hard time. His job at the cotton gin doesn't pay hardly anything. Of course, I feel very lucky having my own house.

ARABELLA: Well, I have a house.

WILMA: Do you own it yourself?

ARABELLA: No. But I live in it.

WILMA: Well, that's hardly the same thing. I own a house, which is very unusual, Aunt Gert says, for a girl of fifteen. I'm a young lady of property, Aunt Gert says. Many's the time I thought I'll just go and live in it all by myself. Wouldn't Harrison sit up and take notice then? Once when I was thirteen and I was very fond of my cousin Neeley I thought I'd offer it to him to get through law school. But I'm glad I didn't since he turned out so hateful. (A pause.) Do you remember when I used to live in my house?

ARABELLA: No.

WILMA: Well, it's a long time ago now, but I still remember it. My mama and I used to play croquet in the yard under the pecan trees. We'd play croquet every afternoon just before sundown and every once in a while she'd stop the game and ask me to run to the corner without letting the neighbors know what I was doing, to see if my father was coming home. She always worried about his getting home by six, because if he wasn't there by then she knew it meant trouble. My mother always kept me in white starched dresses. Do you remember my mother?

ARABELLA: No. But my mother does. She says she was beautiful, with the disposition of a saint.

WILMA: I know. Her name was Alice. Isn't that a pretty name?

ARABELLA: Yes. It is.

WILMA: There's a song named "Sweet Alice Ben Bolt." Aunt Gert used to sing it all the time. When Mama died, she stopped. My mama died of a broken heart.

ARABELLA: She did?

WILMA: Oh, yes. Even Aunt Gert admits that. Daddy's gambling broke her heart. Oh, well. What are you gonna do about it? Boy, I used to hate my daddy. I used to dream about what I'd do to him when I grew up. But he's sorry now and reformed, so I've forgiven him.

ARABELLA: Oh, sure. You shouldn't hate your father.

WILMA: Well, I don't now. Do you know something I've never told another living soul?

ARABELLA: What?

WILMA: Swear you won't tell?

ARABELLA: I swear.

WILMA: I love him now. Sometimes I think I'd give up this whole movie star business if I could go back to our house and live with Daddy and keep house for him. But Aunt Gert says under the circumstances that's not practical. I guess you and everybody else knows what the circumstances are. Mrs. Leighton. She's got my Daddy hog-tied. Aunt Gert says she isn't good enough to shine my mother's shoes, and I think she's right.

A YOUNG LADY OF PROPERTY
by Horton Foote

American (Southern): Two Females

THE PLAY: Young Wilma Thompson dreams of flying away to Hollywood, but the home her mother left her holds her closer to reality. As the people in her life come and go and swirl her dreams all around, she continues to search for the calming sanctity of the swing on "her" front porch.

THE SCENE: The arrival of the letter from Mr. Delafonte (from Hollywood) brings Wilma and Arabella (both 14) one step closer to their dreams —but which ones?

TIME AND PLACE: Harrison, Texas (a fictional East Texas town). 1930s. Wilma's yard. Early evening (twilight).

They both sit dejectedly at the table. The lights fade in the area downstage left as they come up on the area downstage right. Wilma comes in from upstage center of the down right area. It is the yard of her house. She sits in the swing rocking back and forth, singing "Birmingham Jail" in her hillbilly style. Arabella comes running in right center of the yard area.

WILMA: Heh, Arabella. Come sit and swing.

ARABELLA: All right. Your letter came.

WILMA: Whoopee. Where is it?

ARABELLA: Here. *(She gives it to her. Wilma tears it open. She reads:)*

WILMA: "Dear Miss Thompson: Mr. Delafonte will be glad to see you anytime next week about your contemplated screen test. We suggest you call the office when you arrive in the city and we will set an exact time. Yours truly. Adele Murray." Well . . . Did you get yours?

ARABELLA: Yes.

WILMA: What did it say?

ARABELLA: The same.

WILMA: Exactly the same?

ARABELLA: Yes.

WILMA: Well, let's pack our bags. Hollywood, here we come.

ARABELLA: Wilma . . .

WILMA: Yes?

ARABELLA: I have to tell you something . . . Well . . . I . . .

WILMA: What is it?

ARABELLA: Well . . . promise me you won't hate me, or stop being my friend. I never had a friend, Wilma, until you began being nice to me, and I couldn't stand it if you weren't my friend any longer . . .

WILMA: Oh, my cow. Stop talking like that. I'll never stop being your friend. What do you want to tell me?

ARABELLA: Well . . . I don't want to go to see Mr. Delafonte, Wilma . . .

WILMA: You don't?

ARABELLA: No. I don't want to be a movie star. I don't want to leave Harrison or my mother or father . . . I just want to stay here the rest of my life and get married and settle down and have children.

WILMA: Arabella . . .

ARABELLA: I just pretended like I wanted to go to Hollywood because I knew you wanted me to, and I wanted you to like me . . .

WILMA: Oh, Arabella . . .

ARABELLA: Don't hate me, Wilma. You see, I'd be afraid . . . I'd die if I had to go to see Mr. Delafonte. Why, I even get faint when I have to recite before the class. I'm not like you. You're not scared of anything.

WILMA: Why do you say that?

ARABELLA: Because you're not. I know.

WILMA: Oh, yes, I am. I'm scared of lots of things.

ARABELLA: What?

WILMA: Getting lost in a city. Being bitten by dogs. Old lady Leighton taking my daddy away . . . *(A pause.)*

ARABELLA: Will you still be my friend?

WILMA: Sure. I'll always be your friend.

ARABELLA: I'm glad. Oh, I almost forgot. Your Aunt Gert said for you to come on home.

WILMA: I'll go in a little. I love to swing in my front yard. Aunt Gert has a swing in her front yard, but it's not the same. Mama and I used to come out here and swing together. Some nights when Daddy was out all night gambling, I used to wake up and hear her out here swinging away. Sometimes she'd let me come and sit beside her. We'd swing until three or four in the morning. *(A pause. She looks out into the yard.)* The pear tree looks sickly, doesn't it? The fig trees are doing nicely though. I was out in back and the weeds are near knee high, but fig trees just seem to thrive in the weeds. The freeze must have killed off the banana trees . . .

(A pause. Wilma stops swinging — she walks around the yard.) Maybe I won't leave either. Maybe I won't go to Hollywood after all.

ARABELLA: You won't?

WILMA: No. Maybe I shouldn't. That just comes to me now. You know sometimes my old house looks so lonesome it tears at my heart. I used to think it looked lonesome just whenever it had no tenants, but now it comes to me it has looked lonesome ever since Mama died and we moved away, and it will look lonesome until some of us move back here. Of course, Mama can't, and Daddy won't. So it's up to me.

ARABELLA: Are you gonna live here all by yourself?

WILMA: No. I talk big about living here by myself, but I'm too much of a coward to do that. But maybe I'll finish school and live with Aunt Gert and keep renting the house until I meet some nice boy with good habits and steady ways, and I'll marry him. Then we'll move here and have children and I bet this old house won't be lonely anymore. I'll get Mama's old croquet set and put it out under the pecan trees and play croquet with my children, or sit in this yard and swing and wave to people as they pass by.

ARABELLA: Oh, I wish you would. Mama says that's a normal life for a girl, marrying and having children. She says being an actress is all right, but the other's better.

WILMA: Maybe I've come to agree with your mama. Maybe I was going to Hollywood out of pure loneliness. I felt so alone with Mrs. Leighton getting my daddy and my mama having left the world. Daddy could have taken away my loneliness, but he didn't want to or couldn't. Aunt Gert says nobody is lonesome with a house full of children, so maybe that's what I ought to stay here and have.

ARABELLA: Have you decided on a husband yet?

WILMA: No.

ARABELLA: Mama says that's the bad feature of being a girl, you have to wait for the boy to ask you and just pray that the one you want wants you. Tommy Murray is nice, isn't he?

WILMA: I think so.

ARABELLA: Jay Godfrey told me once he wanted to ask you for a date, but he didn't dare because he was afraid you'd turn him down.

WILMA: Why did he think that?

ARABELLA: He said the way you talked he didn't think you would go out with anything less than a movie star.

WILMA: Maybe you'd tell him different . . .

ARABELLA: All right. I think Jay Godfrey is very nice. Don't you?

WILMA: Yes, I think he's very nice and Tommy is nice . . .

ARABELLA: Maybe we could double-date sometimes.

WILMA: That might be fun.

ARABELLA: Oh, Wilma. Don't go to Hollywood. Stay here in Harrison and let's be friends forever.

WILMA: All right. I will.

ARABELLA: You will?

WILMA: Sure, why not? I'll stay here. I'll stay and marry and live in my house.

ARABELLA: Oh, Wilma. I'm so glad. I'm so very glad.

(Wilma gets back in the swing. They swing vigorously back and forth.)

APPENDIX

CLASSROOM EXERCISES

BRITISH (STANDARD AND COCKNEY) EXERCISES

British Experts/Cockney Talk Show   On a talk show (especially fun with a Cockney host), two people speaking Standard English are both experts on the same subject but have opposing views; for example, in a show with "rock" experts, one is a legitimate geologist and the other an animator who creates rocks on a computer for such films as *Jurassic Park*. The audience of the talk show is made up of Cockney speakers. The host keeps the conversation going and occasionally allows the audience to participate. Audience members pick a favorite guest and target the other with insulting, banal questions.

Smelly-Sexy-Funny   This is a popular theater exercise that can be used with any dialect, but it works well with Standard British. Four people participate: one person is the host of a party; the other three are the guests. Before the exercise starts, each person silently chooses one person onstage who is "smelly," another who is "sexy," and a third who is "funny." He or she endows these people with his or her choices in a subtle way throughout the scene. After each person has decided (without telling anyone else) who is who, everyone but the host leaves the set. The host mimes setting up for the party. One by one, the guests arrive and are affected by the presence of their smelly-sexy-funny people. The teacher can side-coach by saying make your smelly 100 times more smelly, etc. Each guest will find a reason to leave on his or her own. Afterwards, quiz the audience to find out who was who to each of the actors.

Character Interviews   Two people interview each other in dialect and find out where each other is from, what he or she does, what he or she likes, etc. The interview should be completely spontaneous and will help the actors find the natural cadence of their characters, as well as helping them remember what they learned about the region where their dialect originates. It can be repeated throughout the rehearsal process. Partners are not necessary; the actor could interview him- or herself, aloud.

Character Dream   This personal exercise may need outside coaching. After researching a given dialect, including looking at photos, reading newspaper articles, watching films, and more, the actor goes to a quiet place, closes his or her eyes, and "sees" a place in the country/region being studied. The actor should look for specific details, like the color of the paint that is peeling off the side of an old wooden building. The actor continues to daydream about this place, seeing the people around the area, what they are wearing, how they are walking, etc. He or she then adds the sense of touch and smell, such as sensing what the weather is like. At a certain point in the daydream, the actor must catch a glimpse of him- or herself in a reflective object and see what body type has come to mind. The actor looks for specific details and asks him- or herself: What am I wearing? How do I feel today? As the image becomes stronger, the actor may want to get up and move around the room, allowing the character's body to enter his or her body. After a short time, the voice of the character can reveal itself (in dialect of course), and the actor can begin to talk aloud to whoever is around. If no one is around, the actor can create an imaginary interview and proceed in an improvised monologue.

Character Walk   This exercise does not have to be done quickly; it may take about fifteen to twenty minutes. The teacher asks the students to first walk normally, then to adopt a variety of other walking styles. Following are suggested directions for these various character walks. (This exercise was adapted from a Laban method exercise.)

Without talking, walk around the room the way you normally walk. As you walk, keep your eyes and head up and active. Now walk a bit quicker and see how that changes your thoughts. Now go back to neutral walking. Now walk as if you were walking through very thick mud that covered you up to your chin. Now go back to neutral. Now walk as if you were walking in zero gravity. Now go back to neutral. Walk as if all your moves originated from your stomach. Now back to neutral. Change your center (where all your moves originate) to your toes and lead your walk with your toes. Now back to neutral. Now lead with your chin. Now back to neutral. Keep changing your center to find new ways to walk and constantly check in with what that walk does to your thoughts and sense of self. From neutral, walk with directness. Find a focus and directly go to it. Change direction and keep changing direction, but always with purpose. Then relax and go back to neutral. Now walk without purpose, try to commit, but then change your mind. What does that do to your body? Now go back to neutral. Walk around the room pigeon-toed. And back to neutral. Now walk bow-legged. And back to neutral. Walk as though you are completely bound in duct tape (keep moving); if you fall, try to get back up. And back to neutral. Walk as if every part of your body weighed 500 pounds. And back to neutral. Now, think of three of the ways you just walked (quickly, slowly, zero gravity, stomach-centered, toe-centered, chin-centered, directly, indirectly, pigeon-toed, bow-legged, bound, heavy) and put three of them together and walk around the room. Keep this walk up as you think about the voice that would come from this character (in dialect, of course). Think of this person's name, occupation, etc. Now find a partner and interview each other in these characters.

IRISH EXERCISES

Galway Monologue   A member of the group gets an ordinary object from an audience member and sets it down on a chair. Then, one at a time, group members come to the chair, hold up the object, and sit down and talk about its relevance in their lives. The object may be a book, for example, but the monologist can make the object anything he or she wants (i.e., it can be a monologue about "this pack of gum I got on the Aran Islands"). Monologues should be done for authenticity in the Irish dialect — rhythm, inflection, and sound changes should be the focus — not necessarily for humor. The monologist finishes his or her story after about two minutes, and then sets the object back down on the chair, and another group member comes up to do a different monologue. The monologues are completely improvised. Group members do not have to add onto anyone's story, but reincorporation from an earlier monologue can be creative ("I got this jewelry box from my mom when I was three." And then, from a different person, "I was searching for the perfect gift for my daughter when I found this old jewelry box in my hope chest"). Everyone in the group should rotate through the exercise.

Irish Scene Without I/You   Players speak in their Irish dialect in a scene of their choice (no more than four people should be up at a time due to focus issues). In the course of the scene, no actor may say the words *I, me, my, myself, mine, you, your, yourself,* or *yours*. With this restriction, people will slow down and become creative in their expression. If a player says one of the forbidden words, he or she must leave the scene gracefully, and another member of the class can join in until everyone has been onstage at least once.

Limerick Line   The students line up and, following the pattern of a limerick poem, make up a limerick. The first person in line says the first line of the limerick, the second person continues the limerick, and so on. The rhyming pattern for a limerick is AA BB A. Below is an example of the limerick rhythm.

> There once was a man from Manhattan.
> He had lots of rugs made from satin
> One day someone slipped
> And totally tripped
> (and) his face was suddenly flattened!

(Plus other previously mentioned exercises.)

RUSSIAN EXERCISES

Russian Translation   Two people sit facing each other, while two others stand behind them. The two people standing should maintain completely blank expressions on their faces throughout the improvisation. The two people sitting converse in Russian-accented gibberish. After Russian A (sitting) speaks, Translator A (standing) translates what he or she said into English but with a Russian accent. Then Russian B (sitting) responds in gibberish, and Translator B (standing) translates, and so on. After the scene has ended or been resolved, the sitters and standers switch places and repeat.

Russian Gibberish Warm-Up   The students stand in a circle. One student tosses a ball to a classmate and says a "Russian" word — not a *real* Russian word, just sounds that mimic Russian sounds. The catcher of the ball repeats the "word," and then throws the ball to someone else, saying a different Russian word. The ball toss can be continued for as long as desired. The faster the game goes, the better; do not try to be perfect in this one — it's gibberish!

Russian/Gibberish/Russian   In this exercise, the teacher/director uses a bell to control the language of the actors as they improvise a scene. The actors start out speaking English with a Russian accent. When the bell rings, they must switch to speaking gibberish, or vice versa. Each time the bell rings, the actors switch into whatever vocal direction they are not doing (either gibberish or Russian-accented English). The switch can happen in mid-sentence and should be as flawless and committed as possible.

(Plus other previously mentioned exercises.)

American (New York) Exercises

Brooklyn Bench   This is a rotation exercise. One person sits on a bench; another person enters and strikes up a conversation in a Brooklyn accent — defining their relationship and a need. The first person finds a reason to leave (relatively quickly, keep them short), and the second person remains. A new person enters and strikes up a conversation and develops a relationship that could be completely unrelated. The second person finds a reason to leave, etc. The whole group rotates through the exercise, ending with the person who started sitting on the bench re-entering and ending the scene.

One-Minute Ramble   Students stand in a circle and take turns talking aloud for one full minute, trying to avoid pauses or self-censuring. In a Brooklyn (or any) accent, they may talk about anything that comes to mind. The sentences do not have to be connected; they can ramble about anything. This is a great exercise for figuring where and how students hold their tension and insecurities.

Brooklyn Standing/Sitting/Kneeling   This is another theater exercise that combines the physical lives of the actors with their emotional and verbal lives. Three actors are in this scene. At all times, one actor is sitting, one kneeling, and one standing. The actors can move around, but there can never be two people in the same position at the same time. To keep it interesting and raise the stakes, the audience can give verbal cues (such as groaning or going *oooo*) when two people are in the same position. If two people are caught in the same position for longer than fifteen seconds, their scene is done, and the next group goes up. It is important to keep the narrative going and the character relationships clear.

(Plus other previously mentioned exercises.)

AMERICAN (SOUTHERN) EXERCISES

Southern New Choice   This exercise is controlled by the teacher. Two students get up to improvise a scene. When a person makes an offer ("That's a mighty fine *hat* you're wearing"), the teacher can call out "new choice" and the actor must (without hesitation or breaking character) make a new but related offer, for example: "That's a mighty fine *necklace* you're wearing." (new choice) "That's a mighty fine *belt* you're wearing." (new choice) "That's a mighty fine *purple felt overcoat* you're wearing." The teacher can stop saying "new choice" at any time, and the actor must then continue with the scene and accept what the final offer was. The teacher may call out "new choice" for either of the actors at any time, relating to any choice. This is especially useful in keeping the scenes positive and moving forward, such as: Actor A: "Do you want to dance with me?" Actor B: "No." (new choice) B: "Yes."

Southern Tag Monologue   One person stands and makes up a monologue on the spot (in a Southern accent, of course). When the next actor wants to take over, he or she simply walks up behind the first actor, taps him or her on the shoulder, and continues the monologue without pausing. The whole class takes turns continuing the monologue until the teacher decides it has ended, or it finds its end naturally.

Southern Subtext   This exercise requires some preparation. The teacher writes down subtext suggestions on pieces of paper (i.e., "I hate you" or "I'm afraid to tell you something") and puts them in a bag or hat to be drawn. Two people perform a scene from nothing (although the class may suggest a place or a relationship to get them started). One of the actors draws a subtext paper from the hat and must play that subtext throughout the scene without ever actually saying it. The other actor must attempt, through normal conversation, to figure out what the subtext is. For example, if the subtext is "I'm jealous of you," the other actor could guess by saying "You seem a little jealous of me right now." The teacher may end the scene by a certain time, or the scene can find its own natural ending. For fun, the audience may know the subtext and can give verbal cues to the actor guessing the subtext. When the subtext is correctly guessed, the audience (if they know it) can cheer to signify the end of the scene.

(Plus other previously mentioned exercises.)

Applying Dialect to a Role

Part of the fun in being an actor comes with the research I do for my roles. As one of my actor friends said, "I feel like I can write a thesis about Sweden, and I'm really just playing Miss Julie!" My enthusiasm for research has led me to devise a method for helping my students develop a comprehensive knowledge of the world of the character/accent. The best way to learn a consistent accent is to figure out why the character speaks the way he or she does. The student then becomes invested in creating a *person* rather than just a *sound change*.

In our character research process, the student asks him- or herself basic questions (adapted from Uta Hagen's list in *Respect for Acting*) that can reveal qualities needed for the accent:

- Who am I?
- Where am I?
- What am I?
- Who is around me?
- What is my past (immediate and ancient)?
- What is my future (impending and hopeful)?
- What time is it?
- What do I want in this play/scene?
- Why?
- What do I do to get what I want?

I encourage students to also ask themselves the following specific questions as part of the character-building process:

- What does/did my family do and how much money do I/we make?
- How is my health/energy?
- What is my self-image?
- What is my intellectual level?
- How do I walk?
- How do other people treat me?
- What is my status with the other people in the play/scene?
- What do other people say about me?
- What do I wish were true about me?
- What is my greatest fear?
- What is my greatest triumph?

- What kinds of music do I listen to?
- What do I do for fun?
- What is my religion?
- Where have I traveled?
- What do people in other places say about the way we talk here?
- How does my country/region stand in the great world picture?

Add your own questions!

FURTHER READING

Acting With An Accent and *Dialect Monologues* by David Alan Stern

The Actor and the Text by Patsy Rodenburg

The Actor Speaks by Patsy Rodenburg

Actor's Encyclopedia of Dialects by Donald Molin

American Dialectss and *Foreign Dialects* by Herman and Herman

"Dialect Notes" by Edith Skinner (note collection in A.C.T. library)

Dialects and Accents for Actors by Gillian Lane-Plescia

Dialects for the Stage and *Speech for the Stage* by Evangeline Machlin

The Dialect Handbook by Ginny Kopf

English Accents and Dialects by Hughes and Trudgill

"The History of English" PBS Documentary (video)

Impro by Keith Johnstone

The Joy of Phonetics and Accents by Louis Coloianni

The Need for Words by Patsy Rodenburg

The Right to Speak by Patsy Rodenburg

Speak With Distinction by Edith Skinner, Lilene Mansell and Timothy Monich

Stage Dialects and *More Stage Dialects* by Jerry Blunt

Vocal Direction for the Theatre: From Script Analysis

Voice and The Actor by Cicely Berry

To Opening Night by Nan Withers-Wilson

PERMISSIONS

Every effort has been made to locate the proper copyright holder for each excerpt published in this anthology. Any discrepancies or exclusions are unintentional.

Golden Boy by Clifford Odets. Copyright ©1937 by Clifford Odets; copyright renewed ©1965 by Nora Odets and Walt Whitman Odets. Reprinted by permission of Grove/Atlantic, Inc. All performance inquiries should be addressed to: Robert A. Freedman Dramatic Agency, 1501 Broadway, Suite 2310, New York, NY 10036.

A Handful of Stars by Billy Roche. Copyright ©1989 by Billy Roche. Reprinted by permission of The Agency. All inquiries should be addressed to: The Agency, 24 Pottery Lane, Holland Park, London, England, W11 4LZ.

Home Fires by Jack Heifner. Copyright ©1999 by Jack Heifner. Reprinted by permission of Dramatic Publishing. All inquiries should be sent to: Dramatic Publishing, 311 Washington St., Woodstock, IL 60098.

The Hostage by Brendan Behan. Copyright ©1958, 1962 by Theatre Workshop. Reprinted by permission of Grove/Atlantic, Inc. All inquiries for performance rights should be addressed to: Methuen, 215 Vauxhall, Bridge Road, London, England SW1V 1EJ. All other inquiries should be sent to: Grove Press, 841 Broadway, New York, NY 10003.

The House of Ramon Iglesia by Jose Rivera. Copyright ©1983 by Jose Rivera. Reprinted by permission of Samuel French. All inquiries should be addressed to: Samuel French, 45 West 25th Street, New York, NY 10010-2751.

The Indian Wants the Bronx by Israel Horowitz. Copyright ©1994 by Israel Horowitz. Reprinted by permission of Smith and Kraus Publishers. All inquiries should be addressed to: Smith and Kraus, P.O. Box 127, Lyme, NH 03768.

Inventing a New Color by Paul Godfrey. Copyright ©1989 by Paul Godfrey. Reprinted by permission of The Agency. All inquiries should be addressed to: The Agency, 24 Pottery Lane, Holland Park, London, England, W11 411Z.

Life and Limb by Keith Reddin. Copyright ©1985 by Keith Reddin. Reprinted by permission of Rick Leed Agency for the Performing Arts. All inquiries should be addressed to: Rick Leed Agency for the Performing Arts, 888 7th Avenue, New York, NY 10106.

The Love-Girl and the Innocent by Aleksandr Solzhenitsyn. Copyright ©1969

SPECIAL THANKS AND ACKNOWLEDGMENTS

A.C.T.'s MFA class of 1995, Kate Brickley, Elizabeth Brodersen,
Lia Fischer, Elaine Foreman, Jeffrey Draper, Jennifer Gould,
Kat Koppett, Gillian Lane-Plescia, Domenique Lozano,
Carey Perloff, Pamela Ricard, Joe Rosenthal,
Jack Sharrar, Craig Slaight,
Melissa Smith, John Sugden, Deborah Sussel,
Francine Torres-Kelly, V.A.S.T.A., Gemma Whelan,
All the young conservatory students at A.C.T., and
Dave Hill, the love of my life.